"Compelling. . . . A fascinating ride. . . . Rich in authenticity and detail."

—*The Plain Dealer* (Cleveland)

"*The Anatomy of Motive* finds John Douglas at the top of his form—as always. This is a terrific book for true-crime and mystery lovers alike."

—James Patterson

OBSESSION

"Eye-opening. . . . Douglas's compassion for the survivors of violent crimes seems to equal his understanding of the criminals themselves."

—*Publishers Weekly*

"I rarely use the phrase 'must-read' . . . but I can't think of a book that deserves it as much as *Obsession*. It's a survival handbook."

—*The Register-Herald* (Eaton, OH)

JOURNEY INTO DARKNESS

"An unsparing account of a brutal business. . . . The real genius here lies in the analytical rigor of Douglas's crime-scene investigations. . . . Gutsy, hard-nosed police work of the most difficult—and readable—sort."

—*Entertainment Weekly*

"Passionate, intelligent, and heartbreaking, the message of *Journey into Darkness* is a hard-hitting, no-holds-barred attack on our namby-pamby, wishy-washy, 'politically correct' age."

—*Nashville Banner*

Also by John Douglas

NONFICTION

Sexual Homicide
with Robert K. Ressler and Ann W. Burgess

Crime Classification Manual
with Ann W. Burgess, Allen G. Burgess, and
Robert K. Ressler

John Douglas's Guide to Careers in the FBI

Mindhunter
with Mark Olshaker

Unabomber
with Mark Olshaker

Journey into Darkness
with Mark Olshaker

Obsession
with Mark Olshaker

The Anatomy of Motive
with Mark Olshaker

The Cases That Haunt Us
with Mark Olshaker

FICTION

Broken Wings
with Mark Olshaker

JOHN DOUGLAS

MAN DOWN

A Broken Wings Thriller

POCKET BOOKS
New York   London   Toronto   Sydney

POCKET BOOKS, a division of Simon & Schuster, Inc.
1230 Avenue of the Americas, New York, NY 10020

This book is a work of fiction. Names, characters, places and incidents are products of the author's imagination or are used fictitiously. Any resemblance to actual events or locales or persons, living or dead, is entirely coincidental.

Copyright © 2002 by Mindhunters, Inc.

Originally published in hardcover in 2002 by Atria Books

All rights reserved, including the right to reproduce this book or portions thereof in any form whatsoever. For information address Atria Books, 1230 Avenue of the Americas, New York, NY 10020

ISBN: 0-671-01705-5

First Pocket Books paperback printing March 2004

10 9 8 7 6 5 4 3 2 1

POCKET and colophon are registered trademarks of Simon & Schuster, Inc.

Cover design by Jae Song, image © Joe Patronite/Getty, image © Scott Cunningham/Getty

Manufactured in the United States of America

For information regarding special discounts for bulk purchases, please contact Simon & Schuster Special Sales at 1-800-456-6798 or business@simonandschuster.com.

To the women in our lives—
when times are good, they're great
and when times are bad, they're even better.

Acknowledgments

I want to thank David Terrenoire, the writer who transformed a good idea into a great story; Jay Acton, not only my agent, but my friend; Lisa Drew, who championed this book; Luke Dempsey, our kind and generous editor; Amy Bagwell, an angel who made this book possible; Gina Gallo, an honest cop and a terrific writer; Josh Grier, attorney to the stars; Kathy Ashton, an ER veteran who helped us survive the GSWs; Col. Chris Reordan (USA Ret.), for his understanding of weapons and their development; and Tom and Ray Magliozzi for their roadside assistance with Jake's Aston Martin.

1

From deep in sleep I hear something fall. Something big. It shakes me and I open my eyes to complete darkness. I smell fresh-cut lumber and newly turned earth. Above my face and as far as I can reach, my fingertips touch wood. I'm in a coffin.

An important part of me knows that I am still asleep and that this is a dream. Still, a dark flower of panic blooms inside my chest and I will myself, against my own panicky animal instinct, to breathe slowly and deeply, letting the focus calm me so that I can think of what to do.

There is air enough, brought in by a steel pipe cool to the touch. I don't see it, but I know it is there. I also know the pipe is threaded on both ends. And as my fingers trace the grooves, I know that the killer will soon come and cap this pipe and I will suffocate, slowly. What is worse, I also know that in the final minutes I will try to claw my way out, no longer able to control my instinct. When I am reduced to an animal, blind to everything but bright fear, that moment is when he wins and achieves release.

We don't know for certain, we have no hard evidence, but we believe this end moment is what gets him off. In all the children we've found, not one has been sexually assaulted or even struck. There are no signs of the control fantasies most predators exhibit except, of course, for the imprisonment itself. But there are those final moments when his victim is stripped of humanity and begs for his life. I say *his* life because all of the victims, fourteen that we know of, have been boys. They have all been blond. They have all been taken from their homes and buried alive.

I think of the boys and repeat their names in a murderer's rosary. Saying them gives the victims some dignity, I think, and blunts his power over the lives they had before he took them. In the exercise of memory, it also blunts his hold over me as I lie here in this black box. I go over the details of each case, one by one, reciting their mysteries and praying for an insight that has escaped me before. Each time, the boys were taken from their bedroom. There is no sign of struggle. A personal object is taken. It's never anything of any value except to the victim. A toy, perhaps a photo. It's the single most important detail we've kept from the press. First, because it helps us eliminate the false confessors, and second, we want our killer to hang on to his souvenirs so that when we catch him, he will convict himself with his own sad collection.

No parent had ever heard the scrape of a window or the slide of a dead bolt. No mother had heard her child cry out. No father had heard the floorboards creak under the weight of an intruder. In the morning, all that was found was the killer's calling card.

It was a literal card, a playing card made by Signet Games, makers of dozens of children's games as well as traditional bridge and pinochle decks. But the killer's card was not from a traditional deck. These decks had had a small run and their distribution was limited to Vietnam. The owner, himself a WWII veteran of the OSS, had made them specially for a unit of assassins. There were fifty-two cards in each deck, all with the same design—a single black diamond. When a Vietcong tax collector or political officer was terminated, his killer left one of these black diamonds on the corpse to "spook the gooks."

This was my first unsolved case as a profiler, when the science was still considered voodoo by most of law enforcement. I didn't have the political muscle to break open hidebound bureaucracies. It took nearly a year for the CIA to declassify the personnel list and another eight months for the Bureau to track down all of the squad's surviving members. Most of them had settled down and started families and were angry when we brought out their dark past into the sunlight and laid it on their swept suburban doorsteps.

Others lived on the fringes, a big part of them still in Vietnam. Some of them were downright scary, alone in the woods, hiding from everyone but themselves. All of them had secrets, to be sure, but every one of them was eventually cleared of being the killer.

Over the time it took us to locate and interrogate all of these veterans, six more boys were taken from their beds, buried in plywood boxes, and kept alive for days, after which the killer would cap the air pipe and listen as the boys cried out. We believe he masturbated as they died. It is a detail that sickens me still, even after interviewing some of the most twisted killers on earth. The press had dubbed him, without much imagination, the Black Diamond Killer.

For these reasons—the abductions, the card, the cruel deaths, and that final act, I pushed myself to find him. The case filled my nights, even though I was working dozens of different cases at the time, interviewing murderers for my first textbook, appearing on television shows at the request of the director, and acting as technical consultant to several motion pictures. It was this last, this continual lunching with stars, that led my rivals in the Bureau to dub me, again without much imagination, Hollywood Donovan.

I was exhausted, physically and mentally. I had come down with a case of viral meningitis that I wrote off as a cold, and I flew out to Oregon, site of the abductions, to assist the local police. It was there that I collapsed and nearly died.

Then, as suddenly as they began, the abductions stopped. We don't know why. We suspect the killer died or was arrested for another crime. And now, eighteen years after the last boy, Billy Jimeson, was found, I was dreaming inside a box, my fingertips running over rough plywood, searching for answers.

From far away I heard a phone ring. I tried to holler but the sound that came out of my mouth was an unformed animal grunt. The ringing got louder. I heard the cap thread onto the pipe. I heard it being twisted until it snugged. My flow of air stopped.

The ringing was here, inside the box.

My lungs pulled in what could be my final breath.

Slowly, the darkness fell away and I came up, slick with sweat, twisted in sheets. Katie's side of the bed was cool. I was alone. I fumbled the phone to my ear. "Donovan."

"It's Andrews, Mr. Donovan, from Special Agent Burke's office."

"Yeah, right. I remember."

"I'm outside your door, Mr. Donovan. I've been knocking and ringing your bell."

"What? You're at the door?"

"On my cell phone, yes."

"Okay, okay, I'll be right there."

I threw my feet to the floor and stumbled to the front door, wrapped in a sheet. In the hall was a young man holding his ID so I could see it. I recognized Vince Andrews, a conscientious hard-charger known in the Bureau as a blue-flamer for the fire that shoots out of his ass.

I know the type because I was a blue-flamer once, too. But that was a long time ago. The Bureau, like all institutions, will throw cold water on a flamer faster than a fireman. Most agents with initiative will either get out or give up and join the ranks of gray plodders. Occasionally, someone like Andrews will sneak through and shine like a battlefield flare in the night, making enemies just by his brilliance.

"Come in." Normally, Andrews was buttoned up, a recruiting poster of a guy. This morning he looked as if he'd run through a hurricane. His tie was twisted, his hair blown about.

As Andrews came in and took in the details of my living room—the book on the table, the half-filled glass from the night before—my phone rang again. "Damn, I'm popular this morning."

"Mr. Donovan . . ."

I held up an index finger. "Let me get this."

"Sir?"

"One minute." I answered the phone. "Donovan."

"Jake, have you heard?"

"Katie, where the hell are you?"

"I was at the gym."

There's something wrong with Katie's voice, but I'm not awake enough to figure out what it is.

"You usually wait for me."

"Sorry, Jake, I woke up early. Have you seen the news?"

"What news?"

Andrews interrupted, "Special Agent Burke wants to see you right away."

"Hold on a minute, Katie." I put my hand over the receiver, the full darkness of bad news settling over me. "What's wrong, Andrews?"

"Special Agent Burke wants to see you right away. The whole building is a madhouse."

This was bad. I knew Neil Burke, special agent in charge of the Washington office, and he wasn't someone who would let it turn into anything close to a "madhouse." A recipient of the Navy Cross for valor in Vietnam, Neil faced each and every crisis with calm determination. Katie had once said that if Neil was on fire, he'd politely ask for a glass of water. Neil set the tone for the entire Bureau, and even when the press was howling at the door and heads were rolling down the aisles of Congress, Neil was relaxed, even icy.

"Katie, Andrews from Neil's office is here. I've got to go."

"Okay, Jake. I've got my cell phone if you need me."

"Right, good, see you later."

I wipe the sleep from my face and say, "Okay, Andrews. Do I have time for a shower?"

Andrews shook his head. "I don't think so, sir."

"Damn." I rubbed my beard. "A quick shave?"

"The director asked for you personally."

That sealed it. Whatever had happened was big. Orlando Ravan, a stickler for chain of command, rarely asked to see me, preferring instead to send assignments through Neil. "What's going on, Andrews?"

"You haven't seen the news?"

I glanced at the bedside clock. "I don't usually watch TV at six in the morning."

Andrews went to the window and pulled back the

curtains. From my balcony I have a terrific view across the Potomac. I can see the Jefferson Memorial, the top of the Lincoln Memorial through the trees, and the Washington Monument standing tall in the center of the Mall.

This morning, the lights of police cars, fire trucks, EMS vans, and Park Service patrols bounced off the Monument's sides and filled the cherry trees with cheap lightning. Beyond that, a column of black smoke rose in the air and spread flat over the city, adding a pall to an already overcast day.

"There, sir, the smoke," Andrews said.

I went to the window. "What is it?"

"A plane went down, sir."

"Oh, no. Do we know if it's an accident?"

"No, sir. Right now, nobody knows much of anything. But we think the First Lady may have been on board."

2

I was dressed and striding toward the elevators within two minutes. Andrews hurried to keep up. Inside, I started to push the button for the parking garage.

"I've got it, sir." Andrews reached past me and hit the button for the roof. "The director sent the Black Hawk. The city's sealed off. The traffic's a mess."

"You mean there's a helicopter pad up there?" I had never been up on the roof of my building, but a pad up there wouldn't surprise me. I live in Crystal City, home to some important people, too important to waste their time idling in D.C.'s notorious congestion.

Andrews touched his brow, trying to hide from the news. "Ah, no, sir, there's no pad."

"But, how . . . ," I started, and then knew why

Andrews looked as if he'd dressed in a wind tunnel.

"Hope you've been keeping up with your PT, sir."

On the roof, Andrews keyed his radio, and from below the HRT Black Hawk helicopter rose up and floated to just above where we were standing. The wind tore at my jacket and I thought for a moment that we'd be blown over the edge. The door opened and a ladder tumbled down, twisting back and forth in the prop wash. Andrews grabbed the end. "You go, sir," he shouted. "I'll hold her steady."

It had been a long time since I'd run the course at Quantico, and even then rope ladders were not my favorite obstacle. They're unstable, by nature, and I've seen guys get turned upside down and dropped, guys younger and in better shape than I am. "You sure I just can't meet you there?" I hollered.

Andrews smiled and shook his head. "It's either this or swim the river," he hollered.

"Okay." I grabbed a rung and pulled myself up. The ladder seemed alive and irritated to have a passenger. As I climbed, it bucked and turned. The wind from the prop tore at me, trying to shake me loose, and if Andrews hadn't been holding the ladder at the bottom, I believe I'd have been whipped off and tossed over the side.

It was only a climb of fifteen feet, but it seemed to take forever to reach the door and the helping hands of the crew chief. "Welcome aboard, sir," he hollered.

I looked down and watched Andrews scramble up the ladder as easily as climbing into a top bunk.

Once the door was closed against the noise, I strapped myself in.

The crew chief gave the thumbs-up to the pilot, and the chopper lifted off, turned, and banked over the Potomac. As we entered the highly restricted airspace over the Mall, two marine Black Hawks joined us, one on each flank.

Andrews caught the questioning look and said, "Just a precaution, sir. We don't know why the plane went down."

Black Hawks had been shot out of the sky in Somalia, and the thought of being in someone's sights, inside this flying box, didn't make me feel all that secure.

We flew low over the trees and along the edge of the Mall. Above us, F-16s crisscrossed the sky in close formation. Below us, a pool of people spread across the lawn. All I could think of was how they were trampling my crime scene. In the center of the chaos was the wreckage. The fire was out, but the blackened metal was still smoking.

Four marine and two Metro Police helicopters hovered over the Capitol. Two others flew the length of the river, not more than fifty yards above the water, one on either shore. News choppers zipped along the edges of the restricted airspace, while every bridge, from Francis Scott Key to Francis Case, was choked with traffic. Nothing moved for miles. In the distance, I saw more smoke rising from the east side of the city.

"Looters," Andrews shouted, "taking advantage of the unadvertised specials."

"What about casualties on the plane?"

Andrews shook his head. "I don't know, sir. But it doesn't look like anyone could have survived that."

I got that September Eleventh hole in the pit of my stomach, and I tried to focus on how best the Broken Wings could be used in the investigation. Our strength was in our flexibility and our ability to hit quickly before the suspects went to ground or fled the country. Unlike regular units, we were free of the layers of oversight and the constant stream of paperwork. And in a case this big, there would be paperwork thick enough to cover every bureaucratic backside in triplicate. Freedom made the Broken Wings efficient, but it also made us vulnerable, naked to politics and the press.

The year before we had been targeted by a radio talk jock who accused the team, and me in particular, of squandering taxpayer money on personal luxuries. We were innocent, but the charges were easy to make and hard to explain, so by the time we were cleared, the public's attention had moved on to another manufactured scandal.

Our only shields were competence, the director's clout, and the inside maneuvering of Mrs. Millicent De Vries. Since the death of *Washington Post* publisher Katharine Graham, Mrs. De Vries had become the most powerful woman in Washington, and the Broken Wings belonged to her. Her money made our unit possible, and her influence gave us what slight political cover we had.

There were five of us. Katie McManus and I,

besides being romantically involved, were crime scene investigators. Trevor Malone, former Ranger and member of the FBI's Hostage Rescue Team, was our weapons and tactics expert. Our C-130 carried its own forensics lab, including a morgue, and we had our own medical examiner, Dominic Sanchez, a man who'd spoken for the army of the dead in Detroit. After his wife's death, Dominic had nearly drunk himself onto one of his own slabs, but he was on the wagon and on our team and we were lucky to have him. Jerry Carruthers, our lab specialist and acknowledged genius in the field, I'd plucked from the halls of Harvard.

We called ourselves the Broken Wings, after the Bureau term for agents who could no longer cut it in the field. In the two years we had been together, we had solved a number of high-profile cases including the murder of the former FBI director. As anyone in this town will tell you, success makes headlines and enemies, and we made plenty of both.

No matter how good we were at solving crimes, our wings would have been permanently clipped had it not been for Mrs. De Vries and Orlando Ravan.

The director was an unusual man in Washington. He knew how to play the game, but was immune to the intrigues and backstabbing that surround power like flies on roadkill. He used us when it seemed right and didn't if he thought we were too high profile to conduct a quiet investigation. Because, no matter what the case, we attracted press wherever we went. Sometimes it worked to our advantage, and sometimes it got in the way.

I expected Director Ravan would have his own ideas on where we would be most effective, but I also knew that Ravan listened to suggestions, and if he heard a good idea, he went with it. As someone once said, you can get a lot done in Washington if you don't care who gets the credit, and Ravan honestly didn't care.

There isn't a pad on top of the J. Edgar Hoover Building, so the Black Hawk set down on the Ellipse between the White House and the Washington Monument. Dozens of men in dark suits and sunglasses, their Uzis drawn, created a perimeter around the helicopter as I disembarked. Joe Ripley, Neil Burke's clerk, met me at the chopper door and shook my hand. "That was quick." He tried to make it sound light, but gloom was in the air as thick as the smoke that spread over the Mall.

The helicopter lifted off and the hot wind whipped us. "We'll have to hoof it," Joe said. "The whole city's in gridlock."

We took off at a trot down Pennsylvania Avenue. "Aren't we going to Neil's office?"

"The Hoover Building," Joe said. "He's with the director."

"Any news?" I said.

"I'll let the director fill you in. Who knows what's happened in the past ten minutes."

It was a run of a little more than half a mile, but in the heat of the morning, in a jacket, I was sweating before we reached Fifteenth Street. Everywhere

I looked I saw chaos. Every street was blocked by traffic, every intersection was manned by policemen in riot gear trying to keep drivers from abandoning their cars. Thousands of gawkers choked the streets, trying to get closer to the Mall, while other police tried to hold them back. Sirens split the air and emergency vehicles were forced up onto the sidewalks. As we approached the Hoover Building, we saw more and more armed security. So many policemen were in full riot gear, armed with automatic weapons, it reminded me more of a Central American capital than the capital of the Free World.

Joe took me through the director's entrance. Security checked our credentials three separate times, made two calls, had us clear our weapons and recite Hoover's hat size before we were allowed in.

Inside, the air-conditioning cooled the sweat on my face.

"I see you still carry the Airweight," Joe said, referring to the revolver tucked into my ankle holster.

"Yeah. Katie's always after me to carry something with more firepower, but I tell her that I'll hold off the press if she'll shoot the bad guys." I gave it a beat. "Or was I supposed to shoot the press while she holds off the bad guys? I forget."

Joe smiled at my attempt to lighten the morning. He was polite that way.

We got into the elevator and Joe pressed the button for the top floor. At seven, the elevator doors opened onto a hallway filled with running people.

Phones rang and people barked. Harry Gillette, looking too busy and too important, ran toward us. Harry was Neil's assistant, and even this early, in this pandemonium, Harry was impeccable from his capped teeth to his capped black oxfords, looking like a glossy magazine ad for fussy men whose priorities were hopelessly skewed. Harry didn't like me, and he liked the idea of Broken Wings running investigations outside of his control even less. He pointed at me as if I were a mutt who'd strayed in from the street. "Turn around."

"What?"

He waggled his finger at me. "Go home. We don't need you, Donovan."

"The director sent for him," Joe said.

"And now he's unsending him." Gillette stood, his arms crossed, in the center of the hallway.

"Unsending? Is that a word?" I tried to get past him but Gillette moved to block me. We stood nose to nose, so close I could smell his Old Spice.

"Go out of my space, Donovan."

I pushed in closer, making him step back.

People in the hallway stopped and watched, hoping I'd knock Gillette onto his well-upholstered ass. Harry was the kind of man who inspires applause when he slips on the ice.

Joe Ripley's cell phone rang. "Ripley," he answered. He listened. "Yes, sir. He's right here, sir." Ripley looked at me as if searching for the answer to some question on my face. "Yes, sir. I understand. Yes, sir." Joe closed up his phone. "You have to go home, Jake."

"What?" We were standing at the elevator doors. People eased past us, coming and going, trying not to make eye contact. "What do you mean, I have to go home?"

"That was Neil. He said to send you home."

"But why?"

Joe shook his head. "I don't know, Jake. I really don't know."

Gillette smiled. "Why don't you and your team go find a TV camera to stand in front of."

"Hey, Harry, when you make cases, the news-people come to you. But you wouldn't know that, would you?"

The elevator doors opened. I turned to Joe and said, "How am I supposed to get home?"

Harry laughed and Joe turned red.

"Take the Metro, Donovan," Harry said. "Maybe you'll get to sign a few autographs for the tourists."

I gave Harry a look that, if there had been any justice in the Justice Department, would have set his hair on fire. I stuffed my hands in my pockets. "Uh, Joe?" I half turned, not wanting Gillette to hear me ask, "This is so embarrassing. I mean, I got dressed so quickly. Could you lend me a couple bucks for the Metro?"

Joe handed me a five and said, "Get a cup of coffee, Jake. On me."

I could hear Gillette laughing even after the elevator doors closed.

The Metro platform was so crowded people were in danger of falling onto the rails. I tried to be inconspicuous but at six-four with a face that's been on a dozen crime shows, there's little I can do if someone recognizes me. It took an hour to get home and I must have been asked a thousand times who I thought did it.

When I finally made it into my apartment, Katie was standing in front of the TV drying her hair with a towel. She was dressed in her usual uniform: jeans, sneakers, and a plain white T-shirt. She made dressing down look damn good. In fact, she was a bright spot in what had been a pretty bad morning.

"The First Lady's alive," she said without turning away from the screen. "She was supposed to be on that plane, joining her husband, when it happened. They were on their way to Florida."

"I heard," I said. "The Metro's full of rumors. It was the Iraqis, the Aryan Brotherhood, the Russians, the Afghanis. One guy swore it was Ted Kennedy avenging his brothers. And everyone wanted to know what I thought. Of course, no one believed that I knew even less than they did."

Katie sat on the ottoman in front of the TV and rewound a videotape. "Look at this, Jake."

I sat on the edge of the sofa and rested my elbows on my knees. On-screen a young boy waved at the camera. I recognized the MIA stands. This was shot across the street from the Lincoln Memorial, looking toward the Washington Monument. The sky and the closed MIA stands told me this was shot early in the day.

The cameraman panned left and the Washington Monument came into frame. The camera panned right and high over the Potomac; leaving Reagan National, a small private jet, what we now knew was a Hawker 700A, was just a speck against the gray sky. The cameraman zoomed in. His voice said, "Jimmy, look at that. I bet someone powerful's in there, heading off to do important things. Could even be the president."

A child's voice, brimming with scorn for a hopeless parent, said, "The president flies in Air Force One."

"Maybe the vice president then," the dad said, clueless.

The airplane banked right toward Virginia, and as it leveled off, the tail exploded. The cameraman bobbled the camera and the screen was filled with sky, then grass, then treetops. When the picture settled, the plane had done a one-eighty and was spinning toward the Mall, trailing smoke. It crashed just beyond the Washington Monument and the cameraman whispered, "My God, oh my God. Jimmy, Jimmy, oh my God."

"The guy's already been offered six figures for this," Katie said.

"I'm not surprised." I looked at Katie. "Where did you get it?"

She turned her head and paused for just a beat. "I'd rather not say, Jake. You know the rule."

I nodded. "Never tell where you get your information if you want to keep getting information."

"When you have a need to know, Jake."

"Okay. Any word on why the First Lady was supposed to be aboard?"

"She was hitching a ride with a congressman's wife. It was his plane. Jason from North Carolina. They think he was on board, too."

"Anyone else?"

"The army chief of staff, some aides, others not yet identified. All heading to Florida for a briefing with the president."

I watched Katie fidget with her hair. Something wasn't quite right with her, but I knew better than to ask. Katie gets into these distant moods at times and it's best just to let her find her own way back. "You were at the gym all morning?" I tried to make it sound conversational instead of an interrogation.

Katie's eyes darted left. "Yes, I did a longer run than usual."

"You hear the news there?"

"Am I under arrest, Officer?"

"Yeah, let me go get the cuffs." She laughed and I let it go. Katie was lying, and as an investigator herself, she knew I knew. When people tell the truth, they look right, where memory lives. When they tell a lie, they look left, toward fabrication. It has to do with the map of the brain and how we retrieve memory. It's a good thing to know if you're interrogating a murder suspect, playing poker, or buying a used car.

Katie and I had been together as a couple for almost two years. Before that she had been one of my students at Quantico and then my colleague in the Bureau. She was thirty-one, which meant I had ten years on her in the field and fifteen everywhere else. Like all the Broken Wings, Katie was profoundly independent. While we spent most nights together, she also kept her own apartment in Alexandria. She had been married once before, to another agent, but he had left her for a piece of fluff from Records, and no one who knew Katie could figure out why. She was beautiful, intelligent, and dangerous—an irresistible combination.

But Katie wasn't easy to live with. She could slip into a depression that lasted for weeks. When you spend your days investigating child homicides or, as we'd just done in Virginia, a string of murder rapes that ended with the elderly victims being nailed to chairs and set on fire, the nights can be plenty dark. All of us who do this kind of work live on the edge of a large, black hole, but Katie's seemed darker and deeper than most.

Katie walked into the kitchen and came back with a cup of coffee. "So, tell me about your morning."

I told her about the chopper ride across the river and what had to be the shortest time on an investigation on record. When I got to the humiliation in the hallway, when I had to beg money for the ticket home, Katie laughed out loud. "It made Harry Gillette's whole week," I said, appreciating the humor for the first time that day.

"Yeah," Katie said. "But it wasn't up to Harry to cut you loose."

"I know. But why would Ravan send the Black Hawk for me and then change his mind?"

"You know why."

"He was overruled." I sat back against the sofa cushions and let out a long breath. "Armstrong. It had to be Armstrong."

"Give the man a cigar. He's taking charge of the investigation. It was just announced." Katie nodded at the TV.

Phillip Armstrong was the newly appointed attorney general, head of the Justice Department, and therefore, in charge of the FBI. If he wanted to take over an investigation, he could. If he wanted to close an investigation, he could. If he wanted to assign Scully and Mulder to an investigation, well, he could probably do that, too. There was no question that if he wanted to cut an old adversary out of the biggest case of the century, he had the juice to do it. Armstrong and I had history, and it was ugly.

I was still in the Bureau and had been helping the local police with a triple homicide in Armstrong's jurisdiction. The investigation had turned up evidence in a capital murder case that had cleared a man Armstrong had sent to death row the year before. What was worse, Armstrong had known the man was innocent and had suppressed the evidence.

The more I pulled on that thread, the more Armstrong's integrity had unraveled. I soon learned of several other cases where evidence was lost or witnesses had changed their stories after spending an afternoon with the prosecutor.

One afternoon, I told him in confidence what I had found and warned him that if I could do this, so could a smart reporter, and maybe he should conduct his business with an eye more to the law than to his political career.

As it turned out, however, a friend and former student of mine was preparing to run against him for state attorney general. Armstrong threatened to prosecute me on blackmail charges.

Eventually, Armstrong ran, and when an investigative reporter came across the same evidence I had, he lost. Of course, Armstrong blamed me for feeding the evidence to the press. He even claimed I'd done it in exchange for an appearance on a morning talk show.

Fortunately for Armstrong he had friends in high places, and when the former attorney general had a heart attack, Armstrong received the appointment. Some liberal senators raised questions about his past, but he was in the end approved and the nation's attention moved on to the next fresh scandal.

I had become a Broken Wing by the time Armstrong was appointed attorney general, and thanks to Ravan and Mrs. De Vries, I was protected from any direct retribution from him. But I knew I was high on Armstrong's enemies list, and the way this guy juggled the law, I considered it a source of pride. A man's strength is not measured by his friends, but by his enemies. I think I read that on a place mat at Denny's.

"So, what do we do now?" Katie asked.

"We wait. Something's bound to come up."

"You mean we hope for a homicide? Maybe we should paint a vulture on the nose of the *Broken Wing*."

I rubbed my hand over my unshaven jaw. "Always looking at the bright side, huh, Katie?"

So, as Katie and I contemplated sitting out what could be the biggest case not only of our careers but our lifetime, the phone rang. Our dark prayer had been answered. Someone had been murdered.

3

Katie and I climbed into the Aston Martin and I turned the key. Silence. Katie knew the drill. She reached behind the seat, pulled out an ancient beat cop's nightstick, and handed it to me as I got out of the car.

I opened the hood, leaned close to the fire wall, and gave the starter a hard whack. I climbed back behind the wheel and twisted the key. The Aston Martin started with a roar.

Tucking the nightstick back in its place, Katie asked, "What's wrong with the starter?"

"Bad spot on the armature, I think."

"Why don't you get it fixed?"

"It starts."

"But you have to get out and open the hood anytime you want to go anywhere."

"I like to think of it as an antitheft device." I

threw the little car into gear and headed into the crowded streets.

It took us nearly three hours to drive what should have been twenty minutes up to Cleveland Park, passing through several checkpoints on our way. At Wisconsin and M Street, a cop recognized me and filled us in on the latest rumors. "Ragheads, they think. Lucky for us their intelligence sucks, huh?"

"Yeah," I said. "Lucky for the First Lady."

"Not so lucky for General Buckholz, though."

"No," I said. "Or the others."

The radio reported that the authorities had determined this to be a terrorist act. Ten people were dead including Army Chief of Staff General Sam Buckholz, four other army officers, and three civilian defense workers. Several people on the ground were injured in the explosion, but their current status was unknown. The White House had released a statement saying that the First Lady had been scheduled to be on that flight, but had given up her seat for the general and his people. The press secretary was quoted as saying, "Concern for the security of the United States is always the First Lady's priority. Her heart goes out to the families of the men lost in service to their country."

The president had issued a statement promising to hunt down and bring to justice the people responsible for this attack on his family and the nation, but he had neglected to say who those people might be.

Public radio ran the attorney general's first press conference. Armstrong outlined the investigation so far. There were FBI raids across the nation, hauling in known operatives in fringe movements, from Middle East revolutionaries to homegrown terrorist militia members. The same thing was happening abroad, only with a little less attention paid to civil rights. "Every resource is being called upon to find those who perpetrated this heinous act of cowardice," Armstrong said.

"Not quite," Katie said.

"They will be brought to justice, make no mistake," Armstrong said. "They will discover that this world is not large enough to hide from the United States of America."

"Tell that to Eric Rudolph," I said, referring to the bombing suspect who had eluded the FBI for years in the North Carolina mountains.

"Or J. P. Napoleon," Katie said. J. P. Napoleon was the head of Empire International, a conglomerate with its hands in dozens of legal and illegal industries, from pharmaceuticals to small arms. He was also my own Moby, my white whale, a man I couldn't prove existed, but a man who had haunted my career as surely as the Black Diamond Killer haunted my dreams.

Some people said that Napoleon was actually several men, and others said he was merely the creation of one man's imagination. Still others suspected he was Fletcher De Vries, the former husband of our own financial backer, Millicent De Vries. Supposedly drowned years ago, Fletcher De Vries had been seen at a number of jet-set soirees throughout Europe and the Far East, a remarkable show of social élan for a corpse.

Aside from the traffic, the bullshit coming from my radio, and the thought of Napoleon, my absurdly named nemesis, the drive was pleasant. We drove past Embassy Row and into Cleveland Park, a beautiful neighborhood of steep lawns and stately homes. Mrs. De Vries lived in a spectacular stone mansion just a soul's breadth from the National Cathedral. With the right security clearances and party affiliation, you could walk over to the vice president's residence and chat up energy policy. In the winter, when the trees were bare, you could see the cathedral's rooftop from Mrs. De Vries's driveway.

We were greeted at the front door by Frederick, Mrs. De Vries's right-hand man. He led us into the solarium, dark on this overcast day, and brought us coffee.

"Mrs. De Vries will be right with you," he said, and left Katie and me alone.

Katie had changed into a green blouse that matched her eyes and a gray suit that matched the sky. As we sat among the orchids and rare palms, I realized how much I depended on this beautiful young woman, not just professionally, but how much she had become a part of my life. Until Katie, I hadn't become attached to anyone since my divorce, and now I couldn't imagine what my days and nights would be without her.

She caught me staring. "What? Do I have something on my teeth?"

"No. I like looking at you."

She reddened and turned her face away. "Jake, stop it."

Mrs. De Vries, elegant in dress and manner that comes from high intelligence, old money, and all the right schools, normally blew into a room on an endless supply of energy. But today, her usual sparkle was subdued as she greeted us: "Katie and Jake, the most dangerous couple in the capital. How are you?"

Behind her a man in his forties with an anchorman's hair and the unmistakable smile of a career politician waited to be introduced. I recognized him as David Jason from North Carolina, already on the short list of possible presidential candidates, and the man with the great misfortune of having offered the First Lady a ride on his airplane. From his hair to the toes of his shoes, he looked far too polished to have spent the morning being grilled, but the lines around his eyes were deep, and his face showed signs of fatigue. Mrs. De Vries drew him closer.

"I recognize Mr. Donovan, of course," Jason said, "but I have to say that your partner, Ms. McManus, is the one everyone talks about in Washington." His manner was one of a country boy with a Duke University education, someone as comfortable in boardrooms as he was pressing the flesh at tobacco auctions.

"I am so sorry," Katie said, and held his hand in the two of hers.

He managed a smile, but it was bruised. "Thank

you, Ms. McManus, but we must remember that our country was the target, not me personally."

"Still . . ."

Mrs. De Vries stepped in and took Katie's hand from the congressman's. "You probably don't know."

"What?"

"The congressman's wife was supposed to have been aboard the plane with the First Lady."

"Yes," Katie said, "we heard. I'm relieved to know that you and your wife weren't on board the plane."

The congressman cleared his throat and, for a moment, looked as though a tear or two might come to those blue eyes. "Thank you. But those men . . ." He trailed off.

"They're treating the congressman horribly," Mrs. De Vries said. "And everyone's so security conscious that I can get absolutely no information at all. We were curious to know if you had heard anything, Jake."

Katie and I told what we knew, which was not much, and then Mrs. De Vries told what she knew, which was considerable. The wreckage hadn't stopped smoking and she knew that the First Lady had been whisked off to Camp David; that the initial suspicion was some type of plastic explosive in the baggage compartment of the Hawker; and that a mechanic who worked on the congressman's plane had been found shot in his home. "My contacts didn't know if his murder was connected to the bombing."

"If I had your contacts, I could solve ninety percent of the crimes in D.C.," I said.

Mrs. De Vries, never comfortable with herself as the topic of conversation, said, "That's why we called you, Jake. We need you."

The congressman cleared his throat. "I understand you've been removed from the case."

I nodded. "You know that we can't help you with this. As much as we would like to."

"That's not why you're here, Jake," Mrs. De Vries said, "although I think it's a shameful waste of talent. David here, even in this hard time, heard about my problem and offered to help."

"What problem, Mrs. De Vries?"

"There's been a murder, Jake, and my niece is missing."

David Jason held Mrs. De Vries's hand in both of his. "To not assist this grand lady in her time of need would be a crime in itself." The way his voice dropped to barely a whisper that forced his listeners to lean in closer, the way he looked each one of us in the eye, the sincerity and determination of his tone, made me understand why he was so good at raising money and hopes within his party. I noticed that he wore a class ring and his nails were buffed to a high shine.

The congressman said, "I've spoken to local law enforcement and cleared the way for your involvement. I know how turf is protected and I wanted to make sure you would get all the cooperation necessary to do your job."

"I appreciate that," I said.

"It's a small thing," he said, "but it was a way I could help."

Katie brought us down to business. "You said there's been a murder."

Jason freed Mrs. De Vries's hand so that he could use his own to gently mold his words, as though the substance of his words would cut him. "William Rush, a key man in a technology start-up, has been killed."

"When?" Katie asked.

"The police believe he was killed last night," Mrs. De Vries said.

"The body was found this morning along a jogging trail in Research Triangle Park." The congressman added, "We're quite proud of the park in North Carolina. To have one of our brightest researchers murdered there is, I admit, a rather selfish reason for me to be involved."

"Human nature runs on self-interest," Mrs. De Vries said. "Not all of us are as honest about it as you, sir."

"Especially given your current situation," I said.

Jason shrugged. "There's not much I can do about the explosion this morning, as much as I feel somewhat responsible for what happened."

"Why is that?" Katie said, her concentration focused on the congressman, searching for physical reasons to believe his words or not.

"Because I was the one who extended the invitation to the First Lady."

"You can't hold yourself responsible for what happened, David," Mrs. De Vries said, her hand on his forearm.

"But I can help here. I can use my influence for good here."

That was true. Jason would be kept at arm's length from the federal investigation, but he'd carry a lot of weight with the local police.

"Why do you think the locals need us?"

"Because they've already decided on the killer. There's evidence that William Rush was having an affair with Janice Callahan, a married woman."

"Janice was divorced," Mrs. De Vries said.

"Is she your niece?" Katie asked. "Is she the one who's missing?"

Mrs. De Vries nodded, her eyes closed, her lips tight. It broke my heart to see her in pain.

"But the police have already decided that it was the husband who did this," Jason said.

"He'd be my first choice," I said.

Katie said, "But you obviously think they have the wrong man."

"First, they don't have the husband. Not in custody. He's disappeared. And second, William Rush was involved in some highly classified work. There are a lot of people who might want him dead. Now, I don't know who did it, but I think there are more suspects than just the husband."

"If you mean foreign governments, maybe you should be talking to Orlando Ravan," Katie said.

Jason shook his head. "I'm afraid they've got their hands full at the moment."

"Still, this might be something outside of our capabilities." If this was a hit by a foreign agent, I didn't want the Broken Wings getting mixed up with the intelligence community. Their morals and motives were far too slippery for a team of cops, especially good cops. "Espionage isn't really our specialty. If it is espionage."

"But murder is," Mrs. De Vries said. "And you're damn good at it."

"I'm sorry to ask this," Katie said, "but was your niece having an affair with the victim?"

Mrs. De Vries's face turned to stone. "No. I don't believe that. I can't believe that. That's why I need you to find her, Jake. I'm afraid that whoever did this to William Rush may be after Janice, too."

4

After whacking the starter, Katie and I climbed back into the Aston Martin for the slow trip home. While we were stopped in the city's traffic, I called home and got my voice-mail messages. There were three, all from Toni, my ex-wife. We have a good relationship, considering that our marriage went down in flames and I was the one holding the match. We're raising two good kids: Ali, who has just turned sixteen, and her brother, Eric, who is ten. Toni's voice rang with worry. "Jake, I know you must be busy. Give me a call when you get this, uh, when you can, and, uh, let us know you're okay. Eric and Ali are worried about you."

I hit speed dial and Toni answered. I assured her I was fine and we made small talk about the disaster, and the kids, and the scenes on the news. Toni was not a person for small talk of any kind so I knew that she was warming up to something, and eventually it came out.

"Jake, I really hate to ask this, especially now, but I have to be in Toronto next week for a psychiatric conference. If you're busy, I'll ask my mother . . ."

"No, no, I'll be happy to stay with the kids. But I can't be sure, Toni, not right now."

"When can you know?"

"In a couple of days. The team is flying down to North Carolina for a case. Once I get a good look at the scene . . ."

"Could you let me know by Monday?"

"Sure, no problem. I should know by then."

I heard Eric in the background.

"Eric wants you to know that Katie is welcome to come down, too," Toni said.

"Eric says hi," I said to Katie. Eric suffered from a preadolescent crush and would do anything to be in the same room, the same planet, hell, the same solar system as Katie.

Katie's relationship with Toni was as good as anyone could expect, considering the circumstances. Katie was twelve years younger than Toni, and while Toni was attractive, Katie turned heads. That Toni didn't harbor homicidal fantasies about Katie was a demonstration of my ex-wife's maturity and self-confidence. I'm not sure I would have been as open-minded if the situation were reversed.

While I was talking to Toni on my phone, Katie was on her phone assembling the team. Dominic Sanchez, our medical examiner, was coming in from a jazz festival in Baltimore. Jerry Carruthers, our forensic lab specialist, had been tutoring a graduate student in Georgetown and was now in his apartment putting his duffel together. Trevor Malone, weapons and tactics specialist, had driven in from Fairfax and was waiting for us at Reagan National along with the flight crew, Scott Kenworthy and Trish O'Connor. By the time all of the Broken Wings were seated around the conference table on board the C-130, it was late afternoon.

The *Broken Wing* was not your stock C-130 but had been a flying executive suite for a prominent Colombian drug cartel before it was seized by the DEA. Drug lords are notorious for their love of luxury and excruciatingly bad taste, but in this case, they had kept their affinity for leopard skin in check. Aside from a padded zebra toilet seat, the rest of the interior was corporate leather and chrome. The plane slept eight, had an executive cabin, a conference room, and a flying forensics lab. This was paid for, in a roundabout way that would take a New York accountant to explain, by Millicent De Vries and the De Vries Foundation.

Scott had filed a flight plan for Raleigh-Durham Airport, and he and Trish were running through the preflight checks when we arrived.

"Departure should be in approximately"—Scott looked at his watch—"twenty-four minutes, Jake."

"Approximately?"

Scott laughed. "Yes, sir. ETA at RDU is twenty-one thirty-four hours."

"Thank you, Scott."

Trevor, as usual, was pacing the length of the small conference room, bulkhead to bulkhead. He was anxious to hear about the case in North Carolina, but was distracted by his anger at being pulled off the attack on the First Lady. "Goddamn, Jake, they need every swinging dick they can get."

Katie cleared her throat.

Trevor waved it away impatiently. "You know what I mean."

I shook my head. "I know, Trevor, and I'm sorry. It's because of me that we're not on the case."

"Dammit." Trevor hit the table with his fist.

Jerry, already highly agitated due to his flying phobia, jumped. "Trevor, please don't do that." Jerry turned to me. "Tell us about this murder in North Carolina."

I pulled out what information I had been able to piece together, which wasn't much. I put a photo on the table and the Wings passed it around. "The victim is a white male, thirty-four years old, a Ph.D. in physics from your old employer, Jerry."

"Harvard?" Jerry squinted at the picture, holding it at arm's length.

Dominic said, "You want to borrow my glasses, Jerry?"

"No, no, I can see." Jerry closed one eye. "I think I know him. William Rush?"

"That's him."

"He was a big deal in Cambridge. Had a reputation for being a little squirrelly, which in the physics department means he was collecting more acorns than usual."

Trevor laughed. "Man, you think someone's squirrelly, they must live in a damn tree."

Jerry straightened up. "In academia, I'm considered extremely well-adjusted."

Dominic harrumphed.

I took the photo from Jerry and looked at the dead man's face. It was soft, and round, almost like a baby's, except for a thin mustache on his lip. His eyes were watery, as if he'd been slicing an onion when the picture was taken. His shirt was a summer print, and the burn across his nose made me think the photo had been taken while Dr. Rush was on vacation. "Does he normally wear glasses, Jerry?"

Jerry scrunched up his face, concentrating on his memory of a man he'd last seen two years before and then only from across Harvard Yard. "I think so, why?"

I handed him the photo again. "He looks like he's wearing contacts, that's all, and isn't quite used to them."

"How was he killed?" Dominic asked.

"Shot," Katie said. "The locals think Dr. Rush was working out some personal physics problems with this woman." Katie pulled another picture out of the file and slid it across the table. The photo was a studio shot of an attractive blond woman seated in front of a large man with a beard, a shirt that strained at the buttons, and a forced smile. "In case you're wondering, that man standing behind her is her husband, estranged, and he's considered the prime suspect."

Trevor shrugged and took a seat at the table.

"Well, that pretty much wraps things up then, doesn't it?"

"Mrs. De Vries doesn't think so," Katie said.

"Why would she think this is more than a man knocking boots with another man's wife?"

"First," I said, "the woman in the picture is Janice Callahan. She's Mrs. De Vries's niece."

"Oh, no." Trevor dropped his head into his hands. "I hate it when these things get personal. It makes everything sticky."

"Ms. Callahan is missing, along with her husband," I said. "So we might be looking at a whole list of things including extortion, kidnapping, blackmail, who knows? That's why she's asked us to look into it."

"It could still be exactly what the police think it is," Katie said, "a jealous husband with a gun."

"There's something else," I said.

Dominic adjusted his glasses. "What's that, Jake?"

"We know that Dr. Rush was working on some classified project, possibly a weapon, so there are people in Washington besides Mrs. De Vries who are interested in our investigation."

The mention of a weapon sparked Trevor's interest. "Do we know what kind of weapon?"

"No," I said.

"Probably from the Buck Rogers collection, considering Rush's research at Harvard," Jerry said.

"You think this might be espionage?"

I shrugged. "You never know."

Dominic shook his head. "I don't like it, Jake.

You know what happens when you get mixed up with politicians. Things get really complicated."

Trish poked her head into the conference room. "We're getting ready to taxi, Jake. You need to move up to the cabin. There's a storm front coming in so we expect to run into some turbulence. Buckle up."

I looked around the table at my team, all highly qualified and all just a bit eccentric, which is how they became Broken Wings in the first place. "I'd say Trish has the right idea."

"Yeah," Katie said, "buckle your seat belts, we're in for a bumpy ride."

Jerry raised his hand. "Can I get a drink before we take off?"

5

We rented two cars at RDU Airport, got directions into Research Triangle Park, and took off. We traveled light, just one bag each except for Trevor, who also carried the duffel held over from his days with the Bureau's Hostage Rescue Team. I had never looked inside this bag, but I guessed enough firepower was in there to take out a small village.

I called our contact, a Detective Weller with the Durham PD, and made a courtesy call to the local special agent in charge, the SAC in FBI parlance, telling him we were in his jurisdiction and what we were doing. People in law enforcement, myself included, are not big fans of surprises, so it's best if no one jumps out from behind the sofa and yells, "Happy birthday!"

Detective Weller said the body was in the morgue at Duke Hospital and invited Dominic in to talk to the medical examiner. He gave Jerry the number of the Crime Analysis Unit, and Katie scribbled down directions to the crime scene.

Katie got behind the wheel, I got in the passenger side, and Trevor climbed in back.

"Figures," Trevor said.

"What's that?"

"We come to North Carolina and you make me ride in the back of the bus."

"It's not a bus," Katie said. "It's a Lincoln."

"Whatever."

"Think of me as your driver."

"That would be okay."

I turned so I could see Trevor spread out in the back. "Just settle back, Miss Daisy, while we carry you to the Piggly Wiggly."

We rolled through gentle hills, dotted with high-tech buildings set back behind a screen of trees, until we came to the exit Weller had instructed us to take. From there a four-lane road, shaded by tall pines, ran past entrances to several Fortune 500 companies plus firms on the bleeding edge of pharmaceutical and high-tech research. Between two landscaped security gates, out of sight of either, was a tan sedan pulled to the side of the road.

"Looks like an official automobile to me," Trevor said.

"And there are two official-looking officials," Katie said.

Two men were standing beside the car, and even from a distance you could see they were plainclothes cops. It's not the look so much as the way they move, slow and easy, as if they get paid by the hour.

Katie pulled up behind their brown-wrapper sedan and we got out.

The moonlight made the men shadows, and one stepped forward. "Is that you, Agent Donovan?"

"*Mister* Donovan, and you must be Detective Weller."

Weller nodded and introduced his partner, Detective Snead. Snead raised a finger to his brow, but hung back.

"I've read your books," Weller said, "especially *Violent Crime Identification and Investigation*. It's been very helpful."

"I sleep with it under my pillow," Snead said. If he'd been a dog, he'd have snarled. I have that effect on local law; they either love me or hate me, depending on their own confidence, usually.

I introduced Katie and Trevor. We shook hands all around.

"I put together packages for each of you," Weller said, and handed us files. "Inside are photos, initial reports, everything we know about the victim and the man we suspect is responsible for this."

"Thank you, this is really conscientious work, Detective Weller," I said. "But for now, don't tell me anything. I like to see things for myself, okay?"

Weller shrugged. "Suits me."

Even in the dark, I could see the rumple and slump of a cop near the end of a long day. Weller's tie was loosened and his face sagged like a bed with broken springs. But his partner had an edge to him that practically threw off sparks.

"Let's get this over with," Snead said.

We followed the two through the trees, our footsteps cushioned by a blanket of pine needles.

"Things up in D.C. must be in a hell of a stew," Weller said, "what with that attack on the First Lady."

"It's got everyone's attention," I said.

"Except yours," Snead said. "I hear the AG personally pulled your ass off the case."

"You heard right." The admission caught Snead off-balance. Honesty will do that sometimes.

"Wait here a minute." Weller moved down the slope and into the darkness of the woods. A moment later we heard a starter crank, a diesel cough and catch, and then the scene was bathed in light. Below us, an asphalt jogging path ran through the woods. The crime scene itself was in a shallow depression.

As many hours as I've spent around crime scene tape, when it's wrapped around trees, I can't shake the feel of cheap party streamers. The single stand of halogens threw the jogging path into high contrast of bright light and deep shadows.

"We've swept the area," Weller said. "Everything's back at the lab."

Snead shrugged, his hands in his pockets, as if to say that there wasn't anything to see here, but if we wanted to waste our time, he would oblige.

"You can see where they found him." Weller pointed to tape marking out the rough outline of a prone body. "We did that for your benefit," he said, referring to the outline. "Otherwise we wouldn't bother."

"I appreciate it." I knelt by the outline and aimed my flashlight beam. "Has it rained today?"

"No," Weller said.

"Not much blood. What else have you got?"

"One footprint." He stared at the outline with me. "Two shell casings."

"You pick up prints from the casings?"

"No. Clean. He must have wiped them."

"So, the shooter was careful," Katie said. "Except here." She stood over the footprint, marked clearly by the white residue of the plaster cast.

As usual, Katie and I were thinking on the same frequency. The smart criminals, the real professionals who have learned from their mistakes, don't usually give us something so obvious as a shoe print. It didn't fit.

I could see Trevor's flashlight farther down the path. He was looking through the trees toward the building a few hundred feet away. "That where he worked?"

Snead said it was.

I straightened up and Weller straightened with me. "Okay, now tell me what you think happened."

"Callahan killed him and dumped him here," Snead said.

"But we don't know that," Weller said.

"Bullshit, Frank." Snead stepped into the light. His hands were out of his pockets and he counted the evidence off on his fingers. "One, people saw Callahan's car parked up there last night."

"Callahan's the husband," Weller said.

"Two, we found the shoe that matches that print

in Callahan's closet. Three, the casings are nine-millimeter Kurz, not exactly your standard caliber."

"Makarov," Trevor said. He'd come back up the trail and was standing behind Snead.

Snead turned, startled. "Yeah, a Makarov."

"What's that?" I looked up from my notepad.

Snead stared, openmouthed.

Trevor laughed. "Jake isn't up on his esoteric firearms. That's why he's got me. It's a Russian pistol, Jake, KGB tested and approved. Fires a nine-millimeter round slightly shorter than standard."

"Kurz," I said.

"Right. German for 'short.'" Trevor turned to Snead. "Go on. The man's up to speed now."

Snead hesitated, then said, "I just can't believe the great Jake Donovan's never heard of a Makarov."

"He still carries a .38," Katie said.

"Get out."

"Show him, Jake."

I lifted the cuff of my pants so Snead could see the Airweight in its ankle holster. "It's not the caliber of the bullet that counts—"

"—it's the caliber of the man," Trevor and Katie said together.

I ignored them. "So how does this KGB gun play out?"

"It's the law in Durham County to register your handgun," Weller said.

"Although nobody ever does," Snead said.

"It's not exactly a great system," Weller said.

"Papers in a shoebox," Snead said.

"Yeah, practically." Weller shrugged.

"Took us all day to find it," Snead said, "but there it was, a Makarov, made in East Germany when there was an East Germany, and it was registered to Callahan. So, combined with the gun, the car, the shoe, and the fact that Callahan and his wife are both missing, I think you can present this to the congressman as a closed case."

"And, with the pictures, we've got motive," Weller said.

"Pictures?"

Weller sighed and ran his hand over his face. "Yeah, in the victim's computer. Pictures of him and Mrs. Callahan."

For the first time, Snead smiled, revealing small, pointed teeth in a possum grin. "Pictures of them doing the nasty in a number of interesting ways. I'll tell ya, pictures like that would make any husband crazy."

"Jake, could you come here?" It was Katie, outside the roped-off crime scene. I could see her flashlight farther up the slope toward the road.

"Could you excuse me for a moment?" I walked up the rise, following my light, being careful where I stepped. "What have you got?"

"This." Katie's light followed a short pair of furrows, about nine inches apart, through the pine straw. "The pine needles look different here, as if they've been disturbed. Smoothed over, maybe."

"We saw that, too," Weller hollered up to us. "We figure that's where the killer dragged the body down the hill."

"Motive, opportunity, weapon, and witnesses."

Snead smacked at a mosquito on his neck. "I say we're wasting our time out here when we should be looking for the husband."

Katie and I walked back down to the jogging path. "I agree with your partner," I said to Weller. "I think we look at the husband."

Weller worked his jaw muscles a bit and said, "Well, that's what we thought, but the congressman sent in an official request . . ."

"The congressman," Snead interrupted his partner. "That's the only reason Donovan's here. Look, he even travels with his own camera crew."

Above us, a van pulled in behind our rental car. The side door slid open and a cameraman climbed out, followed by the soundman, earphones clamped to his head. Another man got out from the driver's side and waved.

"Damn." I looked at Weller. "This didn't come from us."

Weller nodded, too tired to suspect anything different. "I believe you."

"Excuse me, Agent Donovan?"

It was Spider Urich, a reporter with a hundred-dollar haircut and a million-dollar smile. He was making his way down the slope, slipping on his Italian soles.

Snead cut him off. "This is a crime scene, dickhead, you can't come down here."

"Agent Donovan? Can we have a word?" Behind him, the cameraman had me in his lens, and the soundman aimed his boom mike at my face.

I looked at Weller. "I'm sorry, they follow me like

toilet paper stuck to my shoe." I looked back at Spider and shouted up, "Give us a minute. Okay? But you have to wait by the van."

I knew what Spider was thinking, and that was how waiting by the van might affect his screen time. When he decided it probably wouldn't affect it at all, he said, "Okay." He backed up the slope toward the cars, but the cameraman continued to roll.

"Katie? Go charm Spider for me, okay?"

"Right, Jake."

"And, Katie? If Spider gives you a hard time . . ."

"I'll give him a colonoscopy with the camera."

"The woman can read minds," I told Weller.

As Katie talked to Spider in the glare of the camera lights, Weller and I conferred on the path. "These people could be useful," I said. "He's done favors for me before."

"You mean in getting the husband to turn himself in?"

"Maybe. Or just getting the guy's face on the air and hope a good citizen turns him in. But right now, let Katie feed him a few lines of doodah. She's very good at it."

Weller smiled. "I know I'd watch her."

"She's not hard to look at, is she?"

"No. No, she isn't." Weller turned back to the jogging trail. "So, what do you think?" He nodded at the victim's outline.

I turned my back to the camera, just in case the cameraman wanted to shoot some B-roll to back up Katie's talking head. "It's too early to tell. I want to hear from the ME and forensics and talk to some of the people they worked with. But right now, the husband looks real good for this."

"You think he looks a little too good," Weller said.

"That's what I think."

Snead stepped out from the shadows and joined us. "Come on, Donovan, everything points to the husband."

Weller said, "Except for the shell casings."

"Right," I said. "They probably came from Callahan's gun. But look around here. The shoe print, from a shoe that's put back in the closet where you can find it."

"The car by the road," Weller said.

"It's all pretty sloppy," I said.

Trevor wandered back into our circle. "It's too much like TV," he said. "Only thing he didn't leave behind was his wallet."

"Or a matchbook from a local cocktail lounge," Weller said.

"But he thought enough to wipe his prints from the shell casings," I said. "Inconsistent behavior, don't you think?"

"Everybody makes mistakes. The guy's not a pro."

"And the victim was killed somewhere else and then moved. I want to know where and why."

"But he was shot here," Snead said. "We have the brass."

"The guy might have been shot here, but he wasn't killed here. There's not enough blood. So if he was killed somewhere else, why shoot him again here?"

"You think it was staged?" Weller asked.

"Yeah, and badly."

Snead scratched his head. "So, you think it was someone else?"

I laughed. "No. I think we look real hard at the husband. But this other stuff bothers me. Now, let's get up there before Katie shoots the reporter and we have another crime scene on our hands."

6

Unlike in our days with the FBI, Mrs. De Vries's budget allowed us to put up at a good hotel, one with a comfortable bar and a bartender who poured by feel. Trevor and I settled in for a postmortem of the day, but Katie begged off, saying she was tired. Jerry was in his room and Dominic was still at the morgue.

A woman with teased hair sipped at a cosmopolitan, and a man with no hair gulped Amstels. The TV was on CNN coverage of the plane explosion. They'd even come up with a swell graphic, a Hawker 700 split in half by an orange ball of flame. They were calling the story "Assault on the First Family."

Most of the details were the same as we'd heard before except that they'd identified the explosive.

"Semtex," Trevor said.

The announcer said, "The explosive is believed to have been Semtex, a plastic explosive detonated by a timer."

I looked at Trevor. "How'd you know that?"

"Look, security's tighter than a duck's asshole at National. They have dogs and machines capable of sniffing out last July's firecracker residue. Now, there's only one explosive I know of that you might be able to sneak past those highly trained sniffers. Semtex."

The bartender was at the register with his back to us. While ringing up the cosmopolitan and the Amstel, he said, "From either Romania or Hungary." He turned and placed the change and receipt in front of the customers.

I looked at Trevor again and he shrugged.

The woman with the cosmopolitan said, "They've been developing an odorless version for the past five or ten years."

Her partner, the man with the Amstel and the bad toupee, leaned in so he could see past his companion and said, "It's similar to C-4 except for the odorless part. All you'd need is a quarter pound of the stuff to take out a small jet like the Hawker."

"Is this something everyone knows but me?"

The bartender refilled my Scotch without taking my money. "They will before the weekend's out. It's been all over the news."

Trevor sipped his gin and tonic.

The mechanic who'd been found shot in his apartment had been working at the airport the night before, the anchorman reported. But so far, there was no conclusive evidence that his murder was connected to the bombing of the congressman's plane.

When the eleven o'clock news came on, I asked the bartender to switch it to Fox. As I expected, the first fifteen minutes were a repeat of what we had just seen on CNN with an interview with the Speaker of the House, who hinted that the opposition party's current budget fight had weakened morale and caused our security to be compromised.

The headlines were followed by a nice one-shot of Katie in the camera's glare, answering Spider Urich's questions. She looked beautiful, even without makeup, and I found myself wanting to get upstairs, shower, and climb into bed next to her. There's nothing quite like the novelty of a hotel room to add a gymnastic edge to Katie's sexual appetite. It was the one good thing about being on the road.

Katie was good at giving the usual diplomatic answers to Spider's questions. The attorney general was a former prosecutor and more than capable of directing the investigation, she said. We were here only to assist local law enforcement in a homicide investigation, she said. There was no truth to the rumor that Jake Donovan and his team were taken off the assassination attempt. Yes, Katie repeated, the attorney general was quite capable.

Spider ended the report with insinuations that "Hollywood Jake Donovan and his misfit investigative team" were in exile, consigned to a backwater murder case instead of the "case of the century" where they belonged. That last bit was a nice touch and dropped in, I knew, only because I'd agreed to meet with Spider after the news, a promise I regretted making, knowing that Katie was stretched out on clean hotel sheets upstairs.

Down at the end of the bar, the cosmopolitan and the Amstel were arguing in whispers. I knew what was coming.

"Say," said the Amstel with the toupee, "wasn't that you? Aren't you Jake Donovan?"

Trevor dropped a twenty on the bar and said, "This is where I call it a night."

Spider showed up just after twelve and bought me a double. I let him carry the tab. I had known Spider for a few years, since breaking the missing-intern case, and he had been helpful on more than a few occasions, and a pain in the ass on many more.

"I've always wondered, is Spider your real name?"

"No. My real name's Leonard."

"Was 'Spider' your agent's idea?"

"My own. My agent doesn't have any ideas. What about you, you have an agent with ideas?"

"I have a guy who represents my books, a lawyer, but that's just so the publishers don't steal the gold from my teeth."

"You must do all right. I've seen that little car you drive."

"Yeah, with the bad starter."

The bartender asked if he could change the channel. We said yes and then pretended to watch more talking heads for a few minutes.

"Will you tell me something?" Spider asked.

"That's why I'm here."

"On the record?"

"That depends." I tossed back a few bar nuts, followed by a sip of smooth single malt.

"Does this investigation have anything to do with the attempt on the First Lady?"

I laughed. "Not at all."

"So, this isn't some sort of clever diversion?"

"Not even a stupid one."

"Then why would the attorney general pull you off the case?"

I watched Spider. After years of sitting across from serial killers, arsonists, kidnappers, and rapists, I can tell when a few words of either threat or praise will pop them open like a steamed clam. "Who said the AG pulled me off the case?"

Spider tilted his head in an ah-shucks shrug. "You hear things."

"You're too good a reporter to believe rumors."

It was Spider's turn to laugh. "Jake, if you want my sources, you'll have to do better than that."

I raised my glass. " 'I looked upon all the works that I had labored to do and behold; all was vanity.' "

"Shakespeare?"

"Ecclesiastes."

The Scotch and the late hour and the lull of easy banter oiled the conversation for the next hour, and we talked about family and kids and the stresses of being on the road. Spider was divorced, no kids. After the divorce he had dated a movie star and had gone to the Oscars and the A-list party that followed.

"The former president dropped by, although he wasn't former at the time," Spider said. "I had interviewed him before, so he knew me. When I introduced him to my date, she shook his hand and one of her breasts popped out. Just popped right out, almost hit him in the eye. The president took one look, smiled, and said, 'It's a pleasure to meet you both.' "

Spider was a natural storyteller and he had me laughing pretty hard, my guard down, when he sprung it on me.

"So, why are you and Katie splitting up?"

I dabbed my eyes with a bar napkin and said, "What?"

"It must be hard working so closely with her."

"What are you talking about?" I blinked, trying to follow Spider's question and wondering what this new agenda was. The Scotch only slowed me down. "Katie's upstairs."

"In her own room."

"Look, Urich, what Katie and I—"

"She's been seeing a lot of her ex. Or didn't you know?"

"Rob? What's Rob got to do with this?"

"You didn't know, did you? I guess even the great Jake Donovan, a man who's practically psychic when it comes to serial killers, can still be blindsided by a woman."

I put my glass down and tried to grasp on to something that would tell me that Spider Urich was wrong, was way off base, but the past couple of weeks Katie had been distant. The thoughts of her coming to bed after I was asleep, and being gone when I woke up, made my face go red, as if Urich could read my mind. That just made me want to punch him, but killing the messenger doesn't solve anything. I've been the messenger too often not to know.

Spider put his hand on my shoulder. "I'm sorry, man, honest."

"Yeah, right. I think maybe it's time for bed." I stood up and stuck my hand in my pocket.

Spider stopped me. "I've got this."

I nodded and left. The elevator upstairs seemed to take forever. When it finally reached my floor, I hurried down to my room, fit the key into the lock, and was surprised to find my light on, the sheets turned down, and the mint still on my pillow. I called out, "Katie?" Nothing but the hum of the room air conditioner answered. Then I saw it. On the TV was a note folded neatly into a tent. My name was on the outside. Inside were words no man should ever have to read: "We need to talk."

7

I wanted to call her room right away, but decided I could wait a few hours to get my heart kicked in.

I turned on the TV and watched the news for a while. The experts were coming out of the woods; all the authors, ex-cops, crime victims, and former colleagues of mine were on the air, and they were all talking, and most of them didn't know any more than I did about the attack on the First Lady.

I wondered why no one had called me. Disgusted with myself, I changed the channel to a cable station that runs comforting sitcoms from the black-and-white days, before news became a twenty-four-hour torrent of talk. During a crisis with the Beav, I fell asleep.

I woke up in the box. I had gone way past the point of recognizing this as a dream. This was real. The smell of plywood and dirt and my fear filled the tiny space. My coffin closed in, squeezing me, smothering me. I couldn't breathe. I kicked. I scrabbled at the wood over my face until my nails splintered and tore away. I hollered for help but the words were trapped inside the box with me, smothered by this homemade tomb. I jerked and twisted and screamed out, blinded by panic.

I jerked upright in the hotel bed, gasping for air. A TV voice of opportunity announced a miracle cure for toenail fungus. I turned on the light, and without really wanting to, I checked my toenails. They were pink and healthy.

I turned off the TV, went to the window, and pulled back the curtain. Eight floors below me was a small plaza with fountains and a reflecting pool. Across the street was an insurance building. On the side of the plaza was an old movie theater, its red neon marquee dancing in the waters. They were showing *Vertigo*.

I read for a little while, until the sky began to gray, then changed into my running clothes.

I might not know much about relationships. But I know how to stalk someone and I waited until Katie came out of the elevator in her shorts and T-shirt. She didn't seem surprised to see me.

"Good morning, Jake."

"Mind if I run with you?"

"Can you keep up?"

"We'll see." We fell into a nice easy rhythm to start. Katie ran down the hill and I was grateful.

"You wanted to tell me something."

"I think we should ease up a little, Jake."

"Uh-huh. You mean jogging, or do you mean us, like as a couple?" The sidewalk began to climb up a gentle slope.

"Us," she said softly.

"Does this have anything to do with Rob?"

She glanced at me, then looked straight ahead. "How'd you know?"

"I didn't. Spider Urich told me."

"The fuck. I wanted to tell you myself, Jake. I'm sorry you had to hear it that way."

We topped the rise and headed downhill again. We jogged past brick warehouses, a gas station, and a breakfast place already filling the neighborhood with the smell of biscuits and home fries.

"When? When were you going to tell me?"

"As soon as I got it figured out myself."

"So, Rob's honey let him go?" It popped out before I could think of how cruel I was being, and how childish.

"Jake. Please."

At the bottom of the hill we turned left and ran along the outfield wall of the old Durham Bulls ballpark. Katie picked up the pace.

"How long has he been back? In the picture, I mean."

"A couple weeks." Katie stopped at the corner, her hands on her hips. She looked at me, wanting to make sure I didn't misunderstand when she said, "He wants us to try again."

I tried not to show how hard I was breathing from just this short run. "And?"

She put her finger to the pulse in my neck. "You're out of shape, Jake."

"That's not what's making my heart beat like that."

"I'm really sorry. You want to walk a bit?"

"No. I can keep up and talk at the same time."

"Okay." Katie took off again, up the hill away from the hotel.

I ran alongside her, my thighs beginning to burn. Mercifully, she did most of the talking.

"Rob called me a few weeks ago and asked if we could get together for coffee."

"So you went."

"Jake, I've known Rob since high school."

I wanted to ask if she was sleeping with him, but knew how disgustingly desperate that would sound, so I kept my mouth shut.

"I loved Rob well enough to marry him, Jake, and no matter what he's done, he's still a big part of my life. You should understand. You and Toni talk all the time."

"That's about the kids."

"It's more than that, and you know it."

I nodded. She was right. We turned uphill and ran without a word for another half mile.

At the crest, Katie said, "When Rob left, I felt like I'd failed somehow."

"It wasn't you who failed. You know that."

"Intellectually I know that, but emotionally I still feel like it was me, like I didn't do everything I could, that I worked too hard, or didn't work hard enough. And you know how I hate to fail. So, if I have a chance at making it right . . ."

"You're going back to him?"

"No, I didn't say that. I just need some time to think." Katie paused, poised to drop the other shoe. "That's why I'm moving back to my place. I'd hoped you would understand, Jake. I'd hoped you would react more as my partner than my lover."

We ran into a threadbare neighborhood of scarred yards and faded homes, their windows caged in wrought iron. It was still early on a Saturday morning, and few people were up, but the few who were awake watched Katie and I jog past as intently as if we were kangaroos suddenly bounding through their weekend. At a corner near a convenience store and a check-cashing place, I stopped and arched my back, trying to suck in as much oxygen as my body was screaming for.

I rolled over Katie's news a few times in my head and realized I had two choices: I could be an asshole and drive her away for good, or I could leave the door open for her to come back. I'm no genius, but I'm smart enough to pick which of those options was in my best interest. "I just wish you had told me earlier."

"I know, and I'm sorry. You okay?"

"Yeah, just let me catch my breath."

"You ready to run back?"

"How about we walk?"

Katie laughed. "Are you kidding? Come on, Jake, it's time to burn." And she was off, running down a weedy street next to a long-abandoned railroad track. I knew she was holding back while I was running pretty much full out, an old rhino lumbering after a young gazelle, the only consolation being that the view from back there was terrific. Katie bounded full stride, her ponytail swinging back and forth, her glutes high and tight, the backs of her thighs flexing, her calves taut. Katie was a heart-breaking natural wonder, even when she was running away.

I made it back to the hotel in time to shower and make the team's usual on-the-road meeting over breakfast. Trevor was in his standard black fatigue pants and black pullover. I was surprised he didn't rappel into the room.

Dom was dressed in a gray Armani, red tie, and blue shirt. When he reached for the Sweet'n Low, his cuff links caught the morning light.

"Sorry we're late," I said. "Katie and I did a little PT this morning."

Dominic blanched. "Jake, why do you think it's appropriate to parade your personal life in public?"

Katie glared at him. "Dom, we went running."

We didn't tell the team about our conversation, or our breakup. They would know soon enough and I was sure that Trevor, at least, suspected there was trouble in paradise.

Jerry joined us, his hair wild as if it were growing toward the light. He sat and studied the menu with the same intensity he studied trace evidence.

A family of four took the table next to us. The kids squabbled over the menus while Mom tried to quiet them. Dad, meanwhile, was trying not to stare at us. At first he seemed fixated on Katie, a natural thing, and then he stared at me.

After ordering breakfast we listened as Dom and Jerry told us what they had found the night before. Dom was as fastidious in his notes as in his dress. As a counter to Dom, to keep the universe in balance, Jerry dressed in sweats and scribbled his notes on a legal pad. As Dom turned on his laptop, Jerry pulled pages from his pocket and smoothed them out on the tablecloth.

"The victim was a white male, age thirty-four, five-eight, one hundred ninety pounds," Dom said. "The body was in advanced rigor when discovered. No maggots had hatched as yet . . ."

The kids at the next table stopped arguing. Mom gasped and sat staring, as white as the tablecloth. Dad caught my eye and smiled apologetically.

"Speaking of maggots," Jerry said, "the supervisor of the crime team, Dr. Plessy, wrote a terrific monograph on using maggots in toxicology."

"That was a brilliantly researched and written piece," Dom said, not one to hand out compliments easily.

"I've read about that," I said. "The maggots will ingest any drugs in the body."

"Especially barbiturates," Jerry said. "So by analyzing the maggots, you can see if there were any barbiturates in the victim's system."

"You are what you eat," Trevor said.

"I saw the supervisor," Dom said, raising his eyebrows. "She's very attractive."

Jerry blushed. "Oh, really, I hadn't noticed. We were too busy analyzing maggots."

"Analyzing maggots," Katie said. "Is that what you lab types call it?"

"Oh, baby, show me your maggot," Trevor said, his voice thick with Barry White innuendo.

"Just ignore them, Jerry," I said.

"We're sorry, Jerry," Dom said.

"Yes," Katie said. "We're all happy that you've found someone who shows an interest in your maggot."

That was it. The table lost it, all but Jerry, who blushed all the way to his hairline. When we recovered, I encouraged Dom to continue.

Dom dabbed at his eyes with his napkin and said, "Body temperature was eighty-nine point three." Dom looked up from his screen. "But it was a warm night so . . ." He shrugged and went back to his notes. "I'd guess he'd been killed six to eight hours previous, between midnight and two A.M."

At the table next door, Mom was whispering to her husband. The little boy said, "Murdered?"

The waitress and a busboy brought our plates. Without waiting, the team tucked into bowls of fresh fruit, hash browns, eggs, grits, bacon, sausage, toast, juice, and more coffee. For this team, there was always more coffee.

"The lack of blood at the scene made us think the body had been moved," Katie said.

Dom said, "Yes, Katie, no question. Lividity tells us that the man was reclining for several hours after death. We found shards of porcelain in the exit wound, which suggests a tub rather than a chaise lounge or sofa. That, and there were no fabric impressions in the skin."

"Yet he was found lying facedown on the jogging trail," Katie said.

"What was the cause of death?"

Dom said, "The medical examiner states cause of death as cardiac obliteration."

Trevor looked up from his eggs. "You're kidding."

"No, I'm not. Apparently he was killed by a point-blank shot to the chest. The velocity and expansion of the bullet hammered the victim's heart into hamburger."

"Is that a technical term?" Katie asked, shoveling in a forkful of melon.

"It is in Detroit," Dom said. "Now, according to the detectives, they found two nine-millimeter Kurz casings on the jogging trail. In my opinion, that caliber could not have inflicted this chest wound. My best guess is it was a .357 Magnum, although we can't be sure without the bullet."

"What about the head shot?"

"There were two. Both hours after the man was dead, possibly after the body had been moved."

"You think he was killed somewhere else and then moved to the trail and shot again?"

"That's what it looks like, Jake. Weird, huh?"

"Anything else?"

"We found semen on the end of his penis. We assume it was his but the ME is doing a DNA check, just to be sure."

At our neighboring table, Mom stood up and

pulled the kids up by their hands. I heard her whisper to Dad, "You stay if you want, we're eating in the room."

The kids stopped struggling and in unison shouted, "Yay! Room service!"

Jerry, oblivious to the commotion behind him, shuffled through his pages. "His clothing was brand-new, never been worn. The fabric still contained a large amount of formaldehyde"—he glanced up—"which, as you know, manufacturers use to make cotton wrinkle-resistant.

"There were pine needles and dirt from the trail on the front of his jogging suit, but the back was relatively clean, except for the blood. There were no bullet holes, front or back. This indicates that the victim was either naked when killed or was dressed in other clothes, stripped, then dressed in the jogging suit. Gina did find some fibers . . ."

"Gina?" said Katie.

"Dr. Plessy," Jerry said, blushing again. "Dr. Plessy is looking at the fibers, and some hair we found on the clothing, but that's it."

"His hair or someone else's?"

Jerry looked through his notes again. "We think it's dog hair."

"Huh. Dog hair. Do we know what breed?"

"Not yet, but a guy from the NC State veterinary school is taking a look today."

"Oh, and there was also semen found in the underwear, which would match with Dom's findings. Gina, uh, Dr. Plessy, is doing a DNA match."

"So the guy got his flagpole waxed and his

heart shattered, all in the same night," Katie said.

"It happens to the best of us," Trevor said.

"Don't forget head shots," Dom said. "Even though he was already dead, the two shots inflicted significant trauma."

"Brains for breakfast," Trevor said.

All alone at the table next door, Dad tried not to look too closely at his scrambled eggs. When his imagination got the better of him, he pushed away from the table and started moving toward the elevators, but not before he stopped and said, "Mr. Donovan, I'm a big fan. I've read all your books."

"Thank you," I said. "I'm sorry we drove your family away. We tend to forget that our shoptalk isn't exactly suitable for families."

Dad patted the air with his hands. "No, no, it's okay. I think it's fascinating what you guys do." He smiled an apology. "But my wife doesn't share my appreciation for law enforcement."

"Neither does mine," I said.

For an awkward moment Dad stood there, clearing his throat, looking for more to say and coming up blank, while I waited for him to either say something else or leave, and Dad shifted from foot to foot and finally said, "I guess I better catch up to them."

"Okay, sure."

"It was a pleasure. I'm sorry to interrupt."

"Not a problem."

Dad eased away, and I asked, "Anything else?"

"The shoes were brand-new," Jerry said. "So were his jogging suit, socks, and underwear."

Dom said, "If this guy jogged, it was only to the refrigerator and back. He was a heavy smoker plus his liver indicated daily alcohol abuse."

"Abuse or use?"

"Jake, more than one a day is abuse."

"Remind me to buy a bigger glass," I said.

Dom raised an eyebrow, then looked back at his computer screen. "The only other thing of interest I found was this. Mixed in with the blood were traces of a gritty powder all along the victim's back, his buttocks, thighs, calves, and the soles of his feet. We sent it over to Jerry for a look-see."

Jerry shuffled through more paper. "Here it is: calcium carbonate, sodium carbonate, fragrance, and sodium dichlorotriazinetrione dyhydrate."

"What the hell's that?"

"Cleanser. We haven't narrowed it down to brand, but we're working on it."

Dom said, "So he was lying in a tub, and one that had just been cleaned, but not completely rinsed. That's my guess."

"Someone in a hurry," Trevor said.

Katie nodded. "Maybe a housekeeper or a maid?"

I shook my head. "That's a leap. It could just as easily be a bachelor, like our victim, or a busy mother."

"Bachelors never bother," Katie said. "Have you ever seen a single man's bathtub? You'd get more fungus than cleanser."

Jerry blushed and Dom bristled. "Young lady, that is a sexist stereotype." He gave Katie a slight bow.

"Anything else?"

Jerry smiled, a rare event, meaning he'd found something he knew we'd find interesting. "The shoe. The suspect's shoe. The one he was supposed to have worn when he made this track."

I pulled my file and found the photos of the print and the casting. "This one?"

"Yes."

"You say 'supposed to have worn.' The shoe doesn't match?"

Jerry nodded his head. "Oh, yeah, Jake, they match. If you look at the soles you'll see twelve identifying accidental characteristics, like this cut here and here." Jerry pointed a forkful of grits at matching points on the photos. "And this anomaly in the tread."

"So the killer was wearing this shoe, is that right?"

Jerry shoveled the grits into his mouth. "No, Jake, he wasn't." We waited while Jerry swallowed. "Someone might have been wearing this shoe at the murder scene, but it wasn't our suspect."

"Why not?" Trevor asked.

"The police are looking for the husband, right? The guy this shoe belongs to. And by all accounts he's a big guy, six-five, two-forty, wears a size fourteen."

"You know what they say, Katie."

"No, Trevor, what do they say?"

"Big feet—"

"Big shoes," I said. "Go on, Jerry."

"Thank you, Jake. So the guy's got big feet, and he's heavy. Now, I want you to look at this cast." Jerry pointed a slice of bacon at the impression taken from the trail. "Gina and I went out there last night and did some soil tests."

"Moonlight on the murder scene," Katie said.

"Very romantic," Trevor said.

Jerry ignored them. "Now, we could be wrong here, but we don't think a two-hundred-forty-pound man made this print. We're guessing the person who made this print wasn't wearing this shoe at all. We think he pressed it into the soil with his hand. The weight isn't anywhere close to two-forty, and the distribution is too even. You know how when a person walks, the main weight is in the heel, then the ball of the foot. Well, there's no flex in this impression."

"Man," Trevor said, "someone wanted the husband to take the heat for this real bad."

"It's more than that. It's like the killer's playing games with us," Katie said.

I took the check from the waitress and signed my name and room number. The team waited. When the waitress was gone, I handed out assignments. "Trevor, you go talk to the victim's colleagues, shake the tree a bit, and see what falls out."

"Okay."

A cell phone rang and we all reached for our belts. It was mine. "Donovan."

"Weller here."

"You're up early."

"I investigate homicides. And it's the only exercise I get since my wife left and the dog died. I got something you might want to see."

"What's that?"

"Place I think our tech boy was murdered. Interested?"

8

The motel was located north of town just off the interstate. It wasn't the cheapest place a man could spend his last night, but it was a world away from the Four Seasons. A windowed lobby of plastic furniture and dusty ficus separated the rooms from the parking lot so that anyone entering a guest room had to first walk past the lobby.

On the second-floor walkway, people in summer clothes crowded around one room's door, trying to see past a uniformed officer who did his best to keep them back. If the lobby had had postcards of the murder scene, they would have sold out.

Katie, Jerry, and I got out of the rental. I was relieved to have Jerry in the car with us, because I didn't know what I could say to Katie. Few humans are more pathetic than a man trying to navigate his broken emotions.

Weller and Snead met us in the parking lot. Two TV crews had set up, and when they saw us, they shouted questions.

"Is this a federal case?"

"Is this connected to the assassination attempt?"

Once we were past the reporters, I asked, "Who found it?"

"Chambermaid," Weller said. "We're waiting for one of our bilingual officers to question her."

"You'd think they'd learn the fucking language," Snead said.

Katie cut her eyes at Snead in a way that would have shamed an ordinary man, but Snead was not an ordinary man.

"We get a lot of Mexicans," Weller said. "They come up here for the good life." He put his hands in his pockets and looked over the motel. "If this is the good life, I'd hate to see how they live back home."

"I can talk to her, if you don't mind," Katie said.

Weller shrugged, "Fine. Snead, go with her. She's in the lobby."

On the second floor I let Weller clear a path through the walkway gawkers. As Jerry and I pulled on latex gloves, I heard a man whisper, "That's Jake Donovan, the profiler guy." His wife, a large woman in an Elvis T-shirt, whispered, "Who?"

The room was dark except for the pool of light from the bedside lamp. The heavy curtains were drawn against the sun and to block out the curious. Two crime scene techs were working the room while a supervisor, a pale woman with short, orange hair and small, black-framed glasses, took notes.

I introduced myself and said, "You must be Dr. Plessy. Jerry here has been very impressed with your work."

Jerry blushed and shuffled.

Dr. Plessy didn't shake hands, but her coloring changed, too. "It's an honor to work with Dr. Carruthers," she said, giving Jerry the bright lights, "his thinking is so"—she crinkled her nose, looking for the right adjective—"unorthodox."

"Yes, it is." I nodded toward the bed. "Was it slept in?"

Plessy pulled her gaze away from Jerry. "Uh, it's hard to tell. Semen showed up under the UV, so there was something going on, but I wouldn't call it sleep-related."

"Could it have been solitary?"

"You mean was our Jedi knight polishing his light saber? I doubt it." She looked at her notes. "We've found two sets of pubic hair—one blond, probably bleached, and one brown."

"Bleached pubic hair?"

"Some women like to have the carpet match the curtains. So unless our guy's gone two-tone, I'll bet we get epithelials mixed in with the semen." Epithelial cells are shed by a woman during sex. Finding these cells in the semen would mean that our man hadn't spent his last night alone.

The covers on one of the double beds were pulled back. One of the crime scene techs carefully slipped the sheets into separate paper bags.

"We've got great prints," Plessy said. "A thumb-print on the bed frame. A full set on a glass." She held up a tumbler in a plastic bag.

"We used to have a set of those exact glasses," I said.

"I think the manufacturer limited the run to a few zillion," Plessy said.

"Jerry told me you were good. He didn't tell me you had a sense of humor."

She smiled. "It's a vital part of our tool kit, Mr. Donovan. I don't think we'd survive without it. As for being good, my people can spot the hair on a gnat's behind from across the room."

"Speaking of hair, have you figured out what kind of dog our boy was playing with?"

"John thinks it's a Maltese."

"We have a Maltese." I laughed. "My glass and my dog, maybe I did this."

Plessy straightened from the nick she'd been examining on the credenza and said, "You have your dog with you, Mr. Donovan, we can check his fur against the fur we found, just to rule you out as a suspect."

"My ex-wife got custody."

"Too bad. My ex-boyfriend got the dog in our breakup, the incontinent son of a bitch."

"I hope you're talking about the dog."

"Hope all you want," she said. "You ready to take a look in here?"

From the bathroom came the flash and whir of a photographer snapping pictures. "That the main event?"

Dr. Plessy nodded. "Oh, yeah."

"Lead the way."

We went back to the bathroom. The photographer was taking pictures of the tub. At one end, opposite the faucet, the porcelain was shattered. Inside, the bottom of the tub was a dark mass of congealed blood, almost black.

"This is why there was no blood on the trail," I said.

The rings on the shower rod were bare. "Looks like they used the curtain to wrap the body," Weller said, "and mopped the floor with a towel."

"We'll get in here next," Plessy said, "after the photographer's finished."

"Ready to see some movies, Jake?"

"You've got tape on this?"

"This place has been held up so many times the management installed a surveillance camera. A woman rented this room, Jake. The name on the registration is Janice Callahan."

"The secretary?"

"Yeah. Looks like she rented the room for a little after-school action with the boss, the husband catches them engaged in water sports, and bango, there you go."

"But the tub was dry," I said.

Weller nodded. "So my euphemism isn't quite accurate."

"Can I see the tape?"

"Sure. Let's go down to the lobby."

We left Jerry to follow Dr. Plessy around the crime scene, puppylike, and made our way back through the gawkers and gauntlet of reporters.

"What about yesterday morning? If the victim was killed Thursday night and dumped on the trail early Friday morning, wouldn't the maid have cleaned up the room yesterday?"

"Let's find out," Weller said.

Katie was speaking to a Latina whose face was wet with tears. Standing behind her with his arms crossed was a pinched little man in a polyester tie and a vest, the motel's logo embroidered over his tiny heart. Katie introduced me and said, "Mariposa went in to clean this morning and found the blood in the tub. Mr. Mook here is the night manager."

"Did she take her cart into the room?"

Katie asked the maid and she nodded yes.

I took a deep breath and let it out slowly. I didn't like anything coming into the crime scene, but once in, I wanted it to stay there.

Katie picked up on it. She gave the night manager a hard look and said, "Mariposa told me she was afraid to leave the cart, afraid someone might steal her supplies."

"Her supplies?"

Mook wouldn't look anyone in the eye.

"Apparently," Katie said, "Mook here sells the supplies to the maids."

Mook started to sweat.

"I hope you've skimmed enough to hire a lawyer," I said, my voice flat. I was trying to hold in my disgust. In my career, I've spent more time with criminals than, in retrospect, anyone should, and

Mook here was cut from the same predatory cloth as most of them, different only in degree.

"I didn't do anything illegal," Mook said.

"And I'm sure you declared that income on your ten-forty."

Mook tried to divert this line of questioning by appealing to Weller: "I need to clean that room."

Weller shook his head. "It'll be a while. We have to take the tub and a section of the wall."

"What?"

"It's going to be a few days, at best, until the crime scene people are through with it."

"But we need the room. We're booked full."

I looked out the window at people packing their cars. "You'll have plenty of rooms in a minute, Mr. Mook. Murder tends to create vacancies, in more ways than one."

Mook looked as if he'd found a bug in his arugula. "Corporate's not going to like this. This isn't good. This isn't good at all."

I sat down next to the chambermaid and, through Katie, asked if she was all right, if she needed anything. She shook her head no.

Katie said, "She's pretty shaken up. She says she wants to leave."

"We'll let you go home soon," Weller hollered.

"She's not deaf," Katie said.

"*Lo siento,*" he hollered. To Katie he said, "Tell her she can go home soon, okay?"

Katie translated and Mariposa said, hope in her eyes, "*A México?*"

"No," Katie said, "*a su casa aquí.*"

Mariposa sobbed in disappointment.

"Did you see anyone in that room?" I asked, and Katie translated. Mariposa shook her head no. "What about yesterday morning, when you went to clean the room?"

Mariposa, in between sobs that convulsed her body, told us that a note was on the door.

"What was in the note?"

She looked at the night manager before answering, *"Dinero."* In English she said, "One hundred dollars."

"And the note, do you still have the note?"

"Sí, yes." Mariposa pulled an envelope from her apron pocket.

Still wearing gloves, I carefully opened the note and slid it into a plastic evidence bag.

The note was written in Spanish and Katie translated, "Please do not disturb as my wife is very ill. You may clean up the room tomorrow."

"And you never saw who wrote this?"

Mariposa shook her head no.

"Give that to Dr. Plessy and see if she can raise some prints," I told Katie.

Beyond the lobby desk was a nineteen-inch TV on a rolling cart. Balanced on top of the set was a VCR.

I asked Weller, "The surveillance tape in?"

Weller nodded, picked up the remote, and soon the screen was filled with the grainy black-and-white image of a woman in a large hat and dark glasses filling out the registration.

"Is that her?"

"Callahan?" Weller said. "Can't be sure, not with this, but if it's not her, it's her sister. Who else would it be?"

"Have you checked her signature?"

"We got a copy from the DMV. They matched."

"This doesn't look good." I was trying to figure out a way to break the news to Mrs. De Vries when I spotted something on the screen. "Pause that."

Weller hit the button and the picture froze, jittering on a single frame. "You want me to back up?"

"No, no. Look at this."

Weller knelt next to me. "What? What am I looking at?"

"The paper on the desk. Look at the paper."

"It's too blurry." Weller fished out a pair of reading glasses, perched them on his nose, and got so close to the screen that his breath fogged the glass. "It's a *USA Today.*"

"Mook? You hand out *USA Today?*"

He straightened, proud of the corporate largesse he was allowed to dispense. "It's complimentary with the room."

"But you have a stack on the desk here?"

"Yes, but not today, *USA Today* doesn't print on Saturday."

"That's okay. Do you have Thursday's paper?"

Mook looked confused. "No, I'm sure I threw it away."

Mariposa looked up from her hands and said, *"USA Today?"*

"Sí, tiene usted USA Today?"

Mariposa went to her cleaning cart, into the plastic

trash bag suspended on the handle, and withdrew a paper, stained with coffee. She handed it across the desk to Weller.

"It's from Thursday," Weller said. We looked at the front page of our paper and the front page of the paper on-screen. It was impossible to read the headlines, but we could see the layout, and they weren't the same.

"But if that's Thursday's paper, and that was taped Thursday evening, either someone is reading old news," Katie said, "or this videotape has been switched."

Weller looked at me with a big smile. "God, Donovan, she's not only great looking, she's smart, too."

Katie narrowed her eyes. "Are all men pigs, Weller, or is it just men in law enforcement?"

My cell phone rang. "Jake? It's Trevor."

"You at the tech lab?"

"They stopped me at the security gate."

"Show them your badge."

"I did. We've been locked out, Jake, all of us, due to national security."

"Great."

"It just gets better, Jake. The local FBI office has confiscated all the files."

"What about the employees?"

I heard the rustle and shift as Trevor shouldered the phone and checked his notes. "I got a list of employees from the guard at the gate."

"Good work."

"She thought I was cute," Trevor said.

"We all think you're cute. Have you talked to anyone?"

"The first place I went was the receptionist's, because they know all the dirt. Guess who beat me there?"

"The FBI."

"I got to admit you're good, Jake. A damn psychic."

I ignored the sarcasm.

"They've told all the employees not to talk to us."

"Any other news?"

"Yeah, Jake. I think I found a little birdie up a tree."

"Huh?"

"Call me from a pay phone, Jake." He gave me a number.

9

"Why the cloak-and-dagger?"

"I just have this feeling, you know?"

I've learned to respect Trevor's gut. It's saved me twice. Once, when a man we thought was dead turned out to be very much alive, and once when Trevor talked me out of a car that had been wired with explosives.

When Trevor answered, I heard the thump of dance music in the background. "Where the hell are you?"

"A place in Raleigh." I heard a smile creep into Trevor's voice. "You'll like this, Jake."

"What have you got?"

"I've got Bob Shumfeld, the dead man's partner, that's what I've got. I went to his house, staked it out, and then I followed him, not having anything else to do."

"Okay, so where are you?"

"It's called the Honey Tree."

"Sounds like a strip club."

"How would you know what a strip club sounds like?"

"That's classified." Half an hour later I pulled into the parking lot under a sign that announced a free lunch buffet. The lot was jammed with cars, including Bob Shumfeld's Porsche 911.

Trevor was just inside the door. The beat of the dance music spilled into the lobby, and I had to holler into Trevor's ear for him to hear me. "I figured you'd be inside, dollar bills in your teeth."

"My mama told me that if I ever went into a place like this, I'd see something I shouldn't see. So I went the first chance I got and damn if she wasn't right."

"Yeah? What did you see?"

"My father."

We paid the membership fee, twenty bucks each for the free buffet, and walked into the main room. On one wall was a long bar and steam table. In the center of the room, ringed in tiny lights and dazed men clutching bills, was the stage. A girl, naked except for a sequined G-string, hung upside down in the center of the stage, her legs wrapped around a brass pole. Along the left wall, opposite the bar, were tables.

Trevor pointed out our man. He was small, maybe five-seven, carrying thirty pounds of extra weight and sporting a blond mustache that curled up at the ends. He was shoveling in prime rib as a girl who should have been in school danced between his legs, her breasts swaying just inches from his face. The little man's eyes glittered.

I shouted into Trevor's ear, "When I was working out of the Detroit office, the guys used to cross the river into Canada where the women dance naked. They called it the Windsor Ballet."

Trevor laughed. "But you didn't go."

"I was new to the Bureau, and just married. I don't know who I was more afraid of finding out, Hoover or my wife."

"Well, here you are, Jake, this is what you missed. Nice, huh?"

I grimaced. "It's not the same when you have a daughter. Not the same at all."

We waited until the song ended and the girl left fifty bucks richer. Trevor sat on one side of Shumfeld and I sat on the other. Trevor flashed his federal agent ID and said, "We'd like to talk to you."

Shumfeld looked from Trevor to me, bored. "Can't a guy eat his lunch in peace?"

Another girl approached the table. "Hi, Bob."

"Hi, Mary," Shumfeld said. "Gentlemen, this is by far the finest young lady in the entire South. I get wood just saying her name. Mary, these men here are federal agents."

Mary wiggled, giggled, and said, "Like *CSI?*"

"No, like FBI," Trevor said. "Real cops. Not TV cops."

"How about a table dance? On the house. Nothing but the best for our heroes in blue," Mary said.

"Does your mother know where you work?" Trevor said.

Mary smiled. "You want to meet her?"

Trevor growled and Mary scurried away with a bounce and a rippling finger wave. Trevor stood up, tugging on Shumfeld's arm. "Come on, let's get out of here. She could poke someone's eye out with those things."

"But I'm not done," Shumfeld whined, and grabbed at a plate piled high with cheesecake.

I pulled out a pair of cuffs and let them dangle from my finger. "We can make this real embarrassing, if that's what you want."

"No, no, I'll go. Someone might think I'm into kinky."

"Oh, we wouldn't want that, would we?" Trevor said.

A bouncer the size of Maine came up from the west. "Everything okay here?"

"Yeah, Sammy, everything's fine."

Trevor flipped open his wallet for the third time. "Federal agents, Sammy. We're not arresting anybody, we just want to talk to Bob here. You watch his cheesecake, huh?"

Sammy raised an eyebrow. "You be okay, Mr. Shumfeld? You want me to call someone?"

Shumfeld assured Sammy everything was fine. Trevor and I walked him out into the parking lot, where the sun made us shield our eyes from the glare. The Southern summer air was so thick you could use it for seat covers.

"In the car."

Trevor sat behind Shumfeld and I sat behind the wheel. I cranked the AC and Shumfeld adjusted the vent to blow on his outstretched neck.

"I don't know how much more I can tell you than I told the police."

"When was the last time you saw your partner?" I said.

"Monday night."

"Did you think anything was out of the ordinary?"

Shumfeld thought a moment, then shook his head. "No, nothing."

"How well did you know your partner?"

"Not well. But nobody knew him all that well."

"But you were partners."

"I was the moneyman, that's all. I raised over six point two from VCs."

"Venture capitalists," I said.

"Right."

"What about Ms. Callahan?"

Shumfeld softened. "Everyone loved Janice. She was the sweetest woman I'd ever met. Not to mention cute, like a kitten. The kind you'd like to come home to, you know?"

I noticed he talked about her in the past tense. "But your partner was coming home to her, right?"

Shumfeld snapped back. "Jesus, no way. I mean, they had a great working relationship, but romance, get outta here. My partner was a lot of things, but charming he wasn't. To tell the truth, he didn't take very good care of himself. Brilliant, but not exactly a social animal."

"So why would Mr. Callahan want to kill him?" Trevor said.

Shumfeld looked back, slower this time. "Who knows? Maybe the guy believed those pictures. Christ, he was stupid enough."

"Are you saying those pictures were fakes?"

Shumfeld nodded, as if I were particularly slow. "Yeah, Sherlock, they're fake. Haven't you looked at them?"

"Not closely, no."

"I thought you were a big-shot investigator, Hollywood Jake Donovan, and you couldn't tell those pictures were phony? Jesus."

Trevor leaned forward until his voice was right behind Shumfeld's ear. "I looked at those pictures, and they looked real to me, asshole."

Shumfeld got as far away as the Lincoln's dashboard would let him. "Okay, what about the tattoo?"

"What tattoo?"

"Exactly." Shumfeld smiled and crossed his arms. "No tattoo. That wasn't Jan's body. It was Jan's face, sure, but not her body. Jan had a Carolina Tarheel tattooed on her butt, everyone knew that. It was a big joke in the office because of so many Duke fans, you know?"

"Apparently not everyone knew about the tattoo," I said.

Shumfeld laughed. "And I saw my partner naked in a steam room, once, and trust me, that wasn't his body either. Christ, the guy in the picture was hung like a horse. Made me think of my boyhood back on the farm. And Bill, well, Bill was hung more like a duck."

Trevor stifled a laugh.

"Okay, so they weren't having an affair. Who would benefit from your partner's death?"

Shumfeld snorted. "A lot of people. Competition, foreign governments, anyone who believed in personal hygiene."

"So he had a lot of enemies."

"People didn't like him, Mr. Donovan. He was irritating, you know, like crabs."

"Can you tell us what you're working on?"

"I can't." Shumfeld zipped his lips. "No can do. What I know, which isn't much, is classified. I can tell you that it is a weapon. Space-age, Jetsons stuff. Bill was talking to people in D.C. this week and it looked like we were going to get the green light for a prototype." Shumfeld looked down at his hands, folded together in his lap. "I guess that's all over now."

"What do you mean?"

Shumfeld looked up at me, tears brimming, ready to spill. "Because without Bill, we've got nothing."

"But you must have files, schematics, whatever it is you design with."

Shumfeld clenched his jaw. "We looked everywhere. It's what the FBI is looking for, I'm sure. And believe me, when they don't find Bill's files, I don't want to be there."

"Do you know who he talked to in D.C.?"

"Guy from DARPA."

When I looked puzzled, Trevor said, "The Defense Acquisition Research Project Agency. They're fast-track in weapons systems development."

That fit with what Mrs. De Vries and the congressman had told me. "Do you have this DARPA man's name?"

"Uh, yeah, I think maybe. In my laptop."

Trevor laughed. "You mean Little Miss Teen in there?"

For the first time, Shumfeld seemed to relax. "Ha ha. Right. I get it." He pointed across the lot. "It's right over there, in my car."

We got out of the Lincoln, but before we could move across the lot, three gray sedans pulled in. One stopped in front of us. Two young men in dark suits got out and I could almost smell Quantico Creek on them.

One of the dark suits saluted us, a finger to his brow. "Jake, Trevor, good afternoon. I hope you're enjoying the show." He smiled and glanced up at the Honey Tree sign. "I hear the buffet is excellent."

"Hi, Tim," I said. "How's Margie?"

"Fine, Jake."

"The boys?"

"Tim junior is starting middle school this year. Joseph is in kindergarten."

"They grow up too fast, Tim. Give Margie my best."

"Will do."

The second suit moved in and put a grip on Shumfeld's arm. "We missed you at your house."

Shumfeld looked at me and said, "Merry Christmas, Mr. Donovan."

Four other agents spread out and put us into a nice triangulated kill zone as Shumfeld was stuffed into the back of the first sedan. As quickly as they had come, they were gone, a swift little motorcade hauling away our witness.

"What do we do now?" I said.

"We break into his car and get the laptop," Trevor said.

"Okay. With what?"

Trevor smiled, popped the trunk of the Lincoln, reached into his big black bag, and pulled out a slim jim. "Man's got to be prepared."

10

"That's all he said, 'Merry Christmas, Mr. Donovan'?" Katie was tapping out passwords on Shumfeld's laptop, without success.

"Yeah. In August."

We were back in my hotel room, Trevor and I hunched over Katie's shoulders so close I could smell her shampoo.

"Do you think you guys could give me some air here?"

Trevor and I stepped back.

"Okay," she said. "Let's try, Santa . . . elves . . . stockings . . ."

"Candy cane," Trevor said, "carols . . . holly . . . wreathes . . ."

"Jesus . . . Bethlehem . . . manger," I added. Each time we got INVALID PASSWORD. "I had no idea how much cultural baggage comes with Christmas."

"What if we look at it another way," Katie said. "How about happy holidays . . . season's greetings."

"Feliz Navidad," Trevor said.

"Still nothing." Katie slumped back in her chair. "We could be here until New Year's." She leaned into the keyboard and typed, "Happy New Year." The screen, in response, read INVALID PASSWORD.

I paced from the bathroom to the windows and back. "Wait a minute. Why would a guy named Shumfeld wish me a merry Christmas? Isn't he Jewish?"

Trevor opened his file and found Shumfeld's data. "Yeah. He's Jewish."

"So why would he do that?"

"I'll try Hanukkah." Katie typed it in. Still nothing.

"What about Rosh Hashanah?" Katie and Trevor stared at me. "Jewish New Year. You people need to widen your circle of friends."

"How do you spell that?" Katie asked.

I told her. Katie typed. Nothing.

"Wait a minute. That girl at the club. What was her name?"

Katie looked over her shoulder. "Jake, did you meet a girl at the club? And did she shake her moneymaker?"

"Mary something," Trevor said, ignoring Katie.

"Try Mary Christmas, as in the name Mary."

Katie entered the name, the screen blinked, and up came Mary, the girl at the Honey Tree, dressed in a Santa hat, black boots, and whatever God and a good cosmetic surgeon had conspired to give her.

"Mary Christmas," Katie muttered. "Someone should kick this guy's Christmas ass."

"Nice talk. Can you get his calendar or should we look at Mary a little longer?"

In a few minutes we had Shumfeld's full schedule, including his partner's flights out of town. There were three, all to D.C., all within the past month.

"Get the flight manifests. Find out if Janice Callahan went with him."

Trevor made the call, giving the airline his identification number. "They'll get back to us," he said.

In the meantime, we cruised through Shumfeld's e-mail. There were the usual pornographic sites promising uninhibited farm animals and cheerleaders. Business mail was uninteresting except for one from a man named Ted. In it, there were several mentions of meetings, a restaurant, and reservations for three for the previous Tuesday.

"I know that restaurant," Katie said. "It's in Old Town Alexandria."

"Can we find Ted's full name?"

Katie opened Shumfeld's address book. "Ted Baker. And guess where he works?"

"DARPA," Trevor said.

"DARPA it is."

We called DARPA offices and were told that Ted Baker had been home sick since Wednesday morning. Katie made sympathetic small talk and asked for Ted's home number. With this, we found his address in Alexandria.

"God bless the Internet," Katie said, "the investigator's best friend."

"Not to mention child pornographers'," Trevor said.

"Trevor, Trevor," Katie said, "the glass is always half-empty with you, isn't it?"

I dialed Ted Baker's home number and got his answering machine. His voice sounded young, confident, and all business.

I hung up and Katie said, "By the way, Mrs. De Vries called while you were out. I told her you were at a strip club and would get back to her."

"What did she say?"

"She said she hoped you wouldn't put that on your expense report."

I dialed Mrs. De Vries's number in Cleveland Park. Frederick answered. Mrs. De Vries was out, he told me, but she urgently needed to see me, right away. It was an emergency.

Trevor's phone rang. It was the airline. Janice Callahan and her boss, William Rush, had flown up to Washington on Tuesday morning. Rush had taken the train back on Tuesday.

"That means Janice Callahan is still in Washington," Katie said. "I can start checking hotels."

I paced the room again. "I have to go up to see Mrs. De Vries. I can check on Ted Baker while I'm there, see if he knows where Janice Callahan might be."

"You want us to come with you?"

I rubbed my face, suddenly tired. "No, you two stay and help Jerry and Dom. I'll fly commercial into National and call if I need any help."

"You sure?" Trevor had his "good to go" face on, hard and sharp.

My gut really wanted Katie to fly up with me, but it hurt just being in the same room with her, something I'd have to get past and soon, but I wasn't going to get past it today. "Okay, Trevor, come with me."

Katie pressed her lips together in a thin, hard line, knowing she'd been excluded for all the wrong reasons.

"You stay and help Dom and Jerry. Maybe our husband will turn up."

"Okay, Jake." Katie turned away, so angry that heat waves seemed to radiate from her.

My cell phone rang. "Donovan."

"Jake, this is Jerry. I'm back at the lab."

"Yeah?"

"We ran those prints from the motel and got a match."

"Great."

"Not so great," Jerry said. "They're your prints, Jake. On both the glass and on the bed."

11

As we drove to the airport, Weller said, "I'm going to put it in the report as carelessness at the crime scene."

"You watched me put on gloves," I said.

"Don't tell me that or I might have to turn around."

"I'll be back."

"Good, because my partner wanted to lock you up just for the publicity."

"I appreciate this."

"Hey, it's my turn. Next case, Snead gets to be the good cop."

Security at the airport was tight. Armed National Guardsmen patrolled the terminals as bomb-sniffling dogs snuffled every piece of luggage.

At the counter I booked two seats, first-class, into National.

"They've closed National," the ticket agent said. "I can get you into Dulles. That flight leaves here in three hours, would get you there by eleven-fifteen."

"Fine," I said. "Let's do it."

He typed away at his terminal. "I'm afraid all we have left are in coach."

"Okay."

"Center seat."

"It just gets better and better," Trevor said.

I handed over my credit card. A few minutes later the clerk handed it back, saying, "I'm afraid this card has been refused, sir."

"Try it again," I said. This was the Broken Wings card, backed by Mrs. De Vries's millions; it couldn't be rejected.

"I ran it twice, sir." The ticket agent gave me that deadbeat stare.

Trevor handed him his card. "Use this." Trevor chuckled. "Don't worry, Jake, I'll buy the drinks on the plane, too."

"Gee, thanks, Dad."

We landed at Dulles and caught a cab to Reagan National, where we were stopped by a military roadblock. A young lieutenant took our identification, along with our story, and was gone a long time. After checking us out, he waved us through.

Trevor went into his locker at the hangar and returned with two pistols. He handed one to me.

"Trevor, I don't think we'll need this."

"Tuck it into your belt there, cowboy. I like to know you're strapped when you're on my six."

We climbed into the Aston Martin and I turned the key. Not a single sound disturbed the quiet airport. Trevor handed me the nightstick. I got out, raised the hood, and whacked the starter.

As we pulled out of the hangar, Trevor said, "Why don't you get that thing fixed?"

"What thing?"

It's a short drive from National into Alexandria, particularly on a Saturday night after a terrorist attack. Downtown, the trendy restaurants were open for business, but the wait staffs loitered on the sidewalks, smoking, looking up and down the streets for brave customers.

Old Town Alexandria is as old as the republic and had made the journey from respectable to derelict back to respectable several times over the centuries. The neighborhood close to the Potomac was deep into its respectable phase, and the town homes sported fresh paint in colors approved by the historic restoration board, and golden lights glittered behind ancient panes of glass.

Trevor tried Baker's number on our way and got the answering machine.

We found the address a few blocks from the yacht club and marina, on a street paved with ballast stones and shadowed by oaks as old as our flag. Gas streetlamps gave off lots of nostalgia, but little light. The house was narrow brick, with a small courtyard protected by a wrought-iron gate. A black box was mounted to the wall. I pushed the button and waited. When no one answered, I said, "What now?"

Trevor shrugged. "You want in? I can get us in."

I nodded, happy to see Trevor was thinking along the same lines as I was. "Maybe Ted Baker's sick," I said, "and needs our help."

"That could be. The man could have fallen down the steps and be lying there, waiting for two upstanding citizens to rescue him. And here we stand."

"We could call the police."

"We could," said Trevor. "But who knows how long it will take?"

I nodded, both of us silently agreeing to commit a major felony.

Trevor looked up and down the street and said, "You first, old man."

I stepped into his hands and hoisted myself over the top of the gate and into the courtyard. Trevor scrambled up and over. We waited, watching for lights in neighboring homes.

"You take the back," I said.

Trevor evaporated into the darkness. I went up the steps to the front door. The screen was closed, but the door itself was open. No lights were on inside the house. I called out, "Mr. Baker? Mr. Baker? Federal agents, Mr. Baker, just checking in to see if you're all right." There was no answer. Then I smelled it, lightly at first, just a bad omen on a stale breeze.

I eased into the hallway. The streetlamp threw a dim glow into the living room. Trevor shimmered into view. "The back door was open," he whispered. "There's a car in the garage."

"You smell it?"

Trevor sniffed the air. "Uh-huh. What do you think we should do?"

"Take a look."

"I knew you were going to say that."

Trevor and I took the stairs slowly, each creak sounding as if the floor were falling in. We stopped at the top of the steps. Trevor pulled a handkerchief from his pocket and covered his mouth and nose. He pointed with his pistol toward the front of the house.

The smell here was thick, and the closer we got to the closed door at the far end of the hall, the thicker it got. It clung to our hair and clothes, and filled our mouths and throats. Sweet, but nauseating, with a heavy undertone of human waste and the dusty copper tang of old blood.

I slipped on a pair of latex gloves and carefully opened the door to what was the master bedroom. There were two people, half in shadow on the bed. Both were far beyond our help. From the threshold I whispered to Trevor, "Now we call the police."

12

I spent the rest of the night and on into Sunday morning in an interrogation room. Out of professional courtesy, they brought me lots of bad coffee. They asked me a lot of questions. A young officer asked for my autograph.

By the time they released us, Trevor and I had our own aroma, much like an old ram I'd known back home in Montana. Trevor requested some time to clean up and see his wife. "If I hurry," he said, "I just might make it to church."

I called Mrs. De Vries's number again and Frederick answered. This time she was in.

"Jake, I'm so glad you called."

"I need to see you, Mrs. De Vries."

"Yes, and I you. If you'd like to escort me to church, Jake, I would appreciate the company."

I looked at my watch. "I just got home. Give me time to make myself presentable."

"Certainly."

By ten-fifty I was scrubbed, shaven, and suited up in the third pew of the National Cathedral and praying between Mrs. De Vries and the secretary of health and human services. I prayed for peace and wise guidance along with the president, the First Lady, several clerics of different faiths, and an army of Secret Service men whispering into their sleeves, praying, most likely, for an uneventful day.

I am not a churchgoing man, but I have my faith, hardened by the demons I've studied and the wickedness I've seen. I have spent much of my life in places where God has been conspicuously absent, and I've wondered where He could have been that was more important than by a suffering child's side. But I do believe in something. Just don't ask me to explain it too deeply because mine is not a religion of sweet lambs and fluttering doves.

After the service, I waited as Mrs. De Vries talked with dozens of people, one by one or in pairs, all offering kindness and encouragement. Even the First Lady, home from Camp David, stopped and whispered briefly to Mrs. De Vries while Secret Service men scanned the hedges and rooftops.

Mrs. De Vries suggested we walk back to her house. It was hot, but the air was clean, and to me the whisper of leaves in the wind was much more soothing than the prayers of the powerful.

We walked between a hedge and a line of limousines. Mrs. De Vries rested her hand on my arm. "You've come to give me bad news, haven't you, Jake."

"Yes, ma'am, I have."

"It's about Janice." Her hand on my forearm tightened.

"Yes. I'm sorry." As many times as I've done this, it never gets easy. But I've learned to tell the truth, without preamble. "Your niece is gone, Mrs. De Vries."

She paused in her step, just for a blink, then continued, watching the sidewalk before us. "How, Jake?"

"She was murdered, sometime Tuesday night or Wednesday morning. The Alexandria police will be contacting you today to make an identification. I'll go with you if you'd like."

"She was here, in Alexandria?"

"Yes, ma'am."

"I wonder why she didn't call me." It was a passing curiosity, not a reproach, made while her mind was wrapping itself around the awful news.

"Does she have any family besides you?"

"No. No, we're all alone, Janice and I." She stopped and opened her purse. "I can't seem to find a tissue, Jake." I handed her my handkerchief. She lifted her face and I could see the tears breaking and I hugged her to me and she cried softly against my lapel as the long line of limousines crept slowly by, a dark harbinger of more funerals and heartbreak to come.

She gathered her strength, touched her face with

the handkerchief, and said, "You'll catch the son of a bitch."

"Yes, ma'am, I promise."

We walked the rest of the way in silence. Frederick met us at the door. His face told me that he knew, as Frederick always knew, and he gently guided us into the library and brought us coffee.

Mrs. De Vries took a seat by the window. The light, filtered by the green of the garden beyond, made her look younger, an effect I'm sure she had employed many times in this room, but today it was just a comfortable place in a familiar spot. The walk had restored some of her steel and she sat upright, her hands in her lap, still holding my handkerchief.

"Jake, I'm afraid I have more bad news."

"Yes?"

"My husband, the man who widowed me so long ago that I've forgotten what it is to be married . . ."

"Yes?"

"He's alive."

I nodded. "We've always suspected as much."

"And he's back."

"Back? You mean here in the States?"

"No, unfortunately not, or you might be able to arrest him."

Fletcher De Vries, the former dead husband of Mrs. De Vries, was suspected of being near the top of Empire International, J. P. Napoleon's syndicate, and was wanted for questioning by an alphabet of law enforcement agencies including, but not limited to, the ATF, DEA, FBI, CIA, and FCC.

"So if he's not here, where is he?"

"We believe he's in Uganda."

"Uganda?"

"Yes. I don't know for sure, Jake. But I know where his lawyers are and they've filed a lawsuit for control of all my assets."

"But Empire has already stolen your pharmaceutical company."

Mrs. De Vries lifted her hands from her lap, her palms up. "He wants all of this, Jake. Everything I own."

"But he can't."

"He claims he's had amnesia these past thirty years and only now regained any memory of his former life, and his former wealth, which he wants back."

"He can do that?"

She smiled a thin, helpless smile. "My lawyers don't think he can win, Jake, but in the meantime, all of my assets are frozen." She smiled, but it was low wattage. "If it wasn't for Frederick, well, I couldn't afford this cup of coffee."

"I am so sorry. Is there anything I can do? If you need money . . ."

"Jake, dear, you don't understand. As usual, you think of others first. It's quite admirable, and quite rare, especially in this city."

I blinked, trying to see beyond the news itself, to the implications. Then it hit me. "The Foundation."

"Yes, Jake. Everything is frozen, including the Foundation."

"But how can he do that?"

"I don't know." In that moment Mrs. De Vries

looked lost, unable to see into the next moment, the next day, the next week.

"I'll talk to the director. We won't stop investigating your niece's murder."

She tried to laugh, but it stuck in her throat. "It's odd. He lets me believe he's dead all these years, and then, when I'm used to being a widow, he not only rises from the grave, but he manages to ground my Broken Wings as well." She looked up at me. "The bastard."

13

Katie called about seven Sunday evening, interrupting my dinner of crackers, cold cuts, and a lone beer I'd found in the back of the refrigerator.

"I have news."

"Me, too." I told her about finding Janice Callahan and Ted Baker.

"I know. Trevor called me."

"Did he tell you about the Foundation?"

"He didn't have to. I had my credit card rejected at lunch this afternoon."

"I'm sorry. I had the same thing happen at the airport yesterday. I should have figured it out then. Do Jerry and Dominic know?"

"Yeah. They know."

It was a testament to the strength of our team that no one had called to complain or even ask about expenses. Even grounded, the Broken Wings could fly. "Tell them to keep track of their receipts and I'll make it up."

"No one's worried, Jake."

"Are you still at the hotel?"

"I am, but Dom's staying with his friend, the professor at Central. Jerry"—Katie laughed—"is staying at Dr. Plessy's. God, Jake, he is so infatuated, I think he's floating three feet off the ground."

A less than admirable part of me didn't want to hear about how much Jerry was in love, not after I'd had my heart drop-kicked into the end zone. "I'm happy for him," I said. "He deserves somebody he can discuss random hairs and semen samples with."

"Over a candlelit dinner, how romantic." Katie laughed again and it sounded so good.

I forced myself away from the picture in my head of Katie between the cool hotel sheets. "What's the news?"

"I talked to Weller this evening and the Coast Guard found Callahan's boat sunk off of Okracoke this morning."

"They find Callahan?"

"No, no trace of anyone. And yesterday the crime scene people picked up a few more prints they couldn't place."

"You mean besides mine."

"Yeah. Besides yours. Why didn't you tell me you were leading this double life?"

"Someone's playing with my head, Katie. I can guess who, but I don't know why."

"Napoleon."

"But why?"

"I don't know. Jerry looked at the prints and thought the thumb had been planted. There were paper fibers in the print itself."

"That means someone had access to my fingerprint card."

"Not necessarily. Remember when you did that book signing a few years ago? Instead of a signature you placed a thumbprint inside each one? Couldn't they have used one of those?"

"I don't know. What does Jerry think?"

"He thinks it's possible. But the glass is something else. They're your prints, Jake, no question, and Jerry can't find any fibers in those."

"Any more good news?"

"Weller got a call from the local authorities on the coast. A prostitute was murdered and the locals think it might be connected. Jerry and Dominic are going with Weller and Snead tomorrow morning to check it out."

"Why do they think the prostitute has something to do with this case?"

"She's a bleached blonde, Jake, upstairs and down. And she was killed with a .357 to the heart, sitting in the bathtub."

14

On Monday I packed a bag, threw it into the Aston Martin, whacked the starter with the nightstick, and drove down to Toni's house on the river. On the way I listened to the news. Terrorist cells in Germany were being investigated for connections to the attack on the congressman's plane. The explosive was indeed Hungarian and the dead mechanic was, too, evidenced by his dental work. If this was true, I knew the dental identification was the work of Dr. Stacy Coen, one of the best pathologists in the business and one hell of a racquetball player.

There was nothing on the news about Ted Baker and Janice Callahan being murdered in Alexandria. Anyone who died in the next few weeks would most likely die quietly, without headlines.

I pulled into the long drive that ran through the trees to the Rappahannock. At the end of the drive was the stone house that Toni and I had built near the tail end of our marriage when we thought that building a house together would somehow rebuild our life together. It didn't work. It was still our dream house, only now we had separate dreams.

I parked beside Toni's Volvo and got out as Gadget, our Maltese, raced across the yard to greet me, leaping and twisting in a dance of pure canine joy. I put my bag down, patted my chest, and Gadget jumped into my arms.

Eric came out, trying to be cool, but happy to see me. I knew that wouldn't last more than a few more years, so I enjoyed it while I had it. "Hey, sport." I put Gadget down so I could hug my son. "You ready for school to start?"

Eric groaned, but picked up my bag. It was something he'd done since he was four and able to hoist the bag with both hands. Now he was big enough to carry it in one hand, casually, no big deal.

"How's your mom?"

Eric rolled his eyes. "She's been crazy, Dad. Running around trying to get ready for this conference."

We talked about things we could do this week such as drive up to Baltimore and take in an Orioles game or drive down to the coast for a day at the beach. "You think your sister would like to come?"

"Ali's got a new boyfriend. His name's Raoul."

"Raoul, huh? You like him?"

Eric shrugged. "He's okay." Eric tried to toss off his next question, feigning nonchalance: "Is Katie coming to visit?"

"I don't think so. She's working a case in North Carolina."

"Oh," he said, disappointed. I knew how he felt.

"Hey, Dad?"

"Yeah?"

"Why'd they pull you off the plane bombing? You know, with the president's wife and all?"

We went into the kitchen, Gadget prancing on the tile. Eric put the bag down and Gadget sniffed it, taking in all the scents of all the places I'd been without him.

"Not everyone can be working one case, Eric. Somebody has to investigate all the other crimes. The bad guys don't quit just because somebody tried to kill the First Lady."

"I know," he said, but he was looking at his shoes.

"But what?"

"Well, a guy on TV said it was because you were a hot dog."

"Well, he was right. I am a hot dog. That's why they put me on a case involving a top secret weapon."

Eric looked up, his eyes big. "No kidding? Top secret?"

"The toppest." I opened up the cabinet to get a glass for water and there they were, gleaming, five tumblers in two rows. I opened the dishwasher. The sixth wasn't there.

"What are you looking for, Dad?"

"A glass. One of these." I held out one of the tumblers. "You know what happened to it?"

"It wasn't me."

I laughed. "I know, sport. I'm just wondering what happened to the sixth one, that's all. No one is accusing you of anything."

Eric smiled. "Good, otherwise I'd have to call my lawyer."

I hugged him again. "Where's your mother?"

"Upstairs. She's, like, really nervous about this speech."

Toni would be gone for a week at a psychiatric convention, and just the thought of a week with shrinks would be enough to make anyone crazy. I found Toni in the bedroom, the bed piled with clothes that were waiting to be either selected or rejected for the suitcase.

"How's this look?" She held up a red dress.

"Pretty sexy for psychiatrists, don't you think? Or is this a new therapy, trying to shake them out of their Oedipal fixations?"

"Ha ha. Stick to crime fighting, Jake, and leave comedy to the professionals. How long's it been? When were we in Toronto last?"

I tried to remember when we'd eaten in one of the bistros on Yonge, or window-shopped in the boutiques along Queen. It was when I was working out of the Detroit field office, early in my career. "It's got to be twenty-five years, at least."

"God, am I that old?"

"You don't look a day over thirty, Toni."

"Liar."

"At least on this trip, you'll have money to spend. Not like the last time we were there. Remember?"

Toni stopped packing. When she spoke, her head

tilted a little to the right and her eyes sparkled and I saw a glimpse of the girl I had married a long time ago. "But even broke, we had a really good time, didn't we, Jake?"

"Yeah, we did."

She snapped back to the present and turned away, toward the open drawers, as if turning from the memory of our time together, before I brought home the stink of murder that smothered our marriage. Before I spent more time trying to understand killers than I did my own children.

"I appreciate you doing this, Jake."

"No problem. What time's your flight?"

She looked at her watch. "In three hours. I'd better get moving. Security must be a nightmare."

"It is. Leave your gun at home."

Toni stopped and gave me a long look before saying, "I really do appreciate this, Jake. I know you're on a case."

"I'm looking forward to spending time with Ali and Eric. And whatever we need to do for the case, the team will take care of it."

"How's it coming, by the way?" One of the things that had kept us together for as long as it did was Toni's interest in my cases. I told her everything about the North Carolina murder because she often saw things from a different perspective, a psychological insight that could break open a case or give me a new lead to follow.

"It's confusing," I said. "Everything about it points to the husband. The gun, well, at least one of the guns, belongs to him."

"Callahan shot his wife with more than one gun? Why?"

I shrugged. "Well, first, we don't know he shot Janice Callahan. Second, who the hell knows why anyone would use two guns? It doesn't make sense."

"Unless there are two killers."

I shook my head. "All the evidence points to one person."

"You'll figure it out, Jake. You always do." Toni held up a pair of red shoes and a pair of black shoes. "Which do you think goes better with my green silk suit?"

"The red."

Toni considered it, then said, "I'll take them both," and put them in her suitcase. "I'll read the crowd first before I shock them with red shoes."

"You wouldn't think psychiatrists would be so easily shocked."

"Notoriously so."

I sat down on the bed. I could see Toni's reflection in the mirror as she sorted through her clothes. "Someone's playing a game with me, Toni."

"What do you mean?"

I told her about the print on the motel bed frame. I kept the glass and the dog fur to myself. "Why would someone plant my thumbprint at a crime scene? It's weird."

"Speaking of easily shocked, of all the things you've seen, I'm surprised you find anything weird. It's an encouraging sign, actually, that you haven't let your work warp your basic sense of what's normal human behavior."

I laughed. "Yeah, that's me, the poster boy for mental health."

"But how could your thumbprint be in a motel room you've never seen before?

I told her about Jerry's theory.

"Really? I had no idea you could do that."

"It's fairly easy if you have the fingerprint card."

"Amazing," she said. "You know, I rather miss hearing about the ingenuity of criminals and how you track them down. There was a time I thought I'd never want to hear about another crime as long as I lived."

"I know. And I'm really sorry." The truth was, Toni heard only a bit of what I worked on. It's impossible to come home and talk about a child's rape and murder over pot roast. And my work separated me from my kids' problems and made me callous to their own injuries. For instance, when Ali fell off her bike and needed stitches, I was less sympathetic than I should have been because I'd just come off a child dismemberment. It's understandable, but not to a six-year-old.

So there was much of what I did that I didn't talk about to anyone but other law enforcement people. After a few years of this, if you're not careful, you become completely isolated from civilians, including your family, and this isolation, this inability to talk about work at the end of the day, is one reason cops have such a high divorce rate. It's also why cops have such a low regard for the human race. When all you see are criminals, you begin to think that everyone should be locked up but you and your partner, and sometimes, you're not too sure about your partner.

"Where's Ali?"

"Out with a friend. She should be home for dinner."

"Raoul?"

Toni nodded. "So, you've already gathered your intelligence. Have you started a file on him yet?"

I laughed. "Not yet, but when he comes over, I'm going to casually clean my revolver."

"He seems like a nice boy, Jake. Don't embarrass Ali, okay?"

"Honey, she's sixteen and I'm her father. I embarrass her with every breath."

The phone rang and I heard Eric answer it downstairs. I couldn't make out what he was saying, but I could tell from the nervous laugh and that studied cool that it was Katie.

"Dad?" he hollered up the stairs. "It's Katie."

I picked up the phone. "Hi. What's up?"

"I tried your cell phone, but there was no answer."

"I left it in the car."

"It's all right, my calling your home, isn't it?"

"Yes, fine. Is something wrong?"

"No, Jake. Everything's okay. But we've found the husband. Or I should say, he's found us."

"That's great." I waited, knowing there was a catch. There always is. I felt Toni behind me, listening.

"He wants a meeting. Tomorrow night."

"Terrific."

"But he'll only meet with me. Alone."

"What? No. No way. It's too dangerous."

I heard Katie sigh, letting me calm down.

"Okay," I said, "but I'm on my way." I heard Toni stop packing and I could feel the heat on my back.

"No," Katie said. "You've got responsibilities there. I'll be fine."

I hated this. I hated being away from the team, putting them in danger and in situations I couldn't control.

"You stay with the kids. They need you more than I do."

"Okay, but I'm sending Trevor."

"Jake, there will be snipers from the SWAT team covering me. Weller has assured me that I'll be safe."

"I don't like this."

"I've already agreed, Jake. It's happening tomorrow night in Beaufort, on the coast."

I rubbed my face, trying to get hold of my fear. "Katie, I'd feel better with Trevor there. Give me this one."

"Fine. Send him."

"Okay. I'll talk to you again tomorrow."

Katie hung up and I punched the off button. When I turned, Toni wasn't looking at me. She was carefully folding a black silk blouse I'd bought for her last Christmas.

"You were just going to leave the children, is that it?"

"No, Toni, I would have asked my mother to

watch them. You know I wouldn't leave them alone. Although Ali's getting old enough . . ."

"How would you know?" Toni looked up, her face set, older than before, the lines around her eyes deeper, her mouth tight. "Just how the hell would you know?"

"I'm not going. I'm staying here."

Toni nodded. "We always come second, don't we, Jake? Always second."

I walked from the room. I knew this argument, line by line, by heart. I didn't need to hear it again.

15

I called Trevor and told him what Katie had told me.

"Beaufort, huh? Where the hell is Beaufort?"

"It's on the coast. Pretty nice town, actually. Can you leave tonight?"

"Yeah, although right now I'm getting the fish eye from my wife. I spend much more time away from home and she's going to forget what I look like."

"Trevor, if this lawsuit with Mrs. De Vries isn't settled, we'll all be spending more time at home."

I heard Trevor cup the receiver in his hand. "Maybe we should go to Nigeria or wherever the hell this Fletcher De Vries is hiding and, you know, permanently adjudicate the proceedings."

"Uganda," I said. Ali walked into the kitchen followed by a tall boy in baggy jeans. He had a bolt through his eyebrow and a blond streak in his hair. He looked scared, and I like that look on boys dating my daughter. I waved. Ali waved back and waited, leaning her hips against the counter.

"Trevor," I said, "if I thought you could get the man in your crosshairs, I'd happily give you the green light. Oh, speaking of that, pick up your black bag before heading to Beaufort. I want you covering Katie at all times, you got that?"

"Yeah, Jake."

"If you even catch the scent of gun oil on the air, you take him out."

The boy's eyes went wide and his mouth hung open.

Trevor laughed. "Oh, yeah, so you can come visit me in the local slam. I may be paranoid, Jake, but I'm not crazy."

"No kidding, Trevor, I want to be in contact at all times, you got that?"

"Will do. I'll call as soon as we're in position."

We hung up and I extended my hand to the boy, who took it. His grasp was adequate, but his palm was wet.

"You must be Raoul."

"Mr. Donovan, it's a pleasure to meet you." He looked like an anarchist, but he talked like a Republican.

Ali was sixteen, and like all sixteen-year-old girls, her shirt was too small and her shorts hung too low, exposing her navel to the whole world, including sixteen-year-old boys who had a hard enough time controlling their hormones.

"Daddy, Raoul's invited me to a party tonight. Is it all right if I go?"

"What kind of party?"

"You know, just hanging out, with music and stuff."

"Where?"

"At Jacob's."

"Do I know Jacob?"

"No. I don't think so."

"Will his parents be there?"

"I don't know, Dad." Ali pushed away from the counter and put her hands on her hips. "You know, you can't just walk in here and start questioning me like I'm some kind of serial killer."

I laughed. "Oh, can't I?"

"Fine, I won't go. We'll stay in my room." Ali took Raoul's hand and started pulling him away.

I stopped her. "Whoa, hold it a minute. First, I didn't say you couldn't go."

"I don't want to go anyway."

"And second, there will be no *we* in your room while I'm on watch. Got that?"

"Now you don't trust me." Ali crossed her arms and Raoul shuffled his sneakers back and forth. Gadget barked at him, and that made me not like the boy.

"I trust you outside, on the deck."

"It's too hot."

"Then watch TV."

"I don't want to watch TV."

I turned to Raoul. "Would you like something to eat while we're working this out?"

Raoul was definitely interested. I haven't known a teenage boy yet who wasn't perpetually horny and hungry, and I hoped to distract him from the former with the latter. I opened the fridge and nosed around the leftovers. "There's some Cajun meat loaf in here, and"—I opened a plastic container—"looks like linguine with some of Toni's mean marinara."

Raoul looked from the food to Ali and back to the food again. "I guess I could eat something, if you don't mind."

"Are you staying for dinner?" I popped the linguine in the microwave.

Raoul sat at the counter. "Sure. I guess."

"If you two fly, I'll buy. You up for Chinese?"

Raoul nodded.

Ali, knowing she'd been outflanked, sat next to Raoul. "So, can we go to the party?"

"What time will you be home?"

"One."

"How about twelve?"

"Mom lets me stay out until one."

"Mom's not here, is she?"

Ali sulked while Raoul ate the linguine and the meat loaf. Then he was ready for the main course.

"Can we take your car?" Ali asked.

Raoul's eyes widened. "The Aston Martin? That's like the coolest car I've ever seen, Mr. Donovan."

I fished the keys out of my pocket and held them out to Ali. "You promise not to give me a hard time the rest of the week?"

"I promise."

I dropped the keys into her palm. A minute later, she was back inside. "The car won't start."

"It does that." I went out to the driveway where Raoul was standing in front of the open hood. "You see anything interesting, Raoul?"

Raoul blinked, his hands in the back pockets of his jeans where they might do him some good if his ass was about to fall off.

"Ali," I said, "there's a nightstick behind the seat. Get that."

She handed it to me as if it were a snake. The stick in hand, I reached inside and tapped the starter. "There, it should work now."

Ali twisted the key and the engine caught.

"Did you see what I did? In case this happens in town?"

Raoul nodded. "Uh-huh."

Ali hollered, "Come on, Raoul, get in the car."

Raoul shuffled a bit more. "I guess I better go."

"Yeah," I said, "I guess you better."

Raoul sank into the passenger seat until all I could see were his eyes, his knees, and the blond streak in his hair. Ali pushed the car into gear and with a wave of her hand they were off, raising dust into the summer trees.

"You trust her to drive your car, Dad?" Eric was standing behind me, a radio-controlled boat in his hand.

"Shouldn't I?"

"She drove Mom's car into some bushes."

I put my hand on top of Eric's head. "That'll teach the bushes to jump out of the way, huh, sport?

Now, let's go get this boat in the water, see what she can do."

I woke up in the box. The coffin seemed smaller this time and the air was gone. Desperately, I tried to fill my lungs as I pushed against the top and beat on the sides, screaming for help.

"Dad!"

I opened my eyes. Eric and Ali were kneeling over me, shaking my arms.

"Dad! You're having a nightmare," Eric said.

I sat up on the couch and gasped. Gadget barked at me. Ali and Eric stared, fear draining the color from their cheeks. "I'm fine. Fine." The TV was on.

"I heard you yelling," Ali said.

"I couldn't wake you," Eric said. "I tried and you wouldn't wake up."

"I'm fine now. I'm okay." I rubbed my face. "What time is it?"

"Twelve," Ali said.

"Oh, right. Good, okay," I said, still stupid with sleep. My heart was pounding against my ribs. "It was just a dream. I'm okay."

The kids asked a dozen more times if I was all right, and after so many reassurances that even I began to doubt them, we all went off to our rooms. Gadget followed me and I had to lift him up onto the bed. He wagged his tail and did a spin on top of the comforter. "I could use the company," I said.

I patted Gadget's head and thought about the dog hairs found at the motel, and that made me think of

Katie and that made me feel as if I'd been sucker punched, so I turned on the TV and watched a guy with a crime show give his opinion on the bombing of the congressman's plane. I knew this guy and he'd been a drug addict and a shyster lawyer before he'd hit it big with reenacted crime. His opinion was about as insightful as my mother's, a woman who believed that burglars all wore striped shirts and skinny black masks and carried their loot away in a big, round bag.

I emptied my pockets, took off my shoes, and laid my revolver on the nightstand. Somewhere in between interviews, I fell asleep and slept straight through to morning, without waking up in that damn Black Diamond box again. For that I was thankful.

As I put the coffee on and let Gadget out, the phone rang.

"Jake, I hope I didn't call too early."

"No, Mrs. De Vries, not at all. What's wrong? You sound worried."

"I heard that Katie was meeting Janice's ex-husband today."

I laughed. "Mrs. De Vries, you have one hell of an intelligence network. What color shirt am I wearing?"

"Blue." She was right. "Jake, I'm worried about Katie. I know she can take care of herself, but I'd feel much better if you were there with her. I'll pay for your airfare, Jake. Fletcher's lawyers haven't found all of my cookie jars just yet."

"No, Mrs. De Vries, you keep your money. Trevor

will be watching. Nothing will happen. And Katie can take care of herself. She'll talk your former nephew into surrendering, you'll see."

There was a pause and I thought we'd been cut off. "Mrs. De Vries? Are you still there?"

"I'm here, Jake. I also got a call from a friend at the Alexandria PD. This is what their investigators think: Janice was sleeping with this man, her ex followed her and killed them in bed. Is that what you think, Jake?"

"I think we should wait for all the facts, Mrs. De Vries."

"My niece wasn't that kind of woman, Jake."

"No one thinks that."

"Yes, they do, Jake."

I hurt for Mrs. De Vries, this tough old woman who'd suffered through so much loss in one lifetime.

Her voice softened. It was almost apologetic. "I just don't want anyone thinking she was like that."

"I understand."

I heard her sigh. "Well, please keep me posted, Jake. Now that I'm poor, people have stopped calling. This town is so predictable. You know what they say about politics, Jake?"

"No, Mrs. De Vries, what?"

"It's show business for ugly people."

I laughed, happy that the old girl still had her sense of humor, and I promised to call just as soon as I knew anything.

The day seemed long, even for a summer's day on the river. Eric and I ate grilled cheese sandwiches on the deck overlooking the water. Eric made the little

RC boat zip back and forth between the banks until the batteries quit and he had to swim out to retrieve it. Ali went off with friends and promised to be home in time for dinner. A paddle-wheel boat filled with Civil War tourists passed by the house and the tour guide pointed me out as "the famous FBI profiler, Jake Donovan." I returned the waves.

Eric giggled. "We should have mooned them, Dad."

"Maybe on their way back."

It wasn't dark, although the sun had dipped below the trees and cast long shadows across the yard, when Trevor called.

"We're all set, Jake."

"Any more word from the husband?"

"Nothing. But we have two men in the coffee shop, two on the street, and three snipers set up around the meet, all with clear lines of fire. I'm on the roof of a hotel across the street from the café."

"What do you think of the locals?"

"I know one from Quantico. Former marine, trained under Carlos Hathcock. Another I've read about. He saved a bank hostage last year with a head shot at seven hundred yards."

"That's two."

Often, what Trevor says is not as important as what he doesn't say. In this case, he was hesitant to judge the third sniper, a man he didn't know. "He seems okay. Maybe a bit too eager."

"What about Katie, is she wired?"

"Yes."

"Can you patch her into the phone?"

"We're working on it."

On cue, Katie said, "Can you hear me? Is it on?" Then her voice was overwhelmed by a wave of static.

"What's wrong? What's happening?"

"I don't know, Jake."

"Can you see her?"

"She's just below me, not more than sixty yards."

"Can you hear her okay?"

"Yes," Trevor said. "It's just the phone connection that's screwed up."

"You're my ears as well as my eyes."

"Roger, Jake."

"Weller and Snead with you?"

"Weller's here. You want to talk to him?"

"Yeah." The phone passed. "Weller, did the lab get the envelope I sent down?"

"Yeah, the courier showed up around four. The lab hasn't had time to look at it yet."

I heard him wait for an explanation. "They're dog hairs. I'm hoping they don't match the hairs found at the motel."

"If they do?"

"It means someone's sending me a very clear message. The glass, the dog hairs, my prints . . ."

"Means someone can reach your family." Weller was quick to get right to the bottom line.

"Anytime they want."

"You have an idea who?"

"Yeah, a good idea. But I don't know how, or why."

Trevor's voice came back online. "Jake, we've got movement."

Katie's voice crackled, "This could be . . . ," and again was swallowed up by static.

"It's a black Isuzu Trooper," Trevor said. "One man behind the wheel. He's parked in the coffee shop lot."

It was frustrating not being there, not watching with Trevor, not adding my weight to Katie's protection.

I heard Trevor's voice relax. "It's not him. It's not the husband."

I sat in a comfortable lawn chair watching swifts perform aerial acrobatics over the slow-moving river and listened helplessly to an operation three hundred miles away. "Stay on him."

"I am."

Katie came through a curtain of noise: "It's not him. It's not Callahan."

"He's stopping." I could hear the edge come back into Trevor's voice.

"Who is it?"

"I don't know. Maybe he's just attracted to Katie."

"Yeah. Stay on him."

"I am." Trevor's concentration behind the scope made me a distant second in his priorities.

The man's voice crackled through Katie's wire like a distant station: ". . . McManus . . . Spider . . . meet you."

"What? What did he say?"

"Jesus, Jake, you're not going to believe this."

"What?"

"Wait a minute."

I stood up and paced the length of the deck and back, listening to static. When I couldn't stand it, I said, "Speak to me, Trevor. What's happening."

"Hold on, Jake."

"I can't hold on." More static. I heard the man say *contract* and *rights* and *Hollywood.* "Who the fuck is he?"

"He's an agent, Jake. He's a literary agent. Set up by Spider Urich."

"What the fuck is an agent doing there?"

"He's representing the husband. He's saying Callahan will give himself up if you and Katie work with him on a book." Trevor laughed. "He says your involvement is critical to selling the publication and film rights. Jesus, Jake, the guy's doing a deal."

I sat back down in the lawn chair and put my head in my hand. "Trevor, this is insane."

"Tell me about it."

Katie crackled over the line, "Where . . . ? Obstruction of . . . Aiding and abetting . . ."

"She's telling him about the Son of Sam law," Trevor said.

". . . can't profit . . . illegal activities," I heard Katie say. Then I heard a pop and Katie said, "Oh . . . oh . . ."

Trevor said, "Shit."

"What?" I was on my feet again, hollering into the phone. "What! What's wrong?"

"There was a shot, Jake. Somebody took a shot." I heard muffled movements and distant men shouting. "She's down, Jake, Katie's down."

"Is she all right?"

"I don't know, Jake. I don't know."

"Who fired?"

"One of the snipers. The man, the agent, reached into his jacket. Christ, Jake, all I can see is blood. The man's down, Katie's down . . ."

"Is Katie all right?"

"I don't know. I'm on my way."

I was left with a silent cell phone to my ear, watching bats come out of the trees and dart through the summer twilight over the river.

16

In only a few minutes Weller was on the phone, reassuring me, telling me not to come down, that everything was under control, but to me it seemed like hours. In those few minutes I pictured Katie lifeless, her blouse heavy with blood, torn by the sniper's bullet. I saw my life without her, and the team shattered, too wounded to look at one another without calling up Katie's face, her voice, her quick hands, her humor and sharp intelligence.

"She's all right," Weller repeated. "The bullet hit the subject in the head and the splatter hit Katie. But she's all right."

"Can I talk to her?"

"They're taking her to the hospital for observation, Jake. I'll have your people call you from there."

"I'm coming down."

"No. Your team can handle this, Jake."

As if on cue, Trevor came on. "Don't come, Jake. You stay with your kids. I'll let you know what's happened as soon as we piece it all together."

I blew out a heavy sigh, dialing down the tension from a twelve to a ten. "Okay. I don't like it, but okay. If anything changes, and I mean anything, I want you to call me. Don't make me sit here like a fat girl before the prom, waiting for the phone to ring."

Trevor laughed. "Don't worry, baby, you're on my speed dial."

"So use it." I hung up.

Eric stood in the doorway to the living room. "What's wrong, Dad?"

"There was an accident."

"Mom?" Eric's face fell open.

"No, no, your mother's fine. It was Katie. But she's all right."

Eric's shoulders quivered. "Are you sure Katie's all right? Where is she?"

"She's fine. She's with Trevor and Jerry and Dom. She'll be fine."

Eric thought about that for a moment. He knew the team as well as he knew his aunts and uncles and, in some ways, was closer to them than to family. "Dad?" He held back a boy's tears, trying to be a man, too tough to cry.

"Yeah, sport?"

"Why can't you get a real job? You know, like other dads?"

"Come over here, okay?" Eric sat next to me and I

put my arm around him and hugged him to me. "I know this has been really hard on all of us: your mother, you, and your sister. But it's what I do, sport. Someone has to catch the bad guys."

"But I get so scared. Ali does, too, I know. And Mom. We're not brave like you and Katie."

I rocked him back and forth, the way I did when he was a baby. "Sure you are. Being scared doesn't mean you're not brave. It's what you do when you're scared, that's what makes you brave or not, and you're as brave as anyone I've ever known. And that's the truth."

Eric curled up against my ribs. "I'm tired, Dad. I'm just really tired."

Eric fell asleep about midnight and I carried him up to bed. I found a biography of John Adams in the bedroom and stretched out on the couch and tried to read. I wasn't very successful. I kept glancing at the revolver within reach on the coffee table, and listening to the sounds a house makes at night.

Around one, Ali eased open the door, followed by Raoul. Gadget barked at him.

"Ssssh! You little hairball," Ali whispered. "You'll wake up Dad."

"I'm awake."

"Uh, hi, Mr. Donovan," Raoul said, his hands in his back pockets. He was edgy, but kept his cool until he saw the revolver. Then his eyes got big and he backed toward the door. "I, uh, guess I better get home," he said to Ali. "I'll call you tomorrow."

"Wait," she said.

I couldn't see them from my place on the couch, but I could tell he was kissing her. My daughter. My firstborn. Only a few years from being a baby. I heard them whisper, then the door closed.

"How was the party?"

Ali sat down across from me and Gadget jumped into her lap. "It was okay." She looked at the pistol. "Did you leave that out for Raoul's benefit?"

I laughed. "No, but I might have if I'd thought about it. Did you have fun tonight?"

Ali shrugged.

"There isn't drinking at these parties, is there?"

"Some. Some of the kids have beer. Some get drunk."

"Do you?"

"I have." Ali gave me a tight-lipped smile. "I don't really like it much. I threw up."

"That's no fun."

"No."

I had plenty of other questions, but I didn't really want the answers, not right then, so I didn't ask.

"You know you didn't have to wait up for me."

"I know. I wasn't really." I put the book on the coffee table, next to my phone. "I've been waiting for a call."

"I knew something was up. I could see it on your face. You get these lines around your eyes. Did you know that?" Ali saw things in people's faces, and read them, just like her mother. Whatever man she chose to marry would have to be honest.

"There was a shooting tonight. Katie was

involved, but she's fine," I was quick to add. "She's just shook up."

"Have you talked to her?"

"No. Not yet. Trevor called and said she was okay, not even a scratch."

"But Katie hasn't called." Ali put her elbows on her knees, her hands together. Like her mother, the shrink. All she needed was the notepad.

"No, she hasn't."

"And that's the call you were waiting for."

"Yeah, I guess so." I looked at my watch, although I knew what time it was. "It's probably too late now."

"Are you and Katie having problems, Dad?"

I nodded. "Yeah." Then I laughed. "Well, not exactly. I think I'm having more problems than Katie. She's, uh, she's gone back to Rob."

Ali straightened. "Her ex? That creep? I mean, he's nice looking, but didn't he run off with some bimbo?"

"Nice to know you still remember him."

"I'm so sorry, Dad." Ali waited, giving the transition some air. She studied my face again. She was an interesting kid, a combination of her mother's analytical skills and my dogged persistence. "I guess maybe you don't know." A kindness was in her voice, and I got another glimpse of the woman she would become in a few short years.

"There's a lot I don't know."

"About Mom. She's seeing someone. A doctor she met last year."

"Oh. That's great," I said. I tried to sound cheerful, but I didn't convince either of us. "You know I want your mother to be happy."

Ali looked at me with what I hoped was more sympathy than pity. "Sure, Dad. I just thought you should know about this other guy."

"I appreciate it."

Ali stretched. "I guess I'd better get to bed. Unless you want to, you know, talk some more."

"No, no. You go. I'll water the dog."

That made Ali smile. She kissed me on the cheek and said good night.

I stopped her at the bottom of the stairs. "Ali? Have you seen any new people in the house lately? Maybe after I was here the last time?"

"Dad, I don't think—"

"I'm not talking about your mother's dates. I'm talking about delivery people, repairmen, strangers asking for directions."

Ali thought, her hand resting on the newel. "No. Nobody unusual. Why? Has someone been in the house?"

"No, just an old cop's paranoia, that's all."

Ali looked straight at me, her head slightly cocked. "That's why the gun was on the table."

"Of course not," I lied. "But if you think of someone, you let me know, okay?"

Ali nodded, stared at me for a moment, then continued her climb up the steps. She hadn't bought my lie for a second.

I looked at Gadget and said, "You ready?" He ran to the door and did his nightly dance.

Out in the darkness, I looked up and saw Mars on

the horizon, a red spark against the black. If I had been more of a classical scholar, I might have seen it as a sign of the violence to come, but as it was, all I saw was a planet, no more a messenger than Saturn or the stars or the satellite making its shiny way across the night.

17

The shooting in North Carolina was headlined on the local news. The story was spun as a fatal blunder by Hollywood Jake Donovan that resulted in the death of an innocent bystander. There was no mention of the SWAT sniper, or local law enforcement. The grim-looking stringer from the coast made no mention of the missing husband, or the reason a literary agent was meeting with "two of Donovan's operatives, Kathleen McManus, suspended from the FBI just two years ago for endangering innocent lives, and Trevor Malone, also suspended from the Bureau for the controversial killing at Owl Creek."

This was followed by a profile of the victim, Sid Whare, representative of athletes and TV stars with literary aspirations as well as a herd of writers specializing in true crime. Mr. Whare was from East Hampton, New York, and, from the reverent tone in the reporter's voice, had apparently walked across the water from Long Island to Beaufort before being cut down in his prime thanks to Jake Donovan's cowboy disregard for public safety.

I turned off the TV. The Black Diamond nightmare had kept me rolling all night long in that place between wake and rest. My eyeballs felt as if they were being sanded smooth by my eyelids, and I could still taste the fear. To wake up to a public pummeling by a perky morning show, sandwiched in between the cholesterol tips and the celebrity news, was more than I could stomach.

I let Gadget relieve himself on Toni's roses, put him back in the house, and took off at a fast jog down the path that runs along the riverbank. This is probably what I miss most about the house. Not the fireplace or the deck on the river, not even the small office I had once lined with the mementos of a lifetime with the FBI. It was this narrow path, crowded on either side by snake berry and poison ivy. The run took me past places where the Union engineers had constructed pontoon bridges, always under Confederate sniper fire. On the far side of the river was the railroad, and a pyramid erected by Union veterans to mark the forward line of the assault. It was there that Union victory seemed possible until Jackson's reinforcements drove Meade's men back across the Rappahannock.

I lost myself in the rhythm of the run, and the lingering spirits of brave men captured in the rising mists of the river. I ran until the fear was gone and the nausea I'd felt watching the news was replaced by anger, and the commitment I'd need to see the investigation through in spite of everything, including my screwed-up personal life.

At the third mile mark, I turned around and ran home. The trip back was harder than I'd remembered, and by the time I reached the yard my shirt was soaked through and I was seriously winded. I walked around, catching my breath and stretching my muscles. Eric was up and throwing a stick for Gadget. I settled into a lawn chair on the deck and wiped the sweat from my face.

"Hi, Dad."

"Hey, sport. What's up?"

"Nothing." He fell into the chair next to me. "You working today?"

"Some. Why? You want to do something?"

"Nah. Just wondering."

"You see the news this morning?"

"No. Why?"

I told him that he might hear some pretty rough things about his old man in the next few days. He took it well. He'd grown up with so much bad news that once he'd known Katie was unhurt, the rest seemed to roll off.

That was until Rob McManus came roaring into our driveway and skidded to a stop. Before I could stand, Rob was out of his SUV and striding across the lawn toward me, his hands clenched into fists.

"Hi, Rob," I said, looking up at him. His face was red and specks of spittle dotted the corners of his mouth.

"You son of a bitch." He jabbed at me with his finger. "You could have gotten Katie killed."

I tried to stand up but Rob crowded me and I couldn't rise without his backing off, something he had no intention of doing. "Look, Rob, I understand why you're upset, but this is Katie's job. You, of all people, should understand that." Had Rob been a civilian, I might have been a bit more consoling. Had Rob not been a prick, I might have been a bit more sympathetic. Had Rob not taken Katie from me, I might have been a bit more patient. As it was, I didn't care much for Rob, or his tender feelings.

Rob shoved his finger in my face. "It isn't Katie's job to get shot over your hotdogging, Donovan."

I held down my anger and said, as evenly as I could, "She was covered, Rob. It was one of the locals who pulled the trigger."

"Just like Owl Creek. You and Malone."

That did it. I stood up, forcing Rob to step back. "You know what happened at Owl Creek, McManus. That was a clean shoot. Now I suggest you get your philandering, phony, self-righteous ass out of my yard and back to the Bureau where you might do somebody some good."

Gadget barked at us from the driveway and then lifted his leg on Rob's tire. I couldn't help it; I laughed. Which left me completely off guard when Rob took a swing. The throw was short and his fist went zipping past my nose. I backed up, all my attention focused on Rob, younger than I and in better shape, and said, "Rob, don't do this." He stepped in and shot another short jab at my ribs. This one I blocked.

"Eric, go inside," I said as Rob and I circled each other on the lawn.

"Should I call the police, Dad?"

"No. Agent McManus was just leaving."

Rob threw a left that I sidestepped. When his fist went past my face, I grabbed his wrist, planted my other hand against his elbow, and pushed Rob to his knees. I thought that might take the fight out of him, and I let go. Rob came up, intent on tackling me, and I had to pivot out of the way. I hit him just behind the ear as he went past. It wasn't hard, but Rob fell to his knees again. His anger was making him sloppy.

"Rob, don't do this. Go home."

Rob went into a low stance, his arms up, and came at me with a few short kicks followed by a two-shot punch, one aimed at the bridge of my nose, the other at my throat. The punches caromed off my forearms and I hit him once.

Rob backed away, his hand at his eye.

"I'm asking you to go home, Rob, before one of us gets hurt."

He seemed to consider it.

Eric came outside. "I called the police, Dad. They're on their way."

"Rob, go home before the police get here. I'll tell them it was a mistake. You don't want another letter in your file, Rob. Go before they get here."

Still holding his eye, Rob backed up to his SUV and got in. From the safety of his car he said, "Stay away from Katie, old man. It's disgusting."

"Go tell your friends how an old man just kicked

your ass," I hollered, my anger rising. "Oh, that's right. You don't have any friends."

Rob drove off, throwing gravel into the grass. Gadget barked until the SUV was out of sight.

"Are you okay, Dad?"

Eric stood in the doorway, and in an instant I remembered the first time I'd ever seen my father in a fight. It was with a neighbor, over what I didn't know, and it didn't last any longer than a minute. I still remember the awful smack of fists on flesh and I remember being terrified. I hugged Eric's shoulders as he wrapped his arms around my waist. "I'm sorry you had to see that, sport."

"What are you going to tell the police?"

"That it was just a fan wanting an autograph, that's all." It was a credible story. The local police had come out several times to calm down avid followers of serial murder. One fan, sure that I had souvenirs of Ted Bundy, Manson, Gacy, and other killers I'd interviewed, even broke into the house hoping to add to his own collection. He didn't believe me when I told him all I took from those men, besides information, was disturbing dreams.

My hand began to throb. "I better put some ice on this"—I laughed—"or I won't be able to open that spaghetti sauce in the pantry."

Toni called that afternoon, just to make sure we hadn't set the house on fire. "Everything all right there?"

"Fine here." I shifted the phone to my left hand

so I could keep my right in the ice bucket. "How is it in Toronto?"

"There was an intriguing presentation on Native American psychoactive therapies."

"Peyote."

Toni sighed. "Always the cop. No, it was about meditation. How tuning your inner rhythms to the natural rhythms of the world aligns your neural activity. There was quite a bit about menstruation." She laughed. "You would have hated it."

"Probably."

"There was no single malt involved."

"Yeah, I would have hated it."

"Ali up yet?"

It was past two. "She rolled out of bed about an hour ago."

"Anything else you'd like to tell me?"

"Not a thing."

"Not even"—Toni's voice slipped into all-business—"about your partner, your girlfriend, who was almost killed last night?"

"You saw."

"Of course I saw, Jake. Toronto may be in another country, but they have news. In English and French." She waited for me to say something but I came up short. "You weren't going to tell me."

"I didn't want to worry you." Even as I said it, I knew it wasn't going to cover the situation. So I tried a quantity of words over quality: "I thought the news would ruin our vacation."

With a great deal of patience Toni said, "I know Katie. And what's more important, she's a big part of your life, and whatever affects your life affects all of us. Does Eric know?"

"Yes. We talked about it."

"How's he taking it?"

"He's fine."

She let some of the anger boil off. "He has such a crush on her. It's a good thing I'm not a Freudian, Jake, or who knows how this twisted little Oedipal fixation would play itself out."

"Maybe, instead of a college fund, we should start saving for therapy. Maybe you could get a discount from your new boyfriend."

There was a long silence on Toni's end. "That was pretty clumsy, Jake."

"Sorry."

"We're still talking about you, Jake, not me."

"I know."

"My personal life doesn't involve snipers, Jake."

"You're right."

"I haven't been shot at since, oh, let me see— *ever*, Jake. People don't shoot one another in my life, and that's the kind of life I'd like for my children. Is that too much to ask?"

"No."

"What was that, Jake? I couldn't hear you."

"No," I said, louder this time. "It's not too much to ask."

"Good. I'll be home on Friday. Try not to get into any gunfights in the yard until then, okay?"

"What about fistfights?"

"If you must. Call me if you need me. I've got to go."

"Okay, and don't worry. Everything's fine here."

"Sure. I'll call later to talk to the kids."

We said our good-byes and she hung up. Before I could cradle the receiver, it rang in my hand. "Hello?"

"Jake. Spider Urich."

I made a note to screen my calls. "What do you want?"

Spider ignored my tone. "I want you to use me, Jake, abuse me, make me write filthy limericks on men's room walls."

"I didn't peg you for an obscene caller, Urich. You know that's punishable by a ten-thousand-dollar fine and time alone with your cell mate."

"Ha ha, Jake, always the cop."

"I've heard that."

Spider rattled on, "I saw the news, and I think you're getting a raw deal, buddy."

"Gee, thanks, buddy." The sarcasm bounced off Spider's hide. "I can see you're in mourning over your agent."

There was the briefest pause before Spider said, "Yeah, that was a shocker, wasn't it? Who knew?"

I couldn't help laughing at Spider's chutzpah. "You're telling me that you didn't put the late Mr. Whare in touch with our fugitive? Is that what you're saying?"

Spider went into heavy CYA. "Look, I just took a call and made a call. What they talked about after that was between them."

"But you didn't call the police."

"Jake, in this business, you call your agent first and the police second."

"Today isn't a very good time to be making that kind of joke, Urich."

"Right. Because of what happened. Right. And I'm torn up about Sid. Really. He and I'd been together for eight years. I was at his son's Brith, for Christ's sake."

That struck me funny, or maybe I just needed some kind of release, but I laughed. "Okay, Spider, what do you want?"

"The reason I'm calling, Jake, is I want to give you a chance to clear things up and tell your side of what happened last night."

Sid Whare isn't dead twenty-four hours and Spider's working the angles. It didn't surprise me. I'd known Spider to plant a microphone at a grave site to catch the words of the bereaved and just maybe the confessions of a killer. "Thanks, but no thanks." I started to hang up, then stopped. "Spider, you still there?"

"Yeah, Jake, I'm still here."

I gave myself one more time to think about the downside of going public. I decided that with the Broken Wings funding frozen, my team scattered, our political capital spent, and our investigation deeply in the tank, there wasn't much further down we could go. "Maybe I could use some airtime." Maybe, I didn't say, I can get our fugitive husband with literary aspirations to come to me. "When do you want to do this?"

I could hear Spider's million-dollar smile beam over the wires. "That's the Hollywood Donovan we know and love. Let's say tomorrow morning at six, here in the D.C. studio. You'll go on by eight-fifteen. How's that sound?"

"Okay. See you then. And, Spider?"

"Yeah?"

"You sandbag me, for any reason, and you can give my condolences to Sid, personally."

"Gotcha, Jake. I'll be a damn Boy Scout."

Before I hung up, I got Sid Whare's family's address so I could send flowers and suggested Spider do the same. It hadn't occurred to him.

18

That afternoon, I drove into town and picked up some Italian takeout for dinner.

The owner, a strong woman with a good grip, took my hand and told me to keep my chin up. "God gives us only those things we can bear, and He gives us cannoli to help us with those things we can't. I put a few in with your order, on the house." She patted the back of my hand.

I placed the bag, heavy with hot carbohydrates in tomato sauce, on the floor in front of the passenger seat. Gadget dipped his nose into the top of the bag and I shooed him away with one hand as I turned the key with the other. The Aston wouldn't start. I cursed, warned Gadget away from the takeout, and grabbed the nightstick. I opened the hood and stuck my head inside the engine compartment. Slowly, I got the feeling I was being watched and I looked up.

"You need help?" A man in a red shirt, unbuttoned down to a pair of dog tags, stood behind me, his eyes hidden behind dark glasses. He casually licked at an ice cream cone, dwarfed in his fist.

"No, thanks. It does this all the time." I hit the starter with the nightstick. "That usually works."

"Maybe you should call *Car Talk*. You know, the guys on the radio."

"Yeah, maybe."

"Funny guys."

"Yeah."

Something in his voice made me grip the nightstick a little tighter. I stepped away from the car, just in case I needed room. "Do I know you?"

"No, just a guy on the street."

That's when I saw the prison tattoo on his forearm. The work was good, most likely the artistry of Anson Toller in Leavenworth. It was a flaming cross topped by a halo of barbed wire, the symbol of the Holy Knights of New Jerusalem. This is what you get when you throw the Klan and the Aryan Nations together in a small cell and let them breed. Toss in a little psycho killer just to muddy up the gene pool and you come up with the Holy Knights, a murderous gang of racists suspected of terrorist acts throughout the South and West.

"You take it easy now," the guy said, and touched a finger to his brow. But he didn't move.

I memorized his stats: blond and blue, six-two, two-ten, the prison tat, and scar tissue around the eyes, probably from boxing.

"Dog's in your dinner," he said.

Gadget had his head buried in the take-out bag. "Gadget!" He pulled his head from the bag. Cannoli filling frothed his muzzle.

The man strolled up the sidewalk, in no hurry to get away, one hand in his pocket as if it were Sunday in the park. He tossed the half-eaten cone into a trash can and turned the corner without looking back.

I climbed in, started the car, and pulled into light traffic. As I turned the corner, I looked for the red shirt in the white and tan tourist flow. The Holy Knight had vanished.

But his threat lingered.

I parked the car and went inside the ice cream place next to the restaurant.

"Hi, Jake," the counterman said. "Got some of that pistachio you like."

"Bill, there was a guy in here just now, got a cone. Big guy with blond hair, dark glasses."

"Yeah, is he a friend of yours?"

"No, why?"

"I don't know. Just something he said. We saw your car out there and he asked if you were Jake Donovan, the profiler, and I said you were. You're about the only celebrity we have here, Jake."

"What did he say?"

"Well, we got to talking about your career, and he knew so much, like about that Black Diamond case with all those children missing. He seemed like a real fan."

That made the hair on my neck stand up. "What else did he say?"

Billy shrugged. "Gosh, not much. Oh, yeah, he asked about your family. He seemed to know all about Toni being in Toronto and all, and how she was a psychiatrist, and your kids."

"He asked about my kids?"

"Yeah, even knew their names."

"Thanks." I ran from the shop, leaving Billy standing there, his scoop dripping vanilla onto his smock.

"I hope I didn't do the wrong thing," he hollered after me.

I called home. Eric's voice answered, "Hi, no one can come to the phone right now, but if you leave a message . . ."

I turned left and headed back toward the river. At the bridge I ran the yellow and pushed the speed limit by ten. On the way I phoned the FBI.

"Special Agent Andrews."

"Vince, this is Jake Donovan. I need your help."

"Sure, what can I do for you, Jake?"

"Vince, I need you to trace someone."

"I can do that. Name?"

"I don't have a name. But I think he's done time in Leavenworth, at least that's my guess." I told him about the tattoo and gave Andrews the description. "Between thirty and thirty-five, blond and blue, six-two, two-ten, probably with some boxing experience."

"Professional?"

"I don't know. Maybe amateur. I don't know."

"This might take some time, Jake."

"That's okay." I gave him my phone number. "Just let me know what you find out."

"Will do."

I found Ali on the deck, sunning herself on a chaise lounge.

"Didn't you hear the phone?"

Ali looked up and shielded her eyes from the sun. "What happened to Gadget?"

The little dog's face was still covered in cream filling from eyebrows to chin. It seemed to make him deliriously happy. "He got into the cannoli," I said. "Why didn't anyone answer the phone?"

Ali picked up the cordless phone from the table, turned it on, and listened. "Eric's online. I keep telling Mom we need a DSL, but she says it would just encourage us."

"Ali, I want you to get some things together. You and Eric are spending the night at your grandmother's house."

"What?" She sat up in the chaise, but I didn't stay for the argument I knew was coming. I carried the bag inside and put it on the counter before looking into the office. Eric was at the keyboard, so intent on the screen that he didn't see me.

"Downloading porn or music?"

Eric jumped a foot off the chair. "Jeez, Dad, you scared the heck out of me."

I walked around the desk to see the screen. Eric was playing a shoot-the-terrorist game, complete with Glock recoil and blood spatters. "Nice. Has your mother seen this?"

Eric looked up with a grin. "Are you kidding?"

"I brought dinner home from Lubrano's."

"Cool."

"Then I want you and your sister to pack a bag. You're spending the night at Grandma's." That got his attention.

"What?" Eric's voice rose into a vintage whine. "Every time we stay at Grandma's my clothes stink like cigarettes for a week."

"Come on, it's not that bad."

"You know it is."

"Know what what is?" Ali leaned against the doorjamb, her arms crossed.

"Dad's making us go to Grandma's."

"I know. I told you this would happen." Ali turned and walked up the steps to her room.

I caught up to Ali as she was pulling a duffel from her closet. "What did you mean by that?"

"I told Eric you'd be shipping us to Grandma's. I just didn't think it would be so soon." She threw the duffel on the bed. "It's okay, I know we'll never be as interesting as the Teds." She referred to the men I'd spent years studying, Ted Bundy and Ted Kaczynski. "Maybe Eric and I should plant a few kids in the crawl space."

"That was Gacy."

"Whatever." She tossed balled-up socks from the dresser drawer toward the bag.

"Ali, that's not what's going on here. I'm not trying to get rid of you."

"It's okay, Dad. I understand."

Eric came up the steps, two at a time. "Why do we have to go to Grandma's? She doesn't even have a computer."

I sat down on the edge of Ali's bed. "Look, guys, I'd just feel better if you were over at your grandmother's."

Eric whined, "But why?"

Ali knew exactly why. She stopped sorting through her clothes. "Something happened, didn't it? You heard something. Someone's coming here."

"Ali, please." I didn't want her spooking Eric.

"So, what did you hear? Is it imminent and credible?"

She even knew the code. I shook my head. "It's not even close."

"Then what's the rush? Why right now?"

Eric knew we'd moved beyond the stink of Grandma's cigarettes or her lack of video games. "What's going on?"

"It's nothing. I'd just feel better, that's all."

"What?" Eric insisted.

"Dad thinks someone might come to the house."

"Here?"

"That's why you had your gun on the table," Ali said. "Isn't it?"

"Someone's coming here?" Eric's voice was a whisper, his eyes as big as moons.

"No, no one's coming here."

"Then why can't we stay?" Ali said.

"Listen, I'd just feel more comfortable with you

guys in town, inside an apartment building with a doorman."

"The doorman is Billy Tips, Dad, he went to our school. He can barely open a car door."

"I'd still feel better . . ."

"Think about it," Ali said. "If someone wants to hurt us, where would we be safer, at Grandma's with a dropout at the door or here with you?"

"That's not the question."

"That's exactly the question." Ali stood with her hands on her hips.

"Show him the gun," Eric said.

"Shut up," she snapped.

"No, show him."

I looked from Ali to Eric. "What gun?"

Ali shook her head. "You have such a big mouth."

"*What* gun?"

With a sigh, Ali stuck her arm under her mattress and pulled out a Colt .45. "It was Grandpa's, from the war."

I could see the magazine in the pistol's grip and I said, as calmly as I could, "Ali, please hand that to me. That's very dangerous."

She released the magazine, locked back the slide, and handed it to me, grip first.

"Who taught you how to do that?"

Ali sighed and looked everywhere around the room but at me.

"Who taught you how to clear this pistol?"

"A boy from school. His father's a weapons instructor up at Quantico."

I looked at the hollow-points in the magazine, then sniffed the chamber. All I smelled was gun oil. "Have you fired it?"

"A few times."

"She's really good, Dad." Eric was proud of his sister's ability.

"You've seen her shoot?" I turned back to Ali. "You shot this pistol with your brother around?"

"Just once," she said, as if that made it all right.

"Does your mother know you have this?"

Ali rolled her eyes. "Oh, right. Like she wouldn't go all apoplectic."

I tucked the magazine into my back pocket. "She'd be right to. This is very dangerous, Ali. First, you haven't had the training. And second, do you know how much more likely it is for a weapon to be used against one of the family? This isn't a game, Ali. This is very dangerous."

Ali stuck out her chin, defying me. "You've said that like about a hundred times. I know, Dad. I'm being careful."

"And I'll say it again until you get it." Ali's stance made me back away a bit, not wanting to lose the importance of my point in an argument both of us would lose. I told her to sit with me. When she did, I put my arm over her shoulder. "Think of how you'd feel if you accidentally shot someone with this, like your brother, or even Gadget."

"I said I'm being careful. And with you living up

in the city, and Mom not wanting a gun in the house . . ."

"For good reason."

"Someone had to protect us, in case, you know, one of your murderers came looking for you."

"That's not going to happen."

"You don't know that." Ali was right. In a small town, when you have even the smallest amount of fame, everyone knows where you live.

"The police keep a close watch on all of you when I'm not here," I said.

"Then why do we have to go to Grandma's?" Ali was always the smart one, always the one to exploit an opening.

"Because I'd feel better."

"Are *you* coming?" Eric asked.

"No, I'm staying here. In case someone does come to the house, I want to make sure he's caught."

"So it is imminent and credible," Ali said.

"It's probably just an ex-con trying to rattle my cage." I told them about the man in the red shirt, but not how he gave me that black-hole feeling of fear in my gut, or about the missing glass from their kitchen that had turned up at a murder scene two hundred miles south.

"Look, I'm taking the train into the city tomorrow morning for an interview. I'd feel better if you were at your grandmother's. Do this for me, okay, guys?"

Ali and Eric nodded and let me hug them both. "And as for this pistol, I don't want to see either of you handling a gun again, not unless I'm with you, okay?"

Eric brightened. "Does this mean you'll teach me how to shoot?"

"No. Not until your mother thinks it's all right."

Eric sagged. "Which is never." He was probably right, too.

19

I let Ali drive my car to her grandmother's and I called Toronto. Toni wasn't in her room, but it was dinnertime and I pictured her schmoozing with the other shrinks over cocktails. I told the desk clerk I'd try later and said, "No, no message."

Gadget and I ate a bit of the Italian takeout and then stuffed the remaining cartons into the refrigerator. I couldn't shake the nauseating fear I'd felt when Ali had pulled that semiautomatic from under her mattress. I knew how things could go so wrong, so quickly, when you throw a loaded gun into your average day. I decided to take a walk and check on things while the sun was still up. I dropped my revolver into my pants pocket and went into the yard with Gadget. By the time we'd walked around the yard and up the long driveway, the sun was setting behind the trees. Back in the house, I tried Toni's number again and again got no answer.

The house seemed too big for just a man and a dog, so I tried Katie's cell phone and got her voice mail. I hung up without leaving a message.

I tried Trevor's number and found him at the Beaufort police station.

"Nothing new here, Jake. They're all covering their backsides with one hand and pointing fingers with the other. Reminds me of our days at the Bureau."

"But you and Katie are all right."

"Yeah. Katie's still a little shaken, but okay. What about you? How's the family?"

"I sent the kids to their grandmother's for the night. It's just me and Gadget."

Katie would never have let this pass unquestioned. She would have wanted to know why, and for how long, and when I told her about the man in the red shirt, she would have demanded I call the police. But Trevor wasn't wired that way. He said, "Mm-hmm," and let it go. I would probably have done the same.

"Ali surprised me," I said.

"Yeah? What happened? She graduate from law school over the summer?"

I laughed. Trevor had always been impressed with Ali and credited her intelligence to her mother's side of the family. "No, man, she had my father's .45 tucked under her mattress. And it looks like she's learned how to use it."

"When I was sixteen, I had *Playboy*s under mine."

"I don't know which would disturb me more."

Trevor laughed. "Listen, you want me to take her to the range when I get back?"

"Toni wouldn't have it."

"Yeah. Well, think about it. If the kid's interested, she needs to know how to do it right."

"I'll let you try to convince her mother."

"That reminds me. I promised Valerie I'd call before the kids went to bed. I'll talk to you later, Jake."

"Right."

"Everything's okay up there, right?"

"Everything's fine."

I called Dom and got his voice mail. I told him to call if there was anything new on his end of the investigation.

I called Jerry, and he answered after the third ring and in whispers explained that he was at a movie with Dr. Plessy, and everyone, including Dr. Plessy, was glaring at him and he had to go.

I tried Toni again, but still no answer.

It was dark outside so I turned off all the lights except those in my office and set the alarm. Gadget curled up under the desk. I placed my father's pistol on the desktop. He'd carried it onto Guadalcanal, Iwo Jima, and Okinawa. It was the pistol he'd been cleaning when he'd heard about the Japanese surrender.

The December I was twelve, I'd found it in the back of his closet while looking for Christmas presents. It was in a shoebox with his medals, dog tags, and marine insignia. I remember holding it, feeling its weight, trying to pull the slide back against the recoil spring and failing. I put it back and didn't mention it until that summer when I asked my father to teach me how to shoot a pistol. He said he didn't own one, which was the first and only lie my father ever told me.

Later, after I was in the service myself, eager to go overseas and earn my own medals, I asked him why he'd kept it hidden. He told me about having it broken down in front of him, the parts spread across the pages of a *Stars and Stripes*, when the news came over the radio that the war was over.

"Seemed wrong to reload it," he said. "Like maybe if I had, the war would start up all over again." I didn't understand him then, but I understand him now.

I hefted the pistol, feeling the checked grips under my palm, its balanced weight in my hand. The Colt semiautomatic—official nomenclature, the M1911A1—weighs close to two pounds and feels like three compared to my fifteen-ounce Airweight.

Without really thinking about it, I removed the front bushing and eased the spring assembly out from under the barrel. I continued to break the gun down, letting my mind dig around in the facts of the North Carolina murder while my hands worked the smooth, cool steel of Mr. Browning's timeless design.

We knew that William Rush, the key man with the weapons system, thought he had something that would interest the government, specifically DARPA, the whiz-bang, bureaucracy-leaping techno boys who could green-light funds for promising new ways of killing people and breaking things. So Rush and his secretary, Janice Callahan, had traveled to Washington to meet with a DARPA man. Dr. Rush returned to North Carolina, alone.

That night, Janice Callahan and the DARPA man were murdered in Alexandria. The casings found at the scene pointed to Callahan's ex-husband, pushed off the deep end by jealousy when he discovered his ex and the government man in bed together. At least, that's how it was meant to look.

That left me with these questions: If Mrs. De Vries's niece was sexually involved with the guy from DARPA, was the sex business or pleasure? And was the sex real or was it staged? And if the sex was staged, what was the real motive the staging was meant to hide?

The next night Dr. Rush was shot in a motel bathtub, and his body was moved to the jogging trail near his office. The files relating to the weapons system are gone, along with his laptop computer. Again, the secretary's ex is the most likely suspect based on shell casings, witnesses who saw his car, a suspect footprint, and tire tracks.

But why did Rush go to the motel? Whom was he meeting and who was the woman who rented the room that night? Why did someone switch the security video to make it look as if the secretary had rented the room the night of the murder, the night she was lying dead in a bedroom in Alexandria? And who switched it?

Why had the ex-husband disappeared, and why had he surfaced long enough to engage a literary agent? Was the agent's death an accidental shooting or was it a hit on the wrong man?

Back to the motel: There was a woman there, based on the motel tape, hair samples, and epithelia. But who was she? Could she be the prostitute found murdered in a motel bathtub on the coast? We'd find that out soon enough, once the prints from the two motel rooms were compared.

And speaking of prints, the question digging at me was, who planted that glass at the murder scene? And why? Why add this irrelevant item to an otherwise carefully staged crime scene?

It could only be a message, a pointed warning to me personally, letting me know how easily murderers could reach out and touch my family.

I had reassembled the Colt and was casually working the slide, cocking the trigger, and then lowering the hammer and working the slide again. I had put a name to the mind behind these murders. A name he didn't care if I knew. But knowing Napoleon was behind the killings and finding out why, and what agents he had on the ground actually pulling the trigger, was a whole other matter.

By the time I had worked through the case, probing for more answers and coming up with only more questions, it was a little after twelve. I placed one last call to Toni's room, to tell her where the kids were, and to hear a voice besides my own, one that was familiar and knew how to ease me down from this agitated self-investigation.

"I'm sorry, sir, but there's no answer. Would you care to leave a message?"

"What do you mean there's no answer? It's after midnight."

The hotel operator tried again with the same results. "I'm sorry, sir, but if you'd like to leave a message . . ."

I remembered the man in the red shirt. "Let me talk to the manager."

"Yes, sir."

The manager was patient, but insisted that without proper authority, he couldn't violate a guest's privacy. "All I can tell you is your party is not answering her phone."

Exasperated, I said, "I know she's not answering her phone, dammit. If she were answering her phone, you and I would not be having this conversation."

"No, sir, that's quite right."

I ran my hand over my face, trying to be patient, trying not to get angry. "Okay. Fine. Has anyone seen her this evening? Can you tell me that?"

"I'm afraid not, sir, even if we had. We don't make a practice of putting our guests under surveillance. This is Canada," he said with clear emphasis.

"Goddammit, what can you tell me?"

"Just what you already know, sir. Dr. Donovan is a guest of this hotel and she is not taking any calls."

"Aha! So she is in her room."

"I didn't say that."

"But you said she was not taking calls."

"Please forgive me if I was inaccurate, sir. What I meant was that Dr. Donovan is not answering her phone, sir. For whatever reason is not for me to say."

Desperate, I played my cheapest card. Celebrity. "I'm sorry. Perhaps I didn't make it clear who this is. My name is Jake Donovan. Maybe you've heard of me."

"No, sir, I'm afraid I haven't."

"With the FBI?"

"No, sir."

"Do you watch crime shows on television?"

"I don't own a television, sir."

"But you've heard of the FBI."

"Unfortunately, sir, I was an American citizen until I fled the draft, sir, in 1966. I'm quite familiar with the FBI."

"Oh." This wasn't going at all well.

"Would this be official FBI business?"

"Would it matter if it was?"

"No, sir, not in Canada, sir."

I could hear the smile in his voice and wished my reach were as long as my enemy's. Then I realized that my reach was at least as long as the Toronto police force.

I hung up and called headquarters. With luck and several more calls, I tracked down an old friend and colleague, Inspector Haiki Droon, a former student at one of my classes at Quantico.

"Jake," he said, "are you thinking of emigrating north?"

"Every summer, but change my mind in November."

"So, what can I do for you at"—he paused, presumably to look at his watch—"ten to one in the morning?"

"Haiki, I need you to look in on my wife."

"What's wrong?"

I told him about the man in the red shirt and a little about the case I was working. "I'm just worried that she's not answering her phone, and the hotel manager doesn't want to get off his pale northern ass and knock on her door."

"She could be in the bath."

"Maybe. But I'd like to know."

After a moment, Haiki said, "I'll have some men sent round. I'll call you."

"Thanks, Haiki. Next time you're down this way, I'll buy you a hot dog."

The next hour went by like a week in Biloxi. I paced the room, walked around the yard, turned on lights and turned them off again, checked the dial tone three times to make sure the batteries in the phone were good, and made myself a drink. Okay, two drinks.

About the time Conan O'Brien was saying good night, the phone rang.

"Jake?"

"Haiki, what's up?"

Haiki took too long to answer. It could only be bad news. I waited. "Uh, Jake, she's not in her room."

"I know she's not in her room, Haiki. Where is she?"

Slowly Haiki said, "She's all right, Jake. She's just not in her room."

"Then where is she?"

I heard Haiki let out a long breath that blew

past the receiver and into my ear. "Jake, she is your ex-wife, isn't she?"

"Yeah, so?" Slowly the light began to dawn.

"So, a single woman, alone in a romantic city, who is not in her room . . ."

"Is sometimes in someone else's," I finished for him, just to save him the embarrassment.

"But if you look at this the right way, you should be relieved."

"Yes, of course I am."

"Silver lining, right?"

"Right."

"I'm sorry, Jake."

"No, Haiki, it's me who's sorry. I'm sorry you had to do this. Really, really sorry. Does she know I was looking for her?"

"I'm afraid she does. The officers I sent around explained why they were searching for her."

"Terrific."

"She said she would talk to you in the morning."

"Was she angry?"

"The officers said she was, yes."

Suddenly, J. P. Napoleon took second place on the list of people who wanted me skinned.

20

I didn't sleep much that night. My blunder with Toni and the case in North Carolina kept chasing sleep away with questions and a whole page full of what-ifs. Sometimes, an answer comes to me in those times between being awake and being asleep, but not that night. The few minutes I did drift off put me inside that Black Diamond box again, sealed tight against the night air.

At four, I showered, dressed, called a cab, and joined the other early-morning commuters into Union Station. A network driver caught me before I descended into the Metro. The driver, who identified himself as Henry, escorted me through the station and out to the curb where a limo waited, guarded by a uniformed police officer. Everywhere, National Guardsmen with M16s watched over the crowd while D.C. police randomly searched the bags of anyone who even remotely fit the profile of a terrorist.

The police officer guarding the limo touched his cap. "I'm a big fan, Mr. Donovan. I've read all your books."

"Thanks. Busy day, huh?"

"They're all busy. Catching the bad guys."

"Go get 'em."

Inside the car I said, "Thanks, Henry. Must be tough driving around the city."

"It's not the driving, Mr. Donovan. It's the parking." Henry pulled around a yellow Ryder truck being searched by men with dogs. "You can't stop anywhere for more than a few minutes without someone calling out the bomb squad."

Henry drove up Massachusetts to Dupont Circle, turned up Nineteenth, and parked in front of the studio building. "Here you are, Mr. Donovan. Break a leg."

A few minutes later, just after six, I was in the chair in the makeup department and a twenty-something girl circled me. "Hi. I'm Randi, with an *i*."

"Hi, Randi. I'm Jake with a silent *e*."

"Hi, Jake. Don't worry. We'll make you look like you've just spent the week in Cancún." She circled me again, surveying the wreckage.

"That bad?"

"Honey, I'll tell you a secret, okay?"

"Okay."

"You have to promise, 'cause if this gets out, well, who knows how these TV people might act."

"I promise."

She leaned in close and whispered, "I used to work in a mortician's so I've seen worse. But not much."

I was too tired to make a snappy comeback. I settled for a weak "Ha ha."

"Gotcha." She stretched my skin with her fingertips. "Did you get shoes to match these bags? You know, if I didn't know better, I'd swear you spent the night in a coffin."

I didn't tell her how close to the truth she was.

Urich came in, looked at me, and winced. "Randi, you up to the challenge?"

"Oh, yeah."

"Good. Now, Jake, you know how we do these things."

"You ask the questions and I answer them."

"The man's a pro, Randi, make him look like Clark Gable."

She looked up from her makeup tray. "Who?"

In spite of my reputation, I've never sought out celebrity. I learned a long time ago that newspapers misquote you and broadcast editors cut what you say. This is true across the board, from Pacifica to Fox. On one program I come out sounding like a puppet of the fascist state; on another, an inefficient cog in the bloated federal bureaucracy. So, the only reason to appear on these programs is to take a case public. Sometimes, you need help in finding someone. Sometimes, you want to put out information that will either make the suspect cocky so that he makes a mistake or is convinced that the powers of law enforcement arrayed against him are so relentless that his capture is just a matter of time.

In this case, I wanted to convince Callahan, the missing ex-husband, to contact us again. I needed to reassure him that he would be safe. I only hoped that he was watching TV, wherever he was.

Spider Urich, on the other hand, had a different agenda. I should have known.

The stage manager took me from the artistic hands of Randi with an *i* to a technician who wired me for sound. From there I went to the green room, which is never green but does have bagels, fruit, and a TV set tuned to the morning show. Before she left, I asked Randi if I could change the channel. She said, "No, honey, and believe me, I've tried."

I shared the green room with a gardener and his plants for fall, an author with a book about patriotic weight loss, and an actress who was flogging her new movie, *Stung*. I asked if it was a sequel to *The Sting*, but she said it wasn't.

"It's about love gone bad," she said.

I nodded and tried to look interested. It was six forty-five.

About seven-fifteen, after the actress, but before the author and gardener, the stage manager told me to follow her and I did. I waited in the wings next to the producer, and when the host went to a commercial, the producer took me to a set on the far end of the soundstage. Fake books and four golden Emmys lined shelves behind Spider's chair. I sat on the leather sofa, and a young girl wearing a set of head-phones brought me a cup of coffee.

The floor director said, "We're back in five, four, three . . . ," counted silently down the rest of the way, then pointed at Spider.

Spider smiled. "Good morning. Today I have with me Jake Donovan, famed FBI profiler, technical adviser to numerous Hollywood films, author, speaker, and active investigator. Thank you for being with us this morning, Jake."

I smiled back. "It's nice to be here, Spider."

Spider shifted in his chair and leaned closer to me, a pencil in his hand as if he needed to take notes. "Jake, you and Attorney General Armstrong have worked together in the past, isn't that true?"

I shot him a What-the-hell-is-this? look and answered, "Not directly, no."

"But you were involved in one case, the Little Angel Day Care kidnapping."

"Yes. But the attorney general wasn't on that case." I tried to gently change the subject. "I am working on an interesting case right now."

"But in the Little Angel case, you uncovered some evidence that implicated the attorney general in a criminal conspiracy, isn't that right?"

I smiled again and shook my head. "Spider, I don't know where you get your information . . ." I fired warning shots with my eyes.

Spider ignored them. "Armstrong, as a state prosecutor, purposely withheld evidence so that he could gain a conviction, even though the evidence proved his suspect was innocent."

"Is there a question in there?" I said with a laugh, hoping to lighten up what was heading into a bad situation.

"Come on, Jake, the attorney general illegally prosecuted an innocent man, didn't he?"

"That man was released, and eventually the right man was convicted—by Attorney General Armstrong."

"But only *after* you threatened to go public with what you knew, isn't that right?"

"Spider, this is all history—"

Spider poked the air with his pencil. "Now we come to today, and what is arguably the biggest case since September eleventh, and that's the terrorist attack on the First Lady."

"I'm not assigned to that case." I said.

"Precisely! And why not? Why is one of our finest investigative minds not working an attempted assassination?"

I took a sip of coffee, giving myself a moment, looking for a way to take control of the interview. "There are many good people assigned to the case, so that I can handle other cases, like this one in North Carolina—"

"But the attorney general took you off the case."

"Not directly, no."

"We asked the attorney general earlier and this is what he had to say."

Spider nodded and the monitors above us changed to a shot of Armstrong, who said, "Jake Donovan is only interested in furthering Jake Donovan. He relies on hired help, people who have been dismissed from law enforcement for a variety of reasons, to perform actual investigations. What does he do? He goes on television to promote a book. To call him an investigator is granting him a title he doesn't deserve. Yesterday, Jake Donovan, heedless of the consequences, involved a literary agent, Sid Whare, in a dangerous situation. Tragically, Mr. Whare was shot and killed. So, you want to know why he's not investigating the attack on the First Lady? That's why."

The picture on the monitor changed to a tight shot of me, looking up, and looking shocked and uncomfortable.

"What's your response, Jake?"

The monitor changed again to a two-shot of Spider and me. As calmly as I could, I said, "Mr. Whare was an unfortunate victim of an accidental shooting. And he was there because you—"

Spider interrupted, "There is clearly animosity between you and the attorney general."

"I have no animosity toward Mr. Armstrong."

"When did you change your opinion, Jake?"

That was one of those Have-you-stopped-beating-your-wife? questions. No answer would be the right answer. The floor director raised one finger and signaled Spider to wrap it up.

I looked straight into the camera and said, "Mr. Callahan, if you're watching, I want to hear your story. Please, if you're watching, contact me. I promise you'll be treated fairly."

"Jake? You want to say hello to your mother while you're at it?"

I bared my teeth at Spider and hoped it would pass as a smile.

Spider asked, "So, what do you think of the investigation so far?"

"I can't comment on that, because I haven't seen the files. But I'm certain the attorney general is doing everything he can."

"What would you do differently if you were running the investigation?"

Blame my vanity, or my anger, but instead of giving a safe, political nonanswer, I said, "I'd look at the victims in that Hawker 700 and see if anyone had motive to kill one or all of them."

Spider's voice went up. "So you're saying this wasn't an assault on the first family at all? That the attorney general is on the wrong track completely?"

"I'm sure the attorney general has considered every possibility."

Spider turned to the camera. "A stunning speculation by Jake Donovan, former FBI profiler. The First Lady might not have been the target of the most recent terrorist attack, and the attorney general is completely mishandling the investigation. Back in a minute." And we were out.

I pulled the mike from my shirt and headed for the wings.

Spider caught me by the shoulder. "Jake, that was great! The betrayal, the conflict, and that final revelation. That was terrific. You were terrific. Hell, *I* was terrific."

I tried to back away from Spider but was blocked by the crew carrying a table loaded with pots and dirt for the gardening segment. I was shoved in close to Spider and I said, my voice a whisper between us, "You are a backstabbing son of a bitch, Urich."

"Oh, Jake, hold on a minute."

I pushed into the hallway. The producer stopped me at the elevators. "Mr. Donovan, I am so sorry. I had no idea Spider was going to ambush you with that clip."

"It's okay. I should have seen it coming." I watched the numbers above the door change while she apologized again and promised me a three-minute spot for my next book.

The doors opened and I said, "Do me a favor. Lose my number."

Henry met me in the lobby. "The producer just called. I'm supposed to take you back to the train station, Mr. Donovan."

"Thanks, Henry. But I'll catch a cab." Henry followed me out to the sidewalk where the limo waited by the curb.

"Come on, Mr. Donovan. I don't drive you, I could get in trouble."

I looked up and down the street. I didn't see any cabs for blocks.

Henry held the door to the limo open. "Come on, Mr. Donovan. Hell, I'll drive you all the way home. Door-to-door service, what do you say?"

I thought about it for a moment, looked back up at the studios behind me, and said, "Sure, Henry, let's go." I slid into the rear seat.

Henry started to close the door, stopped. "You don't live in Key West, do you? Someplace like that?"

"No. Fredericksburg."

"Ah, well, a man can dream." Henry closed the door.

When Henry was behind the wheel, I said, "You won't get into trouble?"

"Screw 'em, Mr. Donovan." Henry wheeled the limo into traffic as if the rear end were on fire and he was trying to outrun the flames.

We hadn't made it across the Potomac before my phone rang. It was from Orlando Raven's office.

The operator said, "Please, hold for the director."

I watched the neighborhood creep by, the morning traffic snarled even worse than usual as people tried to find new routes around the streets blocked off by armored cars. Once again I was reminded of a Latin American capital where the oligarchy ruled behind the protective screen of armed men.

"Jake? Ravan here."

"Yes, sir."

"I'm going to make this short, because it's not something I find pleasant."

"Yes, sir."

"I'm pulling your credentials, Jake. You no longer have any official law enforcement function. That applies to your team, too."

"You agree with this, sir?"

"My hands are tied, Jake. And you brought a lot of this on yourself."

"Yes, sir."

"Maybe, after all this blows over . . ."

"So, Armstrong watched the news this morning."

"Jake, I have no way to protect you from this."

"I understand, sir."

"When you and I can talk in private, maybe you can explain why a smart man like you could do something so stupid."

"I'd like to try, Orlando."

"And I'd like to hear it. I'll be in touch."

"Thank you, sir." I hung up. That was it. My funding frozen by lawyers and my authority stripped away by politicians. My phone rang again.

"Jake, it's Katie. Are you all right?"

"You saw the news."

"Yes, my God, how could you let that weasel ambush you like that?"

"It happened."

"Trevor told me you called. I'm sorry I didn't call back, but I was a little shaken."

"It's okay."

Henry stopped the long limo at a roadblock. Men in uniform with no insignia, armed with H&K MP5s, peered into the car as Henry showed his identification.

"And then Rob called," Katie said, her voice almost a whisper.

"Was this before or after the fight?"

"I was so angry with you, Jake Donovan. You and Rob, grown men fighting like teenagers. If I was smart, I'd find myself a nice accountant, someone who doesn't have huge amounts of testosterone sloshing around inside him." She sighed and I pictured her pinching the bridge of her nose because it's what she did when she was exasperated.

"Katie, you need to come home."

"You know I can't. You know that."

"I don't mean it that way. I mean you need to come home. We're no longer part of the investigation." I explained what Director Ravan had done, and why.

"You think this is for good? Or are we just suspended?"

"It sounds permanent to me. Come home and we'll see where we are, okay?"

"Okay."

We said good-bye and I called Trevor and told him the news. I also told him about the man in the red shirt. "And, Trevor, I'm not sure how bad this will get before it gets better, but you should be with your family."

"You think this Holy Knight could come visit my house?"

"Maybe. You might want to call Valerie. See if she and the kids can go someplace until you get home. If not, let me know and I'll set them up at a safe house myself."

"Thanks, Jake. I'll catch the next plane out."

By this time we were on I-95 heading south, away from the incoming flow of commuters, so the road was fairly clear, or as clear as the roads get around Washington at this time of morning. Henry and I talked a little about the traffic and the weather, and I asked about his job.

"I drove a cab for a long time, then a friend got me this, driving celebrities. It's easy and fun. Most famous people are pretty nice. In fact, the bigger they are, the nicer they usually are. The worst are the singers, the divas, you know? Liza Minnelli was nice. Had her last week. But that girl is some kind of homely."

My phone rang again. This time it was Toni.

"What is going on, Jake? First you have the Toronto police track me down, and that is none of your business where I am or with whom, and now I try calling the house and no one is there. Where are you and where are the kids?"

"They're safe, they're at my mother's house. I'm in the city. I just had my ticket pulled."

"What?"

"I no longer have a job. The director fired me about fifteen minutes ago."

"Oh, Jake."

I didn't want to tell her about why the kids were at my mother's place, not over the phone, but the threat of the night before wasn't any less in daylight. "Toni, I need you to watch your back, okay? I need you to be extra careful. That's what last night was about, and I'm sorry if I embarrassed you."

Toni laughed. "You should have seen the guy I was with. He thought the marriage police were busting in on him."

"He's married?"

"Separated."

"Oh." I didn't know what to say to that so I said nothing.

"So, what's the danger this time? Some thug get paroled? You get another fan letter full of white powder?"

"No, it's bigger than that." I told her about the Holy Knight and the car, and how he knew she was in Toronto.

"That explains it," she said.

"What?"

"I've had a police escort everywhere I went this morning. They try to blend in, but once you're married to a cop, you can spot them. It's the shoes."

"If one of them is twenty pounds overweight and has a face like a Latvian bulldog, that's Haiki. Say hi."

"That's okay. I'm catching the next flight home. The seminar's a bore and the city isn't the same. Besides, you scared the hell out of my boyfriend."

"It wasn't intentional."

"I know. I was angry last night. I mean really angry, but I'm over it."

I was enjoying Toni's voice and the memory of our last time in Toronto. "Toni, let me know when your flight comes in and I'll pick you up."

"I have my car at the airport. Really, Jake, I'll be fine. I'll call when I land."

"Okay. But be careful."

"I will."

I stretched out in the rear of the limo and closed my eyes. I tried not to think about the consequences of this morning's interview. Although it was Spider Urich who had let the AG's secrets out for a national audience, I was the one who would get fried. As independent as the Broken Wings are, we still come under the jurisdiction of the Justice Department and serve only under the authority granted to us by the attorney general. I knew that authority had the same longevity as Gadget's attention span, and after Armstrong was finished with us, I'd be lucky to land a job as security guard at the local Bag'n'Go.

Somewhere in the snarl of construction on I-95, I drifted off. A few minutes out of Fredericksburg, my cell phone woke me up.

"Jake, this is Vince Andrews. I got a name on that guy in the red shirt."

"Yeah?"

"He's William Bower. Current address is in Illinois, but he hasn't reported to his parole officer in months. He's a Desert Storm veteran with a Tim McVeigh profile. Heavy training in demolitions. And you were right about Leavenworth. Bower was convicted of transporting explosives in '98, served two years of an eight-year sentence. He's supposed to be an expert at wiring cars and is suspected in the bombing of a minister's car in North Carolina last year. Apparently, that's what he does. He blows up cars."

It took a second to penetrate.

"You haven't tried to start your car this morning, have you, Jake?"

"No, I took the train. I mean I'm in a limo. No, I'm not in my car." My mind was sorting this out, faster than my mouth could keep up.

"Good. I wouldn't try to start her before we've had the bomb squad take a look, understand?"

"My daughter has my car."

There was a long silence on Andrews's end. Then he said, "Call her now, Jake. I'll call the police."

"She's in Fredericksburg." I gave him the address.

"Got it." He hung up.

I leaned forward and said to Henry, "I need you to go as fast as you're comfortable driving, Henry. Can you do that?"

Henry smiled in the rearview. "All I needed was the word." The limo nearly lifted off.

I put on my seat belt and tried my mother's number. The phone was busy. I hit redial and got another busy signal. I told Henry where to exit and he flew down the ramp and took a hard left. The traffic was light and Henry threaded the limo through spaces so narrow I wouldn't have tried it in the Aston Martin.

The Aston Martin. Bower knew my car. That's what he was doing the day before, checking it out, and thanks to my starter he had had a good long look inside the engine compartment. And now Ali had the car.

I prayed I wasn't too late. I prayed that Ali had slept in as she did almost every morning she wasn't in school. I prayed that the sirens I heard in the distance weren't meant for her.

We crested Marye's Heights, which overlook the town. Henry was doing sixty, barreling through intersections, weaving between SUVs as if they were slow-footed cattle. I craned to see over the rooftops, to the apartment building where my mother lived. We cleared the trees, and there, beyond the cemetery, past the battlefield, and over the town's low skyline, I saw black smoke rise up and flatten against the cloudless sky. The sirens grew louder, and their wail told me how I had underestimated the enemy, and how naked I had left my family in a dangerous world.

21

Henry ran a red light and picked up a police cruiser. He glanced at me in the rearview. "You want me to stop?"

"No."

"I didn't think so." Henry pulled the wheel left and the limo rolled around the intersection, the police car close behind, its lights flashing, its siren joining the others on the far side of town.

I pressed my ID against the back window, but didn't expect it to give us any official cover. We were doing sixty-five in a thirty-five and scattering people like birds.

Two blocks from the apartment house, we could smell the heavy stench of burning rubber and gasoline. There was no doubt it was a car fire. Flashing yellow and blue lights chased the shadows from the oaks along the street and sirens filled my ears. A block from the fire, a policeman held up his hand and Henry stopped. I jumped out of the car, flashing my ID as I ran, and sprinted toward the fire trucks, EMT van, and police cars blocking the entrance to the apartment building's parking lot.

I still had hope that this was a simple car fire, but that hope turned to horror when I saw the Aston Martin. The chassis sat on flattened, smoking tires. The hood, torn free, had been tossed twenty feet. The roof was twisted back and the interior gutted. The windows, and the windows of all the cars around it, were gone. In front of the car, all alone, covered by a stained sheet, lay a body.

The windows on the parking-lot side of the apartment building were blown out and paramedics were intent, administering oxygen and kind attention to the mostly elderly residents.

A cop I knew only as Tom put his hand on my chest. "Jake, stop. Stay here."

I blew past him and ran to the body lying still on the pavement. I knelt, held my breath, and drew the sheet back. There was a man whose face had been blown away. The flesh was missing and all that was left were bits of bone, teeth, and shredded flaps of torn muscle. His jaw was gone and one eye seemed to look back at me, surprised at such a hard interruption in such a beautiful morning. Smoke curled from his overalls.

"Jake, she's okay. Your daughter is okay."

Tom had his hand on my shoulder. I heard Ali's voice calling me, "Daddy!" She was running toward me, followed closely by two city police and a paramedic.

I stood and caught her and held her as tightly as I could, for as long as I could, afraid to let go, afraid to look at her. "Oh, sweetheart, are you okay? God, I am so glad you're all right."

"Oh, Daddy." She cried hard against my neck.

"I got here as quickly as I could." I stroked her hair. "I'm so sorry."

"It was so horrible. That poor man."

"Who is he?"

"He's a mechanic. I called them when the car wouldn't start."

My skin tingled, frozen. "You tried to start the car?"

"Yes, to take Eric to his baseball practice."

"You and Eric were in the car?"

"Yes." She wiped her face, smudging it with soot. "When it wouldn't start, we went inside and called the garage."

The thought of how close I had come to losing both of my children made my knees weak. The police and a paramedic stepped closer, and one of the cops said, "The bomb was wired to the hood. That's what we think."

I held Ali's shoulders. "You didn't raise the hood?"

She shook her head and started to cry again. "I didn't want to get my hands dirty."

I hugged her to me again. "Oh, honey, I don't want you to do anything to a car, ever again. I don't want you to even pump your own gas, you hear me?"

Eric ran from my mother's building and hugged me around the waist. The three of us stood there, holding each other for a long time.

I took Ali and Eric into my mother's apartment and sat them on the couch. Both were in the walking trance you see in young soldiers after their first firefight. Both were too young to have their sense of immortality stripped away so suddenly, and so violently.

Even my mother, a tough old girl who had spent a lifetime married to a former marine and union organizer, was knocked sideways. As she lit another cigarette in her chain of three packs a day, her hands shook. "Jake, I'm so sorry."

"There was nothing you could do, Mom."

"If your father had been here . . ."

"He would have lifted the hood, Mom. Don't blame yourself for this. This is my fault. I should have moved everyone to a safe house yesterday."

My mother hugged me and held me as tightly as I'd held Ali and Eric. Scared parents and frightened children. An innocent man blown out of his shoes. The dead stretched from the coast of North Carolina to Old Town. Whatever J. P. Napoleon was after, I hoped it was worth it.

Knowing that my mother would be better off if she was busy, I told her to get her stuff together and to make a list of all the things she'd need to be away for a few days.

While my mother was getting ready to move, I

went down to help Henry with the police. I knew most of the cops on the local force, and those I didn't know knew me. After threatening Henry with numerous felonies and more misdemeanors than I could count, the supervisor let him go with his promise that if he was ever in Fredericksburg again, it would be on public transportation. Several of the street cops expressed admiration for the way Henry had piloted the long black limo through the city streets. "Not that we can approve of such reckless behavior," one cop said through a smile, half-hidden by a styrofoam cup of coffee, "but we have bets that in a previous life you piloted an F-18."

I checked with the primary, Detective James Burdick. Burdick and I had known each other for years. He had taken several classes with me at Quantico, and we'd occasionally had a beer together at a local cop bar and swapped war stories.

Behind us, the criminalists were doing their sketches, logging smoking fragments of evidence from the bomb, and arson investigators were already comparing notes.

"It'll take some time to test what's here," Burdick said, "but we think it's a military type of explosive, detonated by lifting the hood. Like I said, that's preliminary. We'll know more in twelve hours or so." Jim took off his hat and scratched his head. "What can you tell me, Jake, I mean about enemies, anyone who might want to see you dead?"

"That's a pretty long list."

"Let's start with the past forty-eight hours."

I told him about Bower and gave him a description, plus Andrews's number in Washington. "He can send the files," I said.

"Good. Fine." Burdick looked off toward a TV news van that was pulling up at the barricades. "And what are you going to do?"

"Take my family to a safe house."

"Then what?"

"Get something to eat."

"After lunch."

"Maybe take a nap."

"Come on, Jake, you know what I'm saying."

"Jim, you'll understand if I take this rather personally."

"And you'll understand if I ask you to stay away from my investigation."

"Sure, I understand. Ask away."

Burdick looked at me, fixing me with the same stare he used to pin suspects. "This tied into a case you're working?"

"Yeah. I think so." I laid out the North Carolina case, as much as I could in a few moments, gave him Weller's number in Durham and the primary's in the Alexandria murders.

"Body count is adding up," he said.

"I don't think we're finished, Jim. Not by a long shot."

"Any idea yet who's behind it?"

Yeah, I thought, I know who's behind it. He's a phantom with a cartoon name that most cops think is no more of a threat than the monster under the bed. "No, Jim, nothing yet," I said.

* * * *

Henry dropped us off at the house on the river. I gave him all the money I had in my pocket, $63, and apologized for putting his life and his job in jeopardy.

"It's nothing." He wouldn't take the money.

"You told me you were married."

"Twelve years in December."

"And what will your wife say when you tell her you refused a sixty-dollar tip?"

Henry's face split into a wide smile. "Whatever she'd say, I'd be hearing it for the next twenty years." He took the bills.

"You have any trouble at work over this, you let me know."

Henry nodded. "I will. You take care of those children now."

I promised I would.

"You need a ride again, give me a call. You're a lot more fun than Liza Minnelli."

I told him I could sing, too. Laughing, Henry drove up the long drive toward the highway, the radio's bass vibrating the neighborhood.

We loaded the bags and Gadget into the Land Rover and drove into northern Virginia. A town house in Fairfax belonged to a friend of a friend. If the investigation didn't turn up suspects in custody in the next two days, I would move the family again, this time to a place in Montana. That is, if Toni would go along with it.

My mother grudgingly agreed to smoke only on the back deck. Eric pronounced the computer adequate for his games, but just barely: "It's only got one hundred twenty-eight megs of RAM, but it'll be okay."

"Can I call Raoul?" Ali wanted to know.

"You can, but you can't tell him where you are. And don't use the cell phone or the phone here. Go down to the convenience store and use their pay phone."

"What?"

"Just in case. Just for a few days."

Ali didn't argue. "I think I'll take a nap." She walked upstairs taking each step as if she were carrying a great weight.

"Watch her, Mom."

"I will."

I kissed my mother's forehead and let her hug me again. She hung on until I said, "I've got to go, Mom."

"I know."

"Make up a list of groceries you'll need."

"Okay."

"I'll even get your cigarettes, although everyone would be happier if you quit."

My mother stared at me as if I were mentally lacking, a look I've seen a lot in my life. She said, "Like smoking is the most dangerous part of my day."

22

I drove to Crystal City, watching to see if I was being followed. I circled the block a few times and once pulled to the curb to let traffic pass me by. When I felt comfortable, I pulled into the parking garage and backed into a slot. I passed up the elevator, an old habit from my field days when I worked the projects in Detroit. Gangs like to ambush elevators, especially elevators containing cops, as an initiation into the family. Far too many rookies had the doors slide open on a nine-millimeter welcome.

I was alone in the stairwell and in the hallway. I quickly let myself into my apartment, my home with its grand view across the river. I opened the drapes and looked out. The plane wreckage had been cleared but a dark spot of scorched earth still marred the Mall.

I turned from the window and saw the blink of

the answering machine. I hit the play button and listened. There were many requests for interviews, most from the day after the congressman's plane went down. I had a couple of crank calls, as usual, from fans anxious to know if I'd kept souvenirs of any of my interviews with serial killers.

While I was thinking about how strange people were, and how that weirdness had actually made my career, I missed the first part of his message and had to replay it.

"Mr. Donovan. This is Mr. Kurz calling to confirm our appointment for twelve. I'll meet you at the coffee place across the street. If you're held up, I'll wait as long as I can."

A man named Kurz with a Carolina accent. I checked my watch. The call had come in at eight-thirty. It was a little after one o'clock.

I jogged across the street and down the long flight of steps into the underground. The buildings of Crystal City are connected forty feet beneath the surface by walkways lined with shops and restaurants, an underground mall for the commuters who travel the Metro every day.

Coffee. Come across the street for coffee. This wasn't helpful. There were a good half dozen coffee bars, from Starbucks to a start-up called The Buzz. Add to these the coffee stations at deli counters, doughnut shops, burger joints, and the newsstand, and Callahan could be almost anywhere.

Which, I guessed, was his point.

I jogged from coffee shop to coffee shop, searching for a man I knew from pictures and stats—six-five, brown hair, blue eyes, two-forty. The lunch crowd had thinned, but plenty were still stretching out their lunch hour.

Callahan would be tanned. He would probably not be wearing a suit, but casual clothes, even work clothes. He would be by himself with that quick look left and right that betrayed a man afraid to be seen. There would be a tension about him, not only from the risk of being caught, but also from an hour's worth of coffee. That is, if he was still waiting.

I tried to think like Callahan. I needed a spot that gave me a view in as many directions as possible, for as far as I could see. I needed a place with enough exits. For Callahan, only one place fit.

A coffee bar was at the top of the steps that came up from the Crystal City Metro stop. It was darker there, with a constantly moving crowd. The coffee bar was the only place to sit, aside from the shoeshine stand, and any surveillance would stand out by standing still. From this bar, a man could run into a hotel lobby on the right and from there to the street. Or he could run left and into the long mall with numerous places to get lost or get away. Straight ahead was the long climb to the street, and behind was the descent to the Metro platform. Once you made the train, you could be anywhere in Washington in under a half hour, including the airport or Union Station.

Eight stools were at the bar. Three of them were filled. A young woman hit on a double espresso. Next to her was a man in a suit reading the *Washington Times* and sipping a latte. The third drinker was a young guy, dressed like a student and hunched over a thick hardback and a double tall cappuccino. I sat between the *Times* and the hardback and ordered a cup of coffee, black.

The girl got up and walked up the steps, into the sunlight. The three of us watched her go.

"Man," said the *Times*. "She is so fine. I'd do her in a minute."

"Yeah," said the hardback. "That's about all it would take. A minute."

The *Times* glared. "Speak for yourself, freak."

The three of us returned to our coffee. The man with the *Times* got up, tucked the paper under his arm, and walked away, in no hurry.

"Hey," the hardback said. "You're Jake Donovan."

I turned to the kid. He was tall, with baggy pants and a T-shirt that said ANARCHY RULES.

"I like your shirt."

"It's an oxymoron," the kid said.

"Yes, it is."

The kid held up the hardback. It was a copy of my first book. My picture was on the back of the dust jacket. "You wrote this."

"Yes, I did."

"You actually met all those killers, dude?"

I nodded and returned to watching the crowd, afraid I'd missed my opportunity.

"The guy said you'd be here."

That snapped me back. "What guy?"

"The guy who gave me this book. He gave me twenty dollars to sit here and wait for you."

"Where? Where is he?" I stood up and put a five on the counter. "How long ago?"

"Dude, man, take it easy. I was at school, in Georgetown. He stopped me and asked if I'd deliver this." He held up the hardback.

I took the book. "Did he say anything else?"

"Why?" A light went on in the kid's face. "Oh, man, he was a killer, right? Oh, dude, like this is so cool."

"Tell me exactly what he said."

"He said to come over here, sit and drink coffee, and when you showed up, to give you the book."

"That's all?"

"Yeah. That's all."

I gave the kid my card. "If you see him again, call me."

"Sure."

I walked away, looking through the hardback. I didn't know what I was looking for. A note, a card, something scribbled into the margins. I walked up the stairs toward the street, flipping through the pages, quickly at first, then more slowly when I didn't find anything on the first pass.

On the sidewalk, I looked away from the book long enough to cross against the light and into my apartment building. I took the steps again, out of habit more than caution. Inside, I threw what I needed for a few days into a spare duffel, shouldered it, and locked up. I still had the book in my hand, riffling the pages with my thumb. The elevator doors opened; I got in and punched the button for the parking garage.

The book was my first, a biography of sorts, concentrating on my investigations into multiple homicides and serial killers. It gave my mother nightmares. Ali hadn't read it, although I suspected Eric had. There isn't a copy of the book in my ex-wife's house, although the book is what paid for the place.

The elevator doors slid open and there he was, Bower, the man in the red shirt. Now he was dressed in a sports jacket and an open-collared, black polo. He was holding a Browning Buckmark .22, its barrel made even longer by the silencer screwed onto the muzzle. "I missed you, Jake." He fired. I struck out with the only weapon I had in hand: the hardback.

The little gun made a noise no louder than a cough, three times, and the elevator car filled with the stink of gunsmoke. The book jumped in my hands and paper rained down like snow. Something pushed into my shoulder, turning me. I spun the duffel from my shoulder and hit Bower's arm, knocking his aim to the side. The little gun fired twice and cracked the paneling behind my head.

The elevator doors closed on Bower and bounced off. He pulled the trigger three more times, and a flame shot up the side of my neck. I shouldered into Bower's arms, knocking the gun aside, and then I hit him with the book, three times in the face, and the smacks of the hardcover against his forehead echoed through the parking garage. The force of the blows knocked him back a step to the curb, where he lost his balance and fell to the concrete. The gun slid beneath a parked Chevy Suburban and Bower rolled after it. He had his hand on the grip before I could get my Airweight free of the ankle holster. I held the duffel up to my head and ran for the cover of the parked cars. One bullet buried itself in my folded clothing, another must have snicked my can of shaving cream. I could hear the hiss of foam filling all the empty spaces inside my duffel.

Bower dropped the empty magazine and shoved another ten rounds into the pistol grip.

I had my revolver out and shouted from behind a panel truck, "Come on, Bower, give it up. You're explosives. You can't handle a gun."

"Bullshit."

"Come on, you missed with ten shots."

"Fuck I missed. You're bleeding, Donovan. I got you."

I put my hand to my neck, and when I did, the pain in my shoulder made me grunt. My hand came away bloody.

"Starting to feel it, Donovan?"

"The cops will be here any minute." My shoulder began to throb and my head buzzed.

Bower laughed. "Nobody heard those shots. Nobody's coming. Now come out and I'll make this real quick—pop, pop, pop. No pain."

I stayed below the windows and duckwalked around to the rear of the truck. Bower was about twenty feet away, crouching behind the Suburban. He saw me and fired twice. The soft-nosed .22s chipped the concrete and powdered my hair. I fired two times with my .38 and the garage filled with giant claps.

"Someone heard that," I hollered. "It's only a matter of time, Bower."

He didn't answer. I eased around the back end of the truck and saw him, ass in the air, aiming under the cars for my legs.

His gun coughed and the truck tire next to me flattened with a sudden sigh.

I shot twice and heard a high-pitched yelp under the thunder.

I waited, listening. I could hear him swearing. "Did I hit you in the ass, Bower? Did I?" He called me a name that told me all I needed to know. I laughed and that made him swear louder.

He stood up and fired off the rest of the magazine.

I kept my head down until the bullets stopped, then fired back. It was my fifth bullet, and the last in the cylinder. I ducked behind the truck, pushed the brass free, and reloaded. When I looked again, Bower was gone. Blood made a dark, shining trail from the Suburban, around the corner, through the gates, and out into the street. I followed it until it stopped by the curb.

Bower had disappeared.

I went back into the garage and picked up the book. It was shredded near the spine where a bullet had turned my prose into so much confetti. I went to the Land Rover and shoved the book under the front seat.

Yes, I was disturbing the crime scene. Yes, I was

concealing evidence. Yes, I might have even been obstructing justice. But Callahan wanted me to have this book for some reason, and I needed to know what that reason was. And I'd never know if it was locked inside the evidence locker of the local police station.

23

The police took my story eight different times in eight different places, beginning at the parking garage as the EMT stopped the bleeding, then again at the emergency room as the doc sewed me up, and finally at the police station. Each time it came out the same. There was no happy ending.

They kept my pistol. If I'd been without a Virginia carry permit, they would have kept me. But a phone call to Larry Berman, my attorney, got things rolling and I was on my way home five hours later. The docs wanted to give me some Percocet but I told them I had to drive.

In the parking lot, I checked my voice mail. There was a call from Toni. Two calls. Three. Finally, on the fifth message, she was frantic. "Where are you? Where are the children? Goddammit, Jake, I've been calling for hours."

I dialed her number.

"Jake? Where are you?"

"I had a little problem. First, the kids are safe. Everyone's okay. Where are you?"

"I'm home. I called your mother's and there was no answer. I didn't know what to do."

"It's okay. Look, maybe you should go into town and stay in public until I get there. Go to Lubrano's, have a nice dinner."

"You can't tell me where the children are?"

"Not on the phone. I'll take you to them."

"Okay."

"But leave the house now. Okay?"

"I will."

The traffic was the regular glut that clogs the capital's arteries every day of the week. By the time I hit the Fredericksburg exit it was nearly eight. I called Toni at the restaurant and asked her to meet me at the house. Amazingly, she didn't sound angry.

I figured I'd beat her to the house by ten minutes depending on how quickly her waiter brought the check. I parked the Land Rover near the entrance to the driveway and approached the house from the river side. The sun was still up and would be for another hour, but the trees gave me cover. I checked the windows and saw nothing out of place. I looked at each door and there were no signs of tampering. There were no new scratches on the brass locks, but a good lock picker wouldn't leave scratches. Slowly, hearing everything magnified a thousand times, I unlocked the side door and went into the kitchen.

From there I could see the dining room, the living room, and into the hall.

At the end of the hall was the office, and inside the desk, where I'd left it, was my father's .45. I gripped the slide, and pulled it back. The sound of the round chambering filled the house. Safety off, muzzle pointed at wherever I looked, I cleared the rest of the house, room by room, closet by closet. By the time Toni drove up, I was sitting on the sofa with a glass of juice.

"I left my bags in the car. I just need a few more things," she said, walking through the kitchen. "Why did you park by the road?" Then she saw me and stopped. "Jake, what happened to you?"

I touched the bandage on my neck. "You mean here?"

"And your shoulder. What happened?"

I fingered the shredded fabric of my sports jacket, the frayed ends stiff with blood. "Now you see why the kids are in a safe house."

Toni's eyes went wide. "This happened here?" She meant the house.

"No, this happened today in Crystal City. But someone planted a bomb in my car this morning, at my mother's place."

"That explains the stares I got in the restaurant." Toni looked at me, the lines around her eyes deeper than I'd seen them before. "How long? How long do we have to stay away from the house?"

"I don't know."

"Before you catch whoever did this to us?"

I could hear the anger returning to her voice. It

was small, but growing. "Until I believe you're not in danger any longer."

"And how long is that?"

"I don't know."

She looked straight ahead, her face a mask. She turned and paced to the windows and then back. "I'll get my things." She started for the steps, then stopped. "It is safe to go upstairs?"

"Yes, I checked."

"What? You checked? You mean you weren't sure until you swept each of our bedrooms? Each of the children's closets? You weren't sure?"

"Toni, calm down."

"Did you have your gun out, Jake? Were you prepared to kill a man in Eric's room? In Ali's? Were you ready to turn our home, *this* home, into a crime scene?"

"Toni, this will all be over soon."

She shouted, "No! It will never be over! Look at you! Before, Jake, it was always in your head, all the killers, all the crime scenes, and all the victims you carried home to our bed. But now, you've brought them here, to my home. I will not allow that."

"What do you want me to do?"

"I want you to leave, Jake. And tomorrow I'm getting a court order to keep you away from this house." Toni let that settle around the room, then she turned and went up the steps, quickly.

I sat listening to her open and close drawers, slam doors, move from room to room, angry all the way to her footsteps. In all of our years together, even through the divorce, I'd never heard her yell. She'd never lost control, not once. Her voice was always calm, which was much worse than hollering. But this, this was more fear than anger, although there was plenty of that, too, shook loose by a glass or two of Lubrano's Chianti.

She came down with a single overnight bag. She had changed into a pair of jeans and a loose, short-sleeved shirt. Her hair was pulled back and held in place with a silver clip I'd brought back with me from Argentina.

"Tell me where the children are."

I gave her directions and said I'd stop by in the morning to make sure everyone was all right.

"Don't bother. I'm taking the kids with me for a while."

"Where?"

"I don't know yet."

We stood, awkward with the ghosts of my work between us.

"Bye, Jake."

I let her go.

24

A large house seems even larger after a fight, when you're alone with the echoes of an argument and the sound of your own voice in your head. I needed to hear someone with more troubles than I had, so I put Billie Holiday on the turntable.

My father's pistol was digging into my back so I pulled it from my belt and laid it on the coffee table in front of me. I thought of Bower, the showboat, packing a .22. Those were meant for men who did their work quickly and quietly, without a lot of banter. Clowns like Bower needed something bigger to get the job done. Like explosives, or a cannon like this GI, slab-sided .45. If he'd had this pistol this morning, I wouldn't have made it out of that elevator.

What had saved me was the book. I remembered the confetti blowing around the elevator car.

I went out to the Land Rover, pulled the book

from under the driver's seat, and carried it back to the house. The corner, near the spine, was torn off and the pages shredded. Another bullet had lodged into the final chapter and dimpled my photo, right above the left eye, on the rear cover. I sat staring at the book for a long time, then picked it up and opened it. The pages separated stiffly. Those holding the single bullet stuck together in a slab. I riffled the corners with my thumb, as I had that morning. The numbers flew by like gray frames of a film. I turned the book over and did it again. This time the gray sequence changed. Frames had been altered. I stopped at one of the page numbers. Page 373. The 7 had been circled in red ink. I looked at the other numbers. Several had also been circled in red. I wrote down the numbers in sequence, first back to front and then front to back. There were twelve numbers, all single digits. Too many for a phone number. I stared at the two strings, trying to see a pattern, a code. I pulled my cell phone and wrote down letters that corresponded to the numbers. After all the Scrabble combinations I could come up with, the closest thing I got to a message was something about a P-O-E-T's body part. If this was a new type of Rorschach test, I was one disturbed individual. But why the operator's zero instead of the 6, with its alphabetic *O?* Then I saw that the first three digits were 703, the area code for northern Virginia.

I pulled my cell phone and punched in the number. A man answered on the first ring. "Shady Grove Motel."

I hung up. Five minutes later I was standing at a pay phone outside a diner. I called the number again.

"Shady Grove Motel."

"Room twelve, please."

"Hold on."

The phone rang. A man answered, "Took you long enough to figure it out, Donovan. Jesus. I'm about to go crazy in here. They don't even have cable porn."

"Callahan?"

"No time, Donovan. I figure, I got about five minutes to check out of here before some asshole with my Makarov knocks on the door."

"You think someone's tapping your phone?"

"No, Donovan. Your phone."

"I'm at a pay phone. It's safe."

The man laughed. "Nothing's safe."

"Why don't you turn yourself in, Callahan? No one will harm you, I promise."

"Oh, right. Like no one would harm that literary agent I had for about ten minutes. Blew his fucking brains out, man."

"That was an accident."

"Bullshit. They thought it was me, man."

"Why would someone want to kill you?"

"Because I have something. It's my ex-wife's computer. Her laptop."

"Oh."

"It's what they all want. Even that congressman, that smiling fuck."

"You mean David Jason?"

"The guy who hired you. Right. Look, the way I see it, I give you this computer and then it's you they come after. So you want it?"

"Yes. Sure."

"Good. You know where that fish market is, at the end of the marina in D.C.?"

"You mean the one under the Fourteenth Street Bridge?"

"That's the one. Be there tomorrow after three. Look for the squid." He hung up.

I stood by the phone for a minute, the dead receiver in my hand. Then I drove home, checked each room of the house again, and when I felt comfortable that I was alone, poured myself a stiff single malt to soften the throb in my shoulder.

It was after eleven when a car pulled into the driveway and stopped by the garage. When Katie opened the door, she was staring down the barrel of my father's .45.

"Jeez, Jake, is that any way to welcome a partner?"

"Sorry, Katie, but I'm a little on edge."

"What the hell happened to your shoulder? And your neck?" She touched the bandage under my ear and her fingers warmed my skin. I wanted to hold her and let her warmth take away some of the day's pain.

"Jake." Rob stood out on the sidewalk, in the shadows. "I came to say I was sorry. You know, about taking a swing at you."

I saw the encouragement in Katie's eyes, something I couldn't resist, so I said, "That's okay, Rob. I'm sorry, too." We shook hands.

"Trevor's on his way," Katie said, "and Jerry and Dom should be here soon. We all flew up in the *Broken Wing.*"

"How? I thought we were grounded?"

"Frederick, Mrs. De Vries's man, sent us enough money to refuel and fly home. By the way, what is Frederick to Mrs. De Vries? Is he her butler? Driver? Manager? Boyfriend? What?"

"He's her majordomo," I said, "and our angel. Anything else is none of my business."

Katie and Rob sat on the stools at the kitchen counter and let me pour the Scotch, one-handed.

"So, what happened to your wing?"

"A guy shot me," I said, coming to enjoy the surprise on people's faces when I told them. "Shot me twice."

Trevor stuck his head in the door. "Who shot who?"

"Someone shot Jake," Katie said.

"Jake, you all right?"

"Why wouldn't Jake be all right?" Dom came in carrying a pizza box.

"Someone shot him," Trevor said.

"Where?"

"In the parking garage in Crystal City," I said.

"I meant, where on your body?" Dom said.

"Whose body?" Jerry came in carrying a bag full of Chinese takeout. Up until then, I hadn't realized how hungry I was.

"My body," I said.

Jerry stopped, looked at me. "Jake, what happened to you?"

"I was shot."

"Twice," said Trevor, taking the takeout.

"Where?"

"In Crystal City," Katie said, getting out plates and glasses.

"How come everybody knows about this but me?" Jerry said.

"I don't know anything," Dom said.

"We just got here ourselves," Trevor said. "So tell us, Jake, what happened?"

"I was shot."

"Twice," Jerry said. "We know that much."

"Well, have a seat and I'll tell you about the car bomb, too." It took the next hour, with interruptions for drinks, more chicken, and to order a pizza, to tell the story, and to show off my wounds. "One grazed my neck," I said.

"An inch in," Dom said, "and it would have pierced the jugular."

"The other," I said, "bounced off my clavicle and went through my trapezius muscle. Came out the other side."

"Bower is a busy man," Trevor said.

"What do you mean?"

Katie opened her notebook. "The prostitute who was killed at the beach was a Bridget Barton, from Gainesville, Florida. Her prints match the prints found at the motel where William Rush was killed. Bridget's address was twelve Magnolia Lane, University View trailer park in Gainesville."

"Bower's last known address," I said. "She was living with Bower."

"Rush and Barton were both killed with the same .357," Dom added.

"And we found fibers from the first motel in the second motel," Jerry added, "plus, hair from a wig we found at the first motel matches a wig we found in the victim's luggage."

"Weller got the phone records from the motel in Durham and the one on the coast. One number came up in common. An apartment in Durham. Guess who rented that apartment."

"Bower?" Jerry said.

"Not under that name," Katie said. "But we ran his prints, and it was him. Weller showed Bower's picture around the neighborhood and got a confirmed ID."

"The phone records from that apartment led us to the SWAT cop who killed Sid Whare," Trevor said.

"And he's missing," Katie said. "Weller and Snead found out he'd had money problems right up until the day before yesterday. Suddenly, he has ten thousand dollars wired to his account from a bank in the Caribbean."

"Wait a minute." Rob pressed his palms against his temples. "My head's starting to hurt."

"It's simple," Katie said, pulling one last shrimp from the bottom of a carton with her chopsticks. "Bower pays the prostitute to take William Rush—"

"The researcher," Trevor said.

"—to the motel in Durham where Bower kills him. Bower then kills the prostitute and hires the SWAT shooter to kill Callahan, except Callahan's hired an agent, Sid Whare, and Sid gets popped in Callahan's place."

Trevor said, "And we have witnesses who put Bower in Callahan's neighborhood."

"But what about the two people in Alexandria?" Rob said. "If Callahan didn't kill them, and Bower was in North Carolina, who murdered Mrs. Callahan and her government-issue boyfriend?"

"I don't know." I shrugged and it hurt like hell.

"Can I get you something?" Katie put her hand on my unhurt shoulder.

"I have some Percocet here." I fished the bottle out of my jacket pocket.

"I'll get you some water." Katie took away my Scotch.

"What we haven't talked about," I said, "is who is behind this." The team looked somber and nodded. "You all know who I mean."

"Napoleon," Dom said.

"But why, Jake?" Trevor had found the one thing that indicated I might be wrong. "I know you think Napoleon's the only one who would play games like planting your prints at a murder scene, but even if that's true, why in God's name would he hire a clown like Bower?"

"I've been wondering that myself," Katie said, handing me a glass of water and two Percocets. "Bower should have never shown himself to you the day before he bombs your car. That's amateur night."

"And," Dom said, "he comes at you today with a

gun, when all of his experience is in explosives." Dom shook his head. "It doesn't add up. Napoleon would hire a pro. That's what makes him so dangerous."

"I know," I said. "I've been thinking about this and I think Napoleon has contracted this out to someone else, someone who might not have all of his usual connections."

"Somebody with a limited criminal Rolodex," Jerry said.

Trevor nodded slowly. "It could be. But you could also think it's Napoleon because that's what you always think."

"Yeah," I admitted, "I thought of that, too."

"So, what do we do now?" Dom carefully crossed his legs, pulling at the crease so his pants wouldn't bag at the knee.

"I don't know if there is a *we*," I said. "The AG pulled what little authority we had. And there's no money to pay you guys."

Dom snugged his tie. "We were talking about that on the flight up."

Katie said, "We each have money saved. We're prepared to ride this out as long as it takes."

I looked around the living room at my team of Broken Wings: Dom, the impeccable dresser and the man who spoke eloquently for the dead. Jerry, who had cataloged every tire type, fabric swatch, and hair sample in the FBI files. Trevor, a disciplined analyst you could count on to watch your back when things got bad. And Katie, a woman who didn't compete in a man's world because, as she put it, "the only person I care about beating is the person I was yesterday." It's what made her the best there is.

Combined, these four were an investigative team second to none, in or out of the Bureau. I was proud to call them colleagues, and even prouder to call them friends.

Trevor said, "So, what do we do now, Jake?"

I swallowed the Percocets with a gulp of water, then said, "Let's go get the bad guys."

25

Katie would go to Gainesville and see what shook loose around Bower and Bridget Barton's place. Jerry would check in with his colleagues in Alexandria for information from that crime scene. Dom would speak to the ME who had performed the autopsies. I told Trevor to take some time with his family. He nodded, knowing without asking why it was important.

"I can run all of Bower's known associates through the computer at home," he said.

"Good. And speaking of computers, is there anyone we can trust to break into Janice Callahan's laptop?"

That caught them by surprise.

Katie blinked. "You have Janice Callahan's laptop?"

"Not yet. But I will tomorrow. But we need some-one who can get by its security."

Rob said, "I know someone."

I shook my head. "No, Rob, although I appreciate the offer. You're still with the Bureau and doing this kind of favor for us won't exactly earn you any points right now."

Jerry said he had a guy he trusted at Langley.

"CIA?"

Jerry nodded. "He's all right. I trust him."

"Great."

Trevor said, "Are you going to tell us how you've come by this computer, or do we have to read about it in your next book?"

I told them about the phone call. "I'm meeting him tomorrow at that fish market next to the marina."

"You need backup, Jake," Trevor said.

"I can do it," Katie jumped in.

"No, I want you in Florida ASAP. And, Trevor, I want you close to your wife and kids for a few days. This is not negotiable. I'll be fine."

Trevor reached into his jacket, pulled out his SIG-Sauer, and offered it to me, grip first. "Since the cops have your .38, take this."

"No, no thanks. I've got my own." I pulled the .45 from my belt.

Trevor took it, ejected the magazine, cleared the chamber, and sighted on a small china figurine at the far side of the room. "Man, this is a museum piece. Real live Colt 1911, government-issue. Sweet." He pushed the magazine back into the grip and handed me the pistol. "You got a carry permit for the District?"

"Not anymore."

"Yeah," Trevor said, "that's what I thought. Last thing you need is to be caught with that in D.C. without a permit."

"You have an idea?"

Trevor raised an eyebrow. "You know I do." He punched a number into his cell phone and, when his party answered, said, "It's Trevor. . . . Yes, sir." He listened. "I know it's late. . . . Yeah, I got a watch. Let me look at it. . . . Uh-huh. Mine says Patek Philippe on it, what does yours say? . . . That's what I thought." Trevor listened again, scowling. "I won this fair and square, Judge. It's not my fault you back a full house when I'm holding four of a kind." We could hear laughter on the other end. "Listen, I need a favor. You know Jake Donovan? . . . Uh-huh. Right. . . . Deep shit, yeah. That's why I called you. He needs a shield. . . . Uh-huh. Tomorrow. . . . No, no pay. Right. . . . So, swear him in and let him go on vacation." Trevor listened for a long time, pulled out his notebook, jotted down a few lines, and finally said, "Brother, I owe you. . . . Right. . . . What's that?" Trevor laughed. "Oh, no, *I* keep the watch. . . . Right. . . . Uh-huh. And, Judge, don't let the man get you down. Oh, that's right, you *are* the man." More laughter, they made their good-byes, and Trevor hung up.

He handed me the page from his notebook. "Go there tomorrow morning and by lunch you'll be a detective in the Metro Police. Congratulations, Jake, you're getting a gold shield."

* * *

The next day the judge with the bad sense to play poker with Trevor introduced me to a young woman who walked me through the paperwork, and by lunchtime, just as Trevor had promised, I raised my right hand and was sworn in as a detective in the Metro Police.

By two-thirty, I parked the Land Rover in the parking lot of the fish market and got out, the gold shield in my pocket and the .45 hidden inside my sling.

With the Fourteenth Street Bridge high overhead, and tons of sculpted marble within walking distance, the humble fish market sat on the Potomac. It was a square chunk of land, wide as a football field and covered in asphalt, where cabinet members rubbed elbows with taxi drivers and clerks. Covered barges wallowed in the water on three sides, enclosing the space. These barges, tied up forever, had been so completely converted into fish shops that it was hard to tell where they began and the land ended.

This was where local restaurants, good and bad, bought their seafood; where the recently singled staffers found that perfect piece of halibut; and where the intern, fresh from Smith, found the octopus for sushi negri that horrified her parents from Tulsa.

This is also where I was to meet Callahan. He was supposed to be carrying a laptop whose contents, according to him, were worth at least five people's lives.

"Look for the squid," he'd said.

I strolled through the afternoon crowd, looking into the barges below me, their counters crowded, two and three deep. Sea bass and yellowfin, flounder and skate, stared blankly up from iced beds. Mountains of oysters and clams waited for the bag, the boil, or the knife. Some counters served up fresh chowder or stew, poor boys, shrimp, clam strips, or raw oysters. The air was a mix of fish, steam, mollusks, marina water, and diesel.

Look for the squid.

It was shoulder to shoulder in front of the steamed-crab station. One of the men behind the counter, enjoying his work, flirted with the women. "Honey, you don't know how to cook these. Jack come home with you, show you how it's done. You ain't never had it done right till Jack do it." He filled a paper sack with crabs. The women smiled.

Several places had squid, dark and alien. Next to them were coral-colored octopuses, flaccid, draped over the contours of crushed ice. I glanced at my watch. I was early by ten minutes. But I knew Callahan was early, too, checking the crowd for anyone who looked to be hunting rather than fishing.

I went from one squid counter to the next, trying to look inconspicuously conspicuous. I had on a light suit jacket, hot in August, but I needed something to help cover the cannon. I was so used to carrying the Smith that the .45 began to feel like twenty pounds of deadweight in the sling. John Browning didn't design this weapon as a comfortable carry. He had other virtues in mind.

I looked at my watch again. It was three o'clock, straight up. No one in the crowd around me looked to be doing anything other than buying and selling fish. I saw dozens of people with laptops, but no one approached me.

I walked away from the barges and into the small collection of shacks set up by the parking lot. No one looked my way, so I strolled across the grass toward the marina. There, boats worth my first eight years' pay as a special agent were tied up gunwale to gunwale with houseboats and day sailers. It was early and many of the slips were empty, the boats still out on the river or south on the Chesapeake. Nothing to see.

Back at the crab stand, a serviceman pointed and ordered twelve to go. He was a navy officer, an ensign. I wondered where I'd heard his voice before, and as he turned to look at me, I knew it was Callahan. Look for the squid, he'd said. And just as a marine is always a *jarhead*, a sailor is always a *squid*.

Without looking at me he said, "You're slow for someone's supposed to be so smart." He nodded toward the man with the clams. "Cherrystones are always good. You like clams?"

"Yeah," I said.

"I like oysters. All the beds are going to shit, though. Didn't used to be you took your life in your hands when you ate an oyster."

"What are we doing here, Callahan?"

"I'm buying dinner. It's on me." He took his bags,

paid for them. "You know what you're getting? With the laptop, I mean?"

"No. I don't know."

"The only reason I'm giving you this is you seem like an honest guy. I'm not sure what that Rush asshole had figured out, but it was something big. That's what Janice said." Callahan stopped and his voice softened as he talked about his ex-wife. "Janice said she was going to be rich. Said they'd all be rich."

"So where is it?"

"It's coming. You know, the only reason I have it is security at RDU wouldn't let her board with it. Isn't that funny?"

"Callahan, you have to turn yourself in."

Callahan laughed. "Oh, yeah. That'll work." He turned to go and stopped. Without looking at me he said, "I'm going to assume you didn't have anything to do with this."

I looked in the direction of the parking lot and watched two uniformed Metro cops get out of an unmarked car. The driver was young, black, and nervous. He scanned the crowd, the way any cop would, but it wasn't with confidence. A cop's got to own the room, it's what gives him that roll and swagger, aside from the thirty pounds of hardware on his belt. But this kid's belt was so new I didn't have to hear it to know that it squeaked.

His partner looked like three of Nebraska's five front linemen and carried his weight on tiny feet pinched into black Corfam shoes. You could stroll through a pig yard in a pair of Corfams and they'd still hold a shine. They're popular footwear among the deskbound, but here on the street, in August, in D.C., they'd bake your feet like Virginia hams in ten minutes, flat.

"Just walk away, Callahan," I said.

"Roger that."

Callahan casually strolled toward the marina. For a man wanted in two states for murder, he didn't seem to be in any hurry. I had to admire his cool.

The rookie said something to his partner. The two came toward me, the crowd parting like the Red Sea. The rookie hung back and watched Callahan. The side of beef with the badge said, "Donovan?"

"Good afternoon, Officer."

"We're your backup."

"Who sent you?"

"Headquarters."

"Who at headquarters?"

The rookie jerked his attention toward me. "Hey, man, we're just following orders." His partner gave him a look that said shut up, and the kid did.

The Metro PD must have been stretched pretty thin by the terrorism alert to accept these two on the force.

The big guy eyed the crowd again. "You just point out the suspect and we'll take it from there."

The big guy was definitely crowding my personal space, not unusual for a street cop. Anyone who has to confront hard guys every day and make them think twice about starting trouble develops an attitude not endorsed by the etiquette guides. But something was wrong with the way he stepped in, and it took me a moment to get what it was.

Street cops get in a guy's face to throw him off-balance. But, they get too close and they're liable to lose a gun. So when a cop steps in, he fronts the side opposite his weapon, his arms loose, ready to do whatever's necessary to discourage the suspect.

This guy had his arms crossed, his gun side to me, six inches from my hand. I looked at his service pistol. It was a stainless-steel Desert Eagle.

That's when I knew. This wasn't a cop's gun. And these guys weren't cops.

The rookie pulled a photo from his shirt pocket and looked at it. "Hey, Ronnie, I think that's him. That sailor guy." The rookie pointed at Callahan, who was near the marina, his bags of oysters and steamed crab still in his hands.

The side of beef went for his gun.

But I'd beaten him to it. I had the Desert Eagle in my hand, all the blinding light in the universe bouncing off its stainless-steel frame.

"Hey," the side of beef said.

I backed away and held the pistol up, not pointing at anything lower than the Fourteenth Street Bridge. "If you don't mind, I like to see some ID."

People in the crowd gasped and the ripple went outward from the gun.

The rookie pulled his own pistol, a Pacific Rim bargain piece that's no bargain when you need it. Panicked, he looked from me to his partner. "He's got your gun."

The beef said, "I know he's got my gun, you fucking idiot. Shoot him."

The rookie looked at Callahan. "That's the man we supposed to get. And he's getting away."

"We'll get him. But first you have to shoot this guy."

"I can't shoot him. I've seen him on TV."

The big man was quicker than I expected, and he grasped the barrel of the Desert Eagle and started to twist the gun from my hand.

His partner danced from foot to foot, pointing the nine-millimeter in my direction. "Oh, man, what's this shit?"

The big man said, "Go get the sailor." The veins on his neck were as thick as my little finger. "I'll take care of this."

The rookie ran off toward the marina.

I stood face-to-face with the beef. He smiled. "You ain't gonna win this one, Hollywood." He tightened his grip on the big pistol.

What he hadn't seen was my father's .45 in my free hand. I jammed the muzzle into his ribs. "As a police officer, I would advise you to let go of the gun and back away with your hands in the air."

He looked down at the .45.

"You don't let go, I'm going to have to get blood all over my shirt." I poked him again.

He relaxed his grip.

"Now let go, back away, and put your hands behind your head."

He did as he was told. I took the cuffs and keys

and backed him up to a bicycle rack. The crowd watched, stunned, as I cuffed him to the rack.

A man in a brown security guard's uniform said, "Aren't you Jake Donovan?"

"Yes, I am."

He smiled, bright as sunlight, just as if we'd met on the street rather than over a cuffed and swearing uniformed cop. "I've read all your books. I love your work."

"Thank you." I held out the Desert Eagle. "Do you know how to use this?"

"Yes." His eyes were fixed on the pistol.

"Do you know what it is?"

"It's a Desert Eagle, fifty cal."

I handed it to him. "Right answer. Watch this guy and shoot him if he moves." The guard hesitated. "He's not a real cop, either."

"Oh," the security guard said. "That's okay, then."

I ran off toward the marina. Callahan and the other fake cop had disappeared. When I rounded the corner, I saw standing open the gate in the chain link that separates the boat owners from the tourists. At the end of the pier I saw the rookie cop creep down the row of boats, looking one way, then the other.

I ran down the steps and through the gate. "Hold it," I hollered, and leveled the .45 at him.

He turned, the gun still in his hand. He saw me and looked for a way out. But the only dry way out was through me.

I didn't like the look in his eye. "Don't do it."

Slowly, as if underwater, he started to bring his gun around.

I gripped the .45 in both hands, aimed at center mass, and tightened my finger on the trigger. "Don't do it."

Callahan jumped from the deck of a large power-boat and brought the sack of oysters down across the kid's head. The bag broke and the kid fell, surrounded by tumbling bluepoints.

Callahan scooped up the kid's pistol and aimed it at the kid. Then he aimed it at me.

I approached slowly, keeping Callahan in my sight picture. "Don't do this, Callahan. I don't want to shoot you."

Callahan tossed the pistol into the water. "I guess I'll eat takeout." He turned and walked to the end of the pier where a small outboard was tied up next to a thirty-foot sloop.

I followed, my pistol still on him. "Callahan, I can't let you go."

"And you won't shoot me. Looks like you have a dilemma, Donovan." He climbed into the boat and started the motor. "Untie me, would you?" He waited, his hand on the tiller.

"What about the laptop?"

"It's coming. As soon as I'm gone."

I nodded. "And if I keep you here?"

He shook his head. "Won't happen."

I untied the line and tossed it into the boat.

Callahan began to push off, but stopped. He looked up at me. "I want you to find who killed

Janice. That's first. And I want you to make them pay for what they did."

"I'll do my best."

"And if any money does come from that thing, I mean once all the smoke's cleared, maybe I'll get some of that. It's about time something really good came my way."

"Turn yourself in."

Callahan shook his head again. "No can do, Donovan. You find out who killed Janice and maybe I won't have to."

We both picked up the sirens.

"Gotta go, Donovan. You enjoy those clams." He pushed off, turned the tiller hard to starboard, and headed into the channel.

For the second time in two days, I was questioned by the police, although this time, I was the police. The gold shield and support from above made the interrogation short and painless. The witnesses corroborated my story, and the two men impersonating policemen were taken into custody. This time, I got my gun back.

As I walked toward my Land Rover, a young man caught up to me, carrying a small crate. "Mr. Donovan? Don't forget your clams."

"What?"

"Before"—he nodded toward the shop—"you ordered a bushel of cherrystones."

"I did?"

"Yes, sir."

I reached into my pocket. "Okay, how much?"

"They're paid for, sir." He smiled.

"You a friend of his?"

"Yes, sir. Served with him on the *Enterprise.*"

"Tell him to keep in touch."

"Yes, sir, I will."

I opened the back of the Land Rover and the young man put the crate inside.

26

It took me a while to get Jerry to take the clams. I'd caught him in the middle of an experiment with different types of perfume.

"So far I've identified forty-seven different brands by their chemical components."

"Jerry, you're the only man I know with a gas chromatograph in your kitchen."

"Really?"

Distracted by the news that not every home had a lab, he didn't quite catch the significance of the cherrystones.

"But I can't eat clams."

"Feed them to your cat."

He considered it. "But I don't have a cat. I could get a cat, I suppose. Unless there's something in the lease—"

"Jerry, I can't lift them out of my car." I held up my wing in a sling.

"I don't understand. Why are you giving them to me?"

"Because—"

"You know I'm allergic. My throat closes up."

"Yeah. I know. But inside—"

"I couldn't even eat clam chowder in Boston," Jerry said, as if being denied clam chowder in Boston was the greatest injustice that could be visited upon man.

I gripped Jerry's shoulders and forced him into the here and now. "Jerry?"

He blinked. "Yeah?"

"Janice Callahan's laptop is inside the bushel of clams."

Jerry refocused. "Oh. Oh."

"You have a friend at Langley?"

"Oh!" Jerry held up his finger. "Right." He looked at his finger, was surprised to see it there in the air, and put it back in his pocket.

"So, can you get the clams out of my car?" I tossed him my keys.

"Right." He nodded.

"And, Jerry? Don't tell anyone about this. Someone knew I was meeting Callahan today, so let's just keep this between us."

"What about Dominic?"

"Dominic's fine. But just Broken Wings. Okay? And if you do say anything, make sure to watch your security."

Jerry smiled. "Cone of Silence, huh, Jake?"

"Yeah, something like that."

Jerry took the keys and left the apartment.

I watched from the window just in case he got lost. While I was watching, my cell phone rang.

"Jake?"

It was Toni, and her voice sounded strained, almost a whisper. From the ambient noise I could tell she was in the car. "What is it, Toni?"

"I'm being followed."

"Are you sure?"

"Yes, I'm sure," she snapped. "I went back to the house to pick up some things—"

"Toni, you shouldn't have—"

"I know that now." To an outsider, Toni might have sounded impatient, but I knew it was fear. "I just wasn't thinking."

"Where are you?"

"I'm in Fairfax."

"Don't go to the safe house."

"I'm not stupid."

"Do you know where the police station is?"

"No."

"Okay. I'm at Jerry's place in Vienna. It's only a few minutes away. How far are you from the Korean restaurant?"

"I don't know. Which Korean restaurant?"

"Where Trevor took us for dinner last year? The kids thought it was gross?" When she couldn't remember, I gave her the best reminder I could think of. "It was in that shopping strip where you bought those expensive boots."

"Those boots weren't expensive. Those were Manolo Blahniks and I got them on sale."

"Fine. You remember where that was?"

"Yes, I remember. I'm about ten minutes away."

"Good. Go inside and call the police. I'll be there as soon as I can."

We hung up and I ran to the car. Jerry had the bushel of clams on his shoulder, the ice melt soaking his shirt. I grabbed the keys. "Call me when you hear something."

"About what?"

"About the computer, Jerry."

"Oh, right. I will."

The traffic was a mess, as usual. I took chances passing and ran every yellow light. I passed on the right, on the shoulder. I didn't care about picking up a cop; in fact, I welcomed it.

What should have been a ten-minute trip took twenty, and when I pulled into the parking lot I searched for Toni's car. It was parked about fifty yards from the Korean place. Twenty yards from the car was a white van. I could see one man inside.

I pulled to the far side of the van and wrote down the license number. I called Toni's number, and when she picked up, I said, "Are you in the restaurant?"

"No. I'm in the shoe store."

"Why didn't you go to the restaurant?"

"I wasn't hungry, Jake."

"Did you call the police?"

"I did. They said it would be a while. There's an accident on Sixty-six."

"Did you tell them it was an emergency?"

"Yes. They still said it would be a while. They told me to stay where I was. Which is here."

"Okay." We hung up, and the longer I sat there staring at the rear of that van, the angrier I got. In a few short days my family had been threatened; a punk had blown up my Aston Martin; I'd been shot, pulled from the terrorist case, lost my funding, federal authority, and girlfriend; two guys in rented uniforms had tried to kill my witness; and now I had some pervert or worse stalking my wife. My ex-wife. All in all, it had been a bad week, and I just got this feeling that I wanted to take it out on somebody.

I got out of the Land Rover and approached the van from the rear. I put my hand inside the sling and gripped the .45. As I approached the driver's side, I could see the man's face in the rearview mirror. He looked up, saw me, and immediately registered shock. I saw him reach for something and then I was on him, the gun drawn. I jerked the door open and screamed at him to get out and get down on the ground.

Hands in the air, he got out and dropped to his knees.

"All the way down," I screamed, and pointed the pistol at his right eye. He dropped to his face and locked his hands behind his neck.

The van rocked and the rear doors burst open. I was there before the skell's accomplice could clear the bumper. All I saw was a man's head, and his hand, and in his hand it looked like a weapon. It could have been a knife or a gun, but it was happening too fast to be sure. I kicked the van's rear door. It swung in and caught the guy half in and half out. He fell back and slumped to the pavement. The first thing I did was kick the weapon from his hand. But it wasn't a weapon. It was a microphone. Inside the van were racks of cables, mike stands, tripods, lights, and a camera. No perps, pervs, or killers. Just TV equipment.

Then I heard the driver say, "Spider? Spider? Are you all right?" and I saw the bleeding man on the pavement was Spider Urich, and for once he wasn't talking. In fact, he wasn't moving at all.

27

Spider had the concussion; Larry, my lawyer, had the headache. He leaned against the wall and removed his glasses, sighed, and closed his eyes. He sighed again.

"Larry? Are you okay? You look like you're having a stroke."

"Yeah, Jake, I'm fine." He took a moment, put his glasses on, and then spoke carefully, as if the words themselves would split his head open like a melon. "I'm earning my fee," he said, more to himself than to me or the police officers, or the line of prisoners shackled to the benches.

The officer behind the wire handed over the manila folder containing my laces, belt, wallet, and newly issued gold shield. "That's good, Larry," I said. "In these times of terror and uncertainty, it's good to earn a living."

The property officer stopped me. "Agent Donovan?"

"Yes?"

"Would you sign this for my daughter? She just graduated from the Academy." He held out a copy of my latest book.

"I'd be happy to."

While I signed the book, Larry muttered to himself, "Harvard law school was a breeze. The sixteen years I spent as a federal prosecutor were just a warm-up."

The doors whirred open and we walked through two more checkpoints before we hit the parking lot. At each gate I had to stop and talk with the officer. In the parking lot, two policemen got out of their patrol cars, applauded, and gave me a thumbs-up.

"I'm a pretty popular inmate," I said.

"Jake, you're supposed to ask me, 'A warm-up for what?' "

"What?"

"I said, 'My sixteen years as a prosecutor were just a warm-up.' You're supposed to ask me, 'A warm-up for what.' "

I pushed my belt through the loops. "Okay, Larry, a warm-up for what?"

"For this week."

We got into his Mercedes and Larry started the engine. "In less than one week, you break into a home—"

"The door was unlocked."

"You *enter* a home, uninvited—"

"Tough for dead people to ask you in."

"—and discover two bodies. Then there's a Wild West shoot-out in Crystal City, you pull a gun in a crowded fish market in the District—"

"You forgot the guy blowing up my Aston Martin."

Larry negotiated the guard stop, showing ID and waiting for the gate to glide open. He looked both ways, then pulled into traffic. "I didn't forget, Jake. But so far, you haven't been charged with anything in Fredericksburg. But then, we still have the weekend." At a red light, Larry rubbed his temples. "Now you assault a TV news crew. Jake, I had no idea how easy my life was until this week."

"Sarcasm is not a comforting trait in a lawyer, Larry."

Once we reached the interstate, Larry said, "Jake, you know, you could go on the speaking circuit, make good money with tales of homicidal nutcases and sexual deviants. Write more books and let Josh, your other lawyer, earn *his* retainer for a change. What do you say?"

"We don't usually refer to them as 'nutcases' in the Bureau, Larry." I sat back in the seat, folded my hands in my lap, and waited. If I was patient and didn't taunt him, Larry might tell me if I had a future as a free man.

After a long time, Larry said, "Urich doesn't want to press charges."

"That's good. Why do I sense a big *but* coming in this conversation?"

"But his grip does. And is. Pressing charges, I mean."

I jerked upright. "I didn't hurt the grip. I never even touched him."

"It's assault if you brandish a weapon."

"I was pointing it."

"Aiming it. At the man's head, Jake."

"His eye, really."

"That's good, Jake, save that one for the judge." Larry passed a slow-moving bus full of prisoners being transferred to the state prison.

"I get the most interesting fan mail from prison."

"I have no doubt," Larry said. "You know, you're lucky that local law enforcement likes you so much."

"I know."

"And that I'm such a damn good lawyer."

"I know."

"Or you'd be spending the night with a cell mate who wants more than your autograph. Someone who hasn't read all of your books."

"Or worse, someone who has."

Larry laughed for the first time that evening.

"How is Urich?"

"He'll live. The door cracked his skull, but he'll be up and muckraking again in no time. It might even improve his ratings. Look what a chair in the face did for Geraldo."

"Maybe he'll thank me."

"Jake, this is a pretty serious charge."

I sank down into the car seat. "I know, Larry. I know. Did they return my gun?"

"No."

"That's the second one."

"You'll get them back when you stop being a public menace."

As he drove, Larry filled me in on the arraignment dates, pleas, and how we'd handle each of the several charges filed against me. By the time Larry dropped me off at Trevor's house, I knew we'd be spending a great deal of time together, plus I'd be spending a great deal of money. It was a good thing I liked Larry.

At the curb, Larry looked skeptically at the tidy suburban house, the white-faced lawn jockey, and said, "So, this is where the Legion of Justice meets?"

"Yeah, for now. We've had our wings clipped."

Larry put his hand on my shoulder. The sarcasm was gone, as was the professional voice, leaving the encouraging words of a friend. "You'll come out of this just fine."

"Thanks to you."

"As your lawyer, I'd advise you to get drunk and get laid."

I laughed. "Not much chance of the latter."

"Things must be tough in the superhero business. Keep your chin up, Jake. Tomorrow's another day."

I thanked him and watched as he drove off. Before ringing the bell, I rubbed the lawn jockey's cap for luck. Tomorrow was another day; I just wasn't sure what fresh hell it would bring.

28

Valerie opened the door and let the sounds of Coltrane mixed with the aroma of clam chowder drift onto the porch. She gave me a short hug and a peck on the cheek. "Doesn't look like your time in the pen's hardened you any," she said.

"You know, for years I've wondered how someone as humor-impaired as your husband could put that lawn jockey out there."

She smiled. "And now?"

"And now I know it was your idea."

"Took you all this time to figure that out. You're getting slow, Mr. Donovan, very slow."

"That's the second time today I've been told that."

I followed her into the kitchen, where she offered me a bowl of clam chowder and a beer.

"I'll take the beer first. I see Jerry's been here."

"Brought a whole bushel of clams with him. We've got enough chowder to feed the state of Maine."

"Where's Trevor?"

"Back in the den." She handed me the cold beer. "Rob McManus is in there, too, Jake."

I let the cold beer wash away the taste of incarceration. "It's okay, Valerie. I'm getting used to the idea of dying alone." I hesitated, then thought what the hell and said, "I just wish Katie had left me for a better guy."

Valerie put a comforting hand on my forearm. "Jake, he's not so bad. He helped Trevor move Toni and the children today."

"Trevor take them up to the place in Mt. Airy?"

Valerie nodded. "He thought they'd be better off. You know, after what happened."

"I tried calling her cell phone earlier. She didn't answer."

"Toni just needs some time. She'll be all right."

"Pretty mad, was she?"

Valerie shook her head. "Not mad. She's just scared, Jake. You understand."

"Yeah. I do."

I walked back to the den. One wall was covered in awards, plaques, pictures, and official recognition from various law enforcement agencies. A bookcase held shooting trophies.

Within easy reach of the remote and a revolver, Trevor held the line in a recliner. Jerry and Rob sat on opposite ends of the couch. "There's our notorious leader, drawing down on reporters everywhere," Trevor said. "Did they let you watch CNN in stir?"

"No, why? What's happening?"

"Spec Ops raided a terrorist camp in Syria," Trevor said. "On the home front, the attorney general's gone underground. No one knows exactly where he is."

"Amazing. Have there been threats?"

"So they say. I think he and the vice president are bunking together."

"In the meantime," Rob said, "the president greets Girl Scouts in the Oval Office."

"I wonder if he gets free cookies," Jerry said.

"Perks of the job," I said.

I grabbed a straight-back chair from the small desk in the corner of the room and sat next to Trevor. "Has anyone heard from Katie or Dominic?"

Rob jumped in first. "Katie called from Gainesville. Nothing new. Still tracking Bower's known associates."

"Anything from Dom?"

Jerry said, "Dom called. There were marks on the wrists of the victims in Alexandria."

"What kind of marks? Ligature marks? You mean they were tied up?"

"Handcuffed," Jerry said.

"They were cuffed, and then killed? But why?"

"Maybe it was some kind of kinky sex game," Rob said. "The husband catches them, just think how you'd feel."

A wise man told me, never attribute to malice what can be written off as stupidity, so I attributed Rob's personal remark to his being a jerk instead of its being an intentional goad and followed the investigative thread through. "But why would he remove the cuffs after he killed them?"

"There's more," Jerry said. You could see him pick out the information from among the atomic weights, bits of movie dialogue, long-ago phone numbers, pet names, and TV jingles that drifted about his cranium. "They were fully clothed, shot, and then stripped."

"So they weren't in bed."

"They were when they were killed. In the bed. But clothed," Jerry said. "That's what made the crime scene look right when they first examined it. And, oh, yes, there were signs of torture."

"What?"

"Apparently, the UNSUB used a clothes iron, plugged in. The woman, Janice Callahan, had burns on the bottoms of her feet, her thighs, and her"— Jerry looked down at his fingers twisted together— "you know, her vulva."

"Jesus," Trevor said. "What kind of sick bastard . . ."

"Sounds like S and M," Rob said. "You know, with the bondage."

"Or maybe someone wanted information," I said.

"But that doesn't make sense," Rob argued. "Look. The husband follows his wife here, catches her in bed with this government guy."

"He worked for DARPA," Jerry said.

Rob shot him an angry look, and unmasked, stripped of civility, I saw a man I would never like no matter how much I tried.

"As I was saying, Callahan catches them in some twisted S-and-M bondage thing, shoots them, strips them like, you know, stripping them of their dignity, and leaves them like that."

I shook my head. "No. If it was a murder of pure passion, he would have mutilated them, or, if he still loved her, he would have covered her or at least he would have covered her face. And there's one more thing."

"What's that?"

"I met the guy. He's not a killer."

"But doesn't he have his wife's computer? See, that proves right there that he was in Alexandria. How could he get his wife's computer if he wasn't there?"

Trevor nodded. "Good question."

"Then why would he give it to me?"

"To throw us off the trail. To make us think he's innocent. Otherwise, why doesn't he turn himself in?"

"Because he doesn't trust the government. Rightly or wrongly, he doesn't think he'll get a fair shake."

Rob chewed on his thumb, a habit he had had when he was one of my students, and a habit I found even more annoying now. "If only you could have gotten Janice Callahan's computer before you were interrupted by those fake cops. Maybe that would tell us something."

I looked at Jerry and his eyes widened as he caught the message I was sending. "Yeah," he said, "that sure would help."

"Oh," Trevor said, "those two cops were sprung."

I couldn't believe what I was hearing. "What? By who?"

Trevor shrugged. "I don't know. I just got a call from my friend on the force. He thought I'd want to know."

Valerie came in and said she was going to bed. "Jake, I've made up the guest room. I want you to stay the night."

At the moment, the drive into Crystal City, the empty apartment, and Bower still out there thinking of me every time he tried to sit down made Valerie's invitation sound pretty good. "Thanks, Val. I appreciate it."

Trevor grumbled, "You tell me how much you appreciate it when the kids wake you up at oh-dark-thirty screaming for their uncle Jake."

As Valerie made her good-nights, Jerry stood up and stretched. "I better get going, too. It's been a long day." As Trevor walked him to the door, Jerry said, "Did Jake tell you I've identified forty-seven different brands of perfume?"

"Fascinating," Trevor said. "I'm so excited I'll never get to sleep."

When we were alone, Rob stood up and said, "This is the first chance I've had to tell you this, but I appreciate you letting me work this investigation with you guys."

"How are things at the Bureau? Busy, I bet."

Rob laughed. "Oh, yeah, Director Ravan's got us running."

"Glad you can make time to help us out," I said.

"No problem."

We shook hands and I walked him to the door.

With Rob gone and Valerie in bed, Trevor and I settled back in the den. "So, what was that between you and Jerry?"

"You caught that, huh?"

"Only because I know you both. I don't think Rob saw it."

"Good. I want to keep this in the team for now." I pointed to the TV and Trevor turned up the sound. In whispers, I told Trevor about the clams, the computer, and Jerry's friend at Langley.

"Why didn't he tell me?"

"Because you weren't alone."

"It was just Rob, and you really think my house is bugged?" Trevor looked around the room as if the walls might fall in.

I said I didn't know. "But for now, let's keep things in the family, okay?"

Trevor nodded. "Okay. I got it." He turned down the TV and we watched ESPN for another half hour. After the week I'd had, there was no way I could concentrate on the baseball standings, so I said good night and went upstairs to the guest room.

For the first time in what seemed like years, I slept a dreamless sleep, surrounded by the Malones' hospitality and protected by the Broken Wings' extended family. Even now the team was working, investigating murders that had happened on our watch. They worked without pay, authority, or the political cover we needed to protect us in a town where thunderstorms of skunk shit rained down upon the just and unjust alike.

I don't know if I was awake or asleep when I heard the phone ring from far off in the house. I opened my eyes. The gray dawn lightened the window shade and I could feel the vibrations of Trevor's sleepy morning voice answering the phone. Then something in his voice changed and a cold dread settled over my chest. I raised my watch to my eyes. It was nearly six. I had slept like a rock since midnight, but now I was wide-awake, my heart beating loudly in my chest.

Trevor knocked on the door. "Jake?"

"I'm awake."

He opened the door but did not enter. He stood there, holding the phone.

"I'm awake." I sat up on the edge of the bed. "What is it?"

I saw Valerie behind him, looking in. She was clutching her robe and tears glistened in her eyes.

"It's Eric, Jake."

The light closed in. All around me was a long, dark tunnel with Trevor at the very end, talking to me.

"That was Joe, from the director's office. Eric's been kidnapped."

29

The director was sending a helicopter to take us up to Mt. Airy, a small town on Route 40, in the rolling green hills of western Maryland. As Trevor drove to the LZ for pickup, Orlando Ravan told me what he knew, which was not much. "I've sent Andrews up as primary. He's had a lot of experience with abductions, and I know you two respect one another."

"I appreciate that, sir."

"Jake, I can't say how sorry I am. You know you have the full Bureau behind you."

"Yes, sir."

"I'm not just saying that, Jake. When news of the kidnapping got out, every agent in this building volunteered to help, even those who've been working eighteen-hour shifts. Hell, Jake, even Harry Gillette asked to express his support and concern."

"I know we've had our differences. You and I, I mean."

"No, Jake. You've always been stand-up. What's happened recently is just politics, nothing more."

"I appreciate that, sir."

"You call me when you get acclimated. You know I can't have you take any official role in the investigation, but as a parent you can be an invaluable resource."

"Yes, sir."

"Just keep your head about you."

"Yes, sir."

The Bureau's Black Hawk set down on the soccer field of the local elementary school. Trevor and I got in. The crew chief offered his condolences and said, "We'll get him back, Donovan. And we'll get the fuck who took him."

It was a short ride from Alexandria to Mt. Airy. I tried not to think of anything at all, but I kept seeing all of the child murders I'd ever investigated running through my head. The pictures kept coming until I thought I'd jump out of my skin I was so crazy with grief, disbelief, fear, and anger. Once again, I had brought this on my family. I had brought this evil home from the field, and now it had devoured my only son, my boy, my baby.

The Black Hawk set down on a field in back of the house. The entire yard was roped off in crime scene tape. There were two perimeters. One was set fifty yards from the house, and that kept the press and the public from trampling the scene. The second, closer to the house, was for visiting politicians who were quick to express concern and get their faces in the paper.

I was whisked through the first tape. The press had not appeared, but it wouldn't be long. The helicopter coming and going was enough to alert even the sleepiest reporter to the possibility of a story. Soon, every TV and print reporter on the crime beat would be outside this tape shouting questions.

A local cop stopped me at the inside perimeter. "I'm sorry, Agent Donovan. You're supposed to wait for Special Agent Andrews."

A small group of state troopers stood to the side and drank coffee. They wouldn't look at me, and I understood. I had been there. It was a strange cop superstition, that making eye contact would bring the contagion to your family.

I watched Andrews cross the yard, stripping off latex gloves as he came. In all of our dealings before, Andrews had been the subordinate, but today he was the primary, called in to investigate a high-profile kidnapping. And I was no longer a senior agent; I was one of the victims.

"Jake, Jake, I am so sorry." He grasped my hand.

"What's happening, Vince? Where's my wife?"

"Mrs. Donovan is at a local hotel, sir. I'll be happy to have one of the agents take you there right away."

"I'll take you, sir." A trooper touched the brim of his hat.

"Thanks, but I'd like to . . ."

Trevor stepped in to help. "We want to see

the . . . ," he almost said "crime scene," hesitated, and said, "boy's bedroom."

"Of course." Andrews put his hand on my arm and guided me gently across the lawn, as if I had suddenly grown old and fragile. I had done the same for so many numbed parents, so many times before. Each time was hard, and each time the grief and fear were different; just as every crime and every criminal is unique, so are the victims and their reactions. The only thing constant was that this never got easier, no matter how many times you did it.

Before we entered, I put on surgical boots and latex gloves so I wouldn't contaminate the crime scene any more than necessary.

Trevor said he would wait outside. "You need me, you holler."

I nodded and followed Andrews inside. The house was a small cottage, one floor with three bedrooms. The first room was the living room, simply furnished with a couch, a chair, and a small coffee table. No TV, and I thought of how Eric must have complained.

The kitchen was next. The refrigerator was old and rattled when it cranked up. The kitchen was so small, there was just room for the fridge and a Formica dinette set. No dishwasher, and I thought of how Toni must have cursed me when she saw that.

As we passed through each room, the crime techs stopped, out of respect, and I wanted someone to reassure me that my son was not dead and this was not a funeral but a crime scene. Again, people's averting their eyes made me feel even more isolated in my grief and fear.

A short hall led to the back bedroom. It was barely ten feet square with a single bed tucked into the corner. One tech was still taking pictures, and the supervisor asked us not to enter the room itself.

I stood in the doorway. The covers of the bed were turned back, as if Eric had just gotten up to go to the bathroom and would come out, rubbing sleep from his eyes and asking what was going on.

On the nightstand, a Harry Potter book was turned over. A glass of water sat undisturbed next to it. On the pillow was the small hollow made by Eric's head.

Andrews whispered, "Talk to me, Jake, tell me what you see." He was forcing me to think like a cop, making me look through the eyes of a man who had investigated dozens of kidnappings instead of through the eyes of a father who had just lost a son.

"The bed shows no sign of struggle," I said, swallowing hard, forcing myself to catalog the details. The crime tech stopped taking pictures and stood quietly, listening. She made herself nearly invisible. "The window is open. The screen is in place." I mentioned Eric's clothing, casually tossed to the floor. There were no shoes. I wondered if he was even wearing shoes, or if he'd brought the flip-flops I'd seen him wearing before. I asked someone to make a note of it and heard the scratch of a pen on paper behind me.

I looked for anything unusual, anything out of

place. But this was not Eric's room. This was a strange room and what was Eric's would be lightly laid on, a few things carried in from the car. Traveling light.

Eric's backpack was at the foot of the bed. "Have you checked inside?" The tech shook her head no. "You won't find anything. He doesn't leave anything. He only takes things," I said. "He only takes things."

The room was hushed, the air tense with the focused concentration of three disciplined people.

"Have you lifted the pillow?"

"No." The tech looked over my shoulder at Andrews. "Should I?"

"Carefully," Andrews said.

With her thumb and her forefinger she slowly lifted the corner of the pillow. There, tucked between the case and the sheet, was the card.

"I knew it was him," I said.

"Who?" I could feel the gust of Andrews's breath on my neck.

"The Black Diamond Killer. He was here. He took my son."

30

Immediately, a thousand questions piled one on top of the other inside my head. I turned on Andrews. "We need the Black Diamond files."

"You've seen them, Jake. Think about the original crime scenes. Do you think this was staged?" Andrews held a minidisc recorder near his chest, and for the first time, I saw he had been recording our morning. I wasn't a participant in the investigation. I was a victim, a witness, and if Andrews was a professional, I was also a suspect.

I closed my eyes and tried to see the bedrooms of all the boys. All I could see was Eric's room. I tried to see the other boys. All I could conjure up was Eric's face. "I don't know, Vince. I can't think about anything other than how to proceed."

Andrews said, "That's okay, Jake. Walk through

the procedure. Maybe something will reveal itself. We'll get the files. What next?"

"See if any one of those initial suspects have been released from prison recently or returned from overseas." I ran through all of the contingencies I could think of. "Or recovered from an extended illness."

"What else?"

"Check any of their children. Maybe the son has picked up where the father left off." I looked up at Andrews. "It's a long shot, I know."

He put his hand on my arm and led me from the doorway.

"See if anyone's requested a deck of those cards, those Black Diamonds. Could be a museum, or a collector, maybe someone claiming to write a book. The manufacturer is in Cincinnati. His number's in the file."

We stood in the living room, but we could have been anywhere, so blind was I to anything real and solid around me.

"Call the primary on the case. His name's Oskovich. If the Black Diamond Killer is really back, the chances are he didn't start with Eric. See if Oskovich knows of any missing children or runaways recently that might have been abductions." A horrifying thought burst open like a malignant pod. "Jesus, Vince, this guy may have been operating for years, without his calling card, and we just didn't know it. There could be hundreds of new victims."

"We'll follow up, Jake."

"All because I stopped looking. I stopped looking,

Vince, because I thought he had stopped. But he hasn't, has he? He's here, Vince, and he has my boy."

I was holding on to Vince's arms, squeezing, and I realized how crazy I sounded. I tried to control my skittering consciousness and slow my heart rate. Each time I'd begin to level out, a new picture of Eric would leap into my head and I'd be gone again, one fear chasing another down a deep hole.

Calmly, the way you speak to a person in panic, Vince said, "Concentrate on the investigation, Jake. Let things unfold naturally. If you raise questions, those answers might get us closer to the truth."

"What questions, Vince? My head is full of questions. Why now? Why here? Why my son?" I backed away. The crime techs had been staring at me and quickly found other things to look at.

"Jake, let's go outside." Vince's voice was soft, and patient, and I knew that I must have looked like a madman.

"No. Something's not right, Vince. We're missing something. The whole scene just doesn't"—I struggled to find the right word to describe what was so wrong—"*smell* right. Does it to you?"

Vince held my arm and walked me into the middle of the yard.

News crews were beginning to assemble at the outer perimeter. When they saw me, they hollered my name and aimed long microphones in our direction. Vince turned his back to them and hunched his shoulders as if lighting a cigarette in the wind. "Jake, I want you to go to the hotel and stay with your wife and daughter. They need you, Jake."

"But there's so much work to do."

"And we have the best people in the Bureau on it. Director Ravan is making sure of that."

Trevor had been hanging back, giving Andrews and me some privacy. On his own, or perhaps cued by a signal from Andrews that I missed, Trevor came up and put his hand on my shoulder.

Andrews handed him a set of keys. "Take my car, Malone." He gave Trevor directions to the hotel and said to me, "You stay with your family. If you have any ideas or think of something we might have overlooked, call me."

"I will."

"You have my number."

"I do."

"Malone, take good care of him."

Trevor nodded. "Let's go see Toni, Jake. Come on. Ali needs you, too."

"Ali. My God, she must be so scared."

Trevor put me in the car as if I were made of china. He went around the front, got behind the wheel, and slowly drove through the crowd of reporters. "Vultures," he said. "Feeding on misery."

"They're doing their job. Just like us."

"Maybe. But everywhere we go, someone wants a piece of you. Doesn't it get old? Don't you ever want to just punch somebody?"

"Trevor, man, I chose this life. I'm the one who decided to write those books. It was me who agreed to coach actors and help crime writers get it right. I like it, Trevor, and I can't have that without the other."

"Maybe," he said again. "But I'm glad it's you and not me. It was me, there'd be a lot more Spider Urichs in the hospital."

I smiled, and it felt foreign on my face. "I have to admit, slamming Urich's head in that van door may have been the high point of my week."

"Maybe you knocked some goddamn sense into him."

"I'm not counting on it." I slumped in the seat, a knuckle pressed against my lips, and watched the Maryland countryside glide by. "We only have forty-eight hours. That's all he ever lets them live."

Trevor didn't say anything, but I could see his grip on the wheel tighten.

My cell phone went off and I answered it. "Jake, it's Joe again. Please hold for the director."

I waited and then Orlando Ravan came on the line. "Jake, I just talked to Andrews. I can't tell you how sorry I am that your work for the Bureau has somehow compromised your family's security. I want to assure you that we'll find your son, if it takes all of our resources."

"What about my team?"

Ravan paused, putting his words together. "You will have a direct line into the case. Of course."

"But we won't be allowed to work it."

"Jake, no one has more respect for the Broken Wings' abilities than I do. That's the truth. But all of you are far too close to this, and there are things you can't know that would hinder your ability to freely investigate the case."

"You mean the attorney general."

"You have no authority, Jake. You're a civilian."

"According to this shield in my pocket, I'm a detective in the D.C. Police."

"Jake. You're a civilian. That could change in the future, and will if I have anything to say about it, but for now you and that pirate crew you call a team are to turn over any leads to Special Agent Andrews. Do you understand me, Jake? Anything else could seriously jeopardize your future and could hinder the successful conclusion of this investigation."

The successful conclusion of this investigation. When Ravan starts speaking like a bureaucrat, you know the conversation's over. "Yes, sir. I understand."

"I have to go, Jake. Please give my sympathy to Toni and call me anytime you need something. I mean that as a friend, Jake, as well as a colleague."

"Thank you, sir."

We hung up and I told Trevor what Ravan had said.

"He gave us Andrews, Jake. The kid's a real bulldog. Just think, we could have drawn Harry Gillette. That man couldn't find his feet if the directions were written on the floor."

I appreciated the effort, but Trevor's jokes weren't working. Now that I had dug myself into this deep black hole, I wanted to look around for a while, see how dark things could get. "I hope Andrews is better at catching this guy than I was."

"Jake, no one is better than you."

"Once, maybe, but this wouldn't have happened had I been on top of things."

"You have done everything a man could do to protect his family, Jake."

"And it wasn't enough."

Trevor heaved a sigh, looked out the side window and then straight ahead. "Okay, Jake, I've run out of encouraging words. You want someone who'll listen to you beat yourself up, you need a shrink or a priest or something, but you don't need me."

"I'm sorry."

"You better be more than sorry. You better be thinking of a way we can find your boy."

I nodded.

"And you think for one minute the team is going to sit around while someone else works this case? Ain't going to happen, Jake. I don't care how many people tell us to stay away. Even you."

"It wouldn't hurt to follow up on a few things the Bureau can't," I said.

"That's what I want to hear."

"I could call Tommy Wight."

"The private detective?"

"Sure, we could work under his license," I said. "We wouldn't be licensed ourselves, but we would be working under his legal authority."

"Think of it as doing our civic duty. Think of all the agents the Bureau has wrapped up in the terrorist case."

"Absolutely," I said. "And we wouldn't be interfering with anything by asking a few questions."

"Amen, brother."

"We could, you know, start by asking around the

local hardware stores and see if anyone's bought plywood, pipe, and a shovel lately."

"Sounds like a plan."

I felt a little better. I hadn't completely crawled out of that pit, but at least I was looking up instead of down.

The motel was a travelers' rest on U.S. 40, not near enough to Washington or Baltimore to be a destination in itself, and not far enough away to be a welcome stop between there and wherever you were going. This made business an iffy proposition, and the motel looked a season away from Chapter 11.

I knocked on Room 12.

A woman's voice asked, "Who is it?"

I identified myself to the darkened peephole.

Toni threw open the door and I held her as though she would spin off the planet if I didn't. Ali joined us. We three hung together in the doorway until Trevor gently nudged us inside.

"A news van just pulled up," he said.

I looked into the parking lot and a TV news crew was pulling its equipment out and setting up for the vigil, hoping to catch us in time for the evening news.

Toni said, "Jake, I called the police right away. I didn't touch anything."

"I know, Toni."

"I did everything I could think of to do. I called him and called him, and when I knew he was gone, as soon as I knew, I took Ali outside so we wouldn't disturb anything."

"It's okay."

"I should have checked on him earlier."

"You did everything right." I sat Toni on the edge of the bed. With her hands in her lap she seemed to fold in on herself, the pain was so great.

I shook hands with the plainclothes officer, a woman who looked as if she could bench-press Trevor.

"Agent Donovan, I'm Detective Tennyson. Mt. Airy police.

"I'm Mr. Donovan now, Detective."

"I'm here to protect your wife and daughter, sir, but if there is anything else I can do, I am at your service."

"I appreciate that, Detective, and will keep it in mind."

Tennyson knew when to back off, and she did, allowing me to sit with my wife and daughter alone. "I'll be right outside, sir, if you need me."

Toni began to cry again and I held her. Ali hugged my shoulders and we sat like that for a long time, holding on to each other, afraid to let go, afraid of what would come next.

"Orlando sends his support and sympathy," I said. "He's assigned Vince Andrews to the case."

"Do I know him?"

"Young man from Pennsylvania; he brought a box of Krispy Kreme to the house. When we had the picnic, remember?"

"That was a long time ago," Toni said.

"Not that long. What? Six years?"

"Eric was so little."

I let that innocent picture of Eric run through our

memories and said, "I want you to go to Trevor's until we find the person who did this."

Toni jerked out of my arms. "No! I'm not leaving here. I'm not leaving without my son."

"Toni, there will be news reporters camped out in the parking lot."

"I don't care."

"And gawkers."

Toni wiped her eyes and shrugged. "Let them gawk."

"Ali? What about you?"

Ali almost always had a strong opinion about everything. This time, instead of telling us what she wanted, she said, "I don't know, Dad. Whatever you think is best."

"Toni?"

"I want Ali to stay here with me."

"Fine." I knew it was useless to argue. "We'll do it this way. But if there's even a hint of trouble, I'm sending you both to Montana."

The threat was a family joke, like sending someone to stay with my sister was like sending them away to Siberia, but Toni just nodded, her stare fixed on the space between us.

"I better call my family before they see this on the news." Toni got up and went into the next room, closing the adjoining door behind her.

Ali got up. "I'm going to take a shower."

I hugged her. "Everything will be okay, sweetheart."

"Sure, Dad."

"We'll find Eric and bring him home safe."

"I know." She wore the same look she had when I'd told her everything would be fine after the divorce. She didn't believe me then and she didn't believe me now.

"I promise," I said.

Ali opened the door and I could hear Toni's voice talking quietly on the phone. Ali turned to me. "Don't worry, Daddy, I don't blame you for this. I know it's not your fault."

I gave her a tight-lipped smile, barely a glimmer, and thanked her. But I wasn't so sure.

31

I paced the room, mapping out our end of this shoe-string investigation while Trevor sat on the bed making a list.

Trevor liked lists. "Okay, Dom is on his way to help us cover the hardware stores. I chatted up one of the local cops while you were in the house, and she's willing to help."

"She?"

Trevor smiled. "God doesn't hand out all this charm and then expect a man not to use it. But I'm not sure how far this local is willing to go, you know?"

"You mean you don't know if she'll break the law for us."

"Right."

"So you admit your charm is limited."

"I hold back. Like Superman not using his X-ray vision to see through people's clothes."

"Uh-huh." I stopped pacing and looked out the window at the tree line behind the motel. The day was gray and the gloom sucked all the color out of the woods, making the photographer easy to see as he set up his tripod and telephoto lens. "Isn't that one of the tabloids?"

Trevor joined me at the window. "Looks like Barry from the *Weekly World*."

"That means the news has reached Baltimore. And if it's reached Baltimore, it's reached Washington. This place will be a zoo by lunchtime."

I turned away from the window. "Okay, I called Tommy Wight and explained the situation. He's put us all on the payroll so his license covers us to ask questions."

"I brought my black bag," Trevor said.

"I know. What do you have in there, anyway?"

Trevor shook his head. "In light of our current legal limbo, it's best you don't know."

"Okay."

"But I got enough of whatever you need."

My cell phone went off and it was Vince Andrews. I realized that I was almost afraid to hear his voice and knew, for the first time, how the relatives of missing children felt when I called. "You have something new, Vince?"

"I'm more interested in what you have. Or will have soon, Jake."

"What do you mean?" I tried to sound innocent, knowing he'd found out about Tommy Wight and our attempt to flank the Bureau with our Junior G-Man buzzers.

"I'm talking about the file, Jake."

"What file?"

"The Black Diamond file. Hand it over and this will be as far as it goes. No need to involve the director, okay?"

"Vince, I don't know what you're talking about."

"The Black Diamond file. I called Records. The file is missing and the last person to sign for it is McManus."

I took a deep breath, hoping the oxygen to my brain would blow open a door to instant enlightenment—and was instantly enlightened to the fact that I knew no more than before.

"Jake. Don't make this difficult."

"Vince, I understand why you would think it was my team, but I give you my word that we had nothing to do with this. Katie's in Florida."

It was Vince's turn to take a breath and think. My guess is he came up with the same big zero I had. "I didn't mean Katie. I meant Rob. Rob McManus signed for the file."

"When did he do that? I haven't seen Rob since last night."

"You're serious? You had nothing to do with this?"

"On my honor, Vince."

"Uh-huh. Right. Good. Okay. I'll get back to you."

He hung up before I could say anything. I told Trevor about the missing files.

"Maybe Rob is trying to do you a favor," Trevor said.

I shook it off. "If Rob was trying to do me a favor, he would make sure Vince Andrews has the files."

"So, what do we do now?"

I picked up the slim Mt. Airy phone book, flipped to the yellow pages, and ripped out the Hardware and Real Estate sections. "I'm going to start asking around at the hardware stores. You take the real estate offices."

"Real estate?"

"There are vacation cabins for rent around here. Let's see if someone's rented one in the last couple days. If the Black Diamond Killer took Eric, he's going to need a place to build the box. That means electricity. That means a place to stay with a lot of privacy."

"What if he's brought the box with him?"

"Then we hope he's not a camper."

Sometimes, not often, but sometimes, the hardest part of investigating a case is shaking the press. In this case, the reporters were more interested than usual in where I was going and what I was doing, and how I was feeling. They all wanted to know how I was feeling. It took nearly an hour to shake the last of them and I did that in a mall.

Trevor called from the road. "You should have taken the real estate offices, Jake. The last people weren't too happy to see a black man ask about rental property."

"It's those hip-hop vibes you give off."

"Thought I was looking to set up a crack den here in white-bread America, turn their sons and daughters into crack whores."

"Did they give you anything?"

"No. They settled down after I showed them my shield."

"Uh-huh. What shield is that, Trevor?"

"The one from my black bag."

"Okay. So, besides impersonating an officer, did you accomplish anything else?"

"No. They have a few cabins up around South Mountain, they said, but they were rented to families they'd known a long time. Not much in the way of houses in town, either. You having any luck with the hardware stores."

"I haven't been able to talk to anyone. I have this permanent tail."

"Reporters?"

"Uh-huh."

"Where are you now?"

I told him and Trevor suggested he swing by and pick me up. I agreed. "It'll slow us down to work the same side of the street, but at this rate I'll never get away."

"I just talked to Dom. He's on his way, Jake."

"Why didn't he call me?"

"I don't know. He said he couldn't reach you. Must have been in a dead zone or something."

I looked at the mall around me with its fat shops, coffee bars, karate schools, and tire stores. "I'm in a dead zone, no question about that."

Within minutes, Trevor's rental car pulled into

the far side of the parking lot. He cruised until he saw me, picked up speed, and barely slowed down long enough for me to jump in.

We spent the rest of the afternoon checking rental offices and hardware stores between Mt. Airy and Frederick.

A Home Depot manager said, "I saw the news and I'd like to help, I really would. But we sell a lot of plywood and a lot of power tools. I'm not sure how much I can tell you."

"The list would be very specific." For the sixth time that day I ran it down: "Enough plywood to build a box three by five, maybe two feet deep."

"Large enough to hold a boy," Trevor said, driving home the point, just in case this manager had missed it.

The manager's face went white as the visuals kicked in.

"A power saw, nails, possibly a nail gun or at least a hammer, two threaded galvanized pipes and caps, and digging tools—a shovel and maybe a pick or mattock."

"Like I said, we sell a lot of those items, but I'll certainly ask the checkouts. It might take a while to call everyone."

"I appreciate it." I shook the man's hand and we left. On the way to the car I said, "Imagine being a grown man and making your living in an orange vest."

As Trevor slid behind the wheel, he said, "I hate this part of the job. All these dead ends. All these boring people."

"That's why you went HRT. Once you guys are called in, all the footwork's been done by the grunts like me pounding the sidewalk."

"I'm surprised we haven't crossed paths with any of Vince's men."

"Me, too. Or at least the locals."

My cell phone rang. It was Katie calling from Florida. I'd called her earlier to tell her what had happened and had had to persuade her to stay with the investigation in Florida. It took some time, but I finally convinced her to stay on Bower's trail.

"Jake, is there any word yet on Eric?"

"Nothing yet."

"Something will break, I just know it."

"What about you? Anything?"

"I'm so close to Bower's contact I can smell his cologne. Seems Bower had a thing for college girls. A campus cop here, name of Clausen, caught him lurking around the grounds of one of the dorms. He creeped her out, she said."

"She's an excellent judge of character."

"She took him in for questioning and he called someone. Next thing you know, a lawyer's on the phone talking habeas corpus and threatening to sue for unlawful detention, false arrest, civil rights violations, you name it. They had to let him go."

"Have you checked the phone records?"

"I did. Bower's call was to a motel outside of town. I'm on my way there now."

"Good girl. Let me know when you've got something."

"You, too," Katie's voice went from rapid, all-business, hard-nosed cop-talk to soft and concerned with a slight note of worry. "Jake, my heart breaks when I think about what you and your family are going through. As soon as I'm done here, I'm coming up, and you won't stop me from helping, Jake."

"I know, Katie. But right now you're helping me so much, just knowing you're on the job Mrs. De Vries hired us to do."

"I'll call as soon as I know something." Katie was about to hang up when she said, "Jake? Do you know where Rob is?"

"No, why?"

"I tried calling him at the Bureau and he's out sick. So I tried calling home and there was no answer."

"Did you try his cell phone?" I asked, although I wanted to suggest she try the girl from Records' apartment and maybe she'd find Rob there.

"I did, but he's got it turned off or something. I'm a little worried, Jake."

"I'm sure he's fine, Katie, but I'll try him from here if you want me to."

Katie thought about it a moment. "No, that's okay. I'm sure he's fine. Probably just sleeping and has the ringer off."

"That's right."

We made reassuring noises at each other and then signed off. So, not only had Rob taken the Black Diamond file, now he was missing. None of this made me feel any better.

"Rob's missing," I said to Trevor.

"See? Not all the news is bad."

"Katie's worried."

"Maybe he's on his way here."

"Yeah. Maybe."

Trevor shook his head. "I don't get it. Rob is a lightweight compared to you. What could a smart girl like Katie see in such an asshole?"

"Love makes you stupid. Look at Valerie. How long have you two been married?"

"Sixteen years."

"And she's smart."

"Uh-huh. It's nice to work with such a funny guy. Keeps things interesting."

The last real estate office on our list was on the far side of Frederick, a Norman Rockwell town best known as the place where Barbara Frietschie flew the American flag while the Confederates rode through. "Shoot, if you must, this old gray head, / But spare your country's flag," the poem goes, and on every corner of Frederick is a plaque or marker honoring the legendary old broad.

"Woman was suffering from dementia" was Trevor's assessment of Barbara's patriotism.

The real estate office was in the bottom floor of a two-story building off the main street. We caught Mr. Terwilliger at the door just as he was locking up. I introduced myself and it took a moment, and then his face opened in recognition and sympathy. I immediately liked the guy and guessed he did a modest but honest business. He was probably the kind of real estate agent who talked about putting people in homes rather than houses and meant it. At Christmas, I bet he signed all of his agency's cards himself.

He let us into the office and sat at his desk. Trevor and I took the padded chairs across from him, the usual husband-and-wife seats. Terwilliger put his elbows on the desk, hands together in an earnest prayer, and said, "How can I help you, Agent Donovan?"

"We're looking for anyone who might have rented a house or cabin recently. He'd be a single man, white, midthirties to forties, probably driving a van. Someplace that would give him a lot of privacy, maybe with a garage."

"I don't even have to check my files. I rented a place north of here yesterday to a nice-looking young man."

"Did he pay with a credit card or check?"

Terwilliger hesitated and looked from me to Trevor.

"He paid in cash," Trevor said.

"Don't worry. We're not from the IRS," I said.

Terwilliger swallowed once, then spoke in a voice so low that we had to lean forward to hear him. "Two weeks' rent plus a very large security deposit. I know I shouldn't have, but"—Terwilliger searched for an excuse that would give him some moral wiggle room—"business has been so bad lately, what with the economy and no one taking vacations anymore."

"Was there something about this man that made you suspicious?"

"His name." Terwilliger let his fingers fold together and he looked away, ashamed of letting his ethics slide.

"Which was?"

"John Smith." Terwilliger looked at me again. "You'd think he would have come up with something better, out of respect, wouldn't you?"

It was Trevor's turn. "Guess he didn't have to, did he?"

Terwilliger had the decency to blush.

32

Vince didn't even jump on us for working the case. He just took the information, said they would handle it from there, and warned us again to go home and wait for him to call.

"We'll wait, just like you'd wait if it was your boy."

"Jake. I'm grateful for the work you've done. I am. And I understand how you'd want to be there. But think of how you'd feel if this guy sees you and the whole thing goes south. And it could, Jake, in a hurry. You don't believe me, ask your partner there how many times a Hostage Rescue op turns bad. Go ahead, ask him. I'll wait."

"No, Vince. I don't have to. I know you're right. But at least let us come with you. You owe me that, Vince. He's my son."

Vince rolled it over in his head, looking for rough

spots, of which there were too many to count. "One more in the van won't hurt."

"Two more."

"Two more." Vince sighed.

He picked us up an hour later in an observation van. An agent from Washington drove while Vince filled us in. "The house is isolated, which is good, but it's also surrounded by open fields, which gives us no cover."

"So we wait until dark," Trevor said. This was his area, and Trevor knew how to get in and get out of a hostage situation better than anyone else I knew, including his superior officers at Quantico.

"That's right," Vince said. "The locals have all the roads in and out covered so there's nowhere he can go. The HRT will be standing by, just in case negotiations fall through."

"What do you mean, negotiations?"

"Jake, I understand you want to thump some heads. I do, too, but we have to do this by the book. I have the phone number, and when everyone's in place, I call and try to convince him to give himself up. If he doesn't, then we play rough. Okay?"

"You know it's not."

Trevor put his hand on my shoulder. "It's the right way, Jake."

"We'll have snipers with night scopes positioned, and go teams ready to bust in if I even think things are heading into squirrel town."

"Squirrel town? You get this snappy stuff from a comic book?"

In a John Wayne voice, Trevor said, "I been to squirrel town, mister, and believe me, it's no place to be after dark."

"Amen," I said. I put my head down and prayed that things would stay as far away from squirrel town as possible. I looked up in time to see the driver's eyes in the rearview mirror. He was looking back at us as if we were brain-damaged, and he was probably right.

"Remember," Vince said, "you two are not even here. So I don't want anything remotely cowboy out of either of you or I might as well apply for that night shift at the 7-Eleven right now. The director would have my ass in a sling if he knew I'd let you two do a ride-along."

Trevor crossed his heart. I promised I'd behave.

The van stopped at the intersection of two country roads. All around were open fields, broken by small stands of hardwoods and rolls of cut hay. We got out and the heat wrapped us up. The gloom of the morning had lifted and been replaced by a yellow sun in a cloudless sky. I immediately began to sweat. Neither of us had changed clothes since we'd rolled out of bed at Trevor's place fourteen hours before, but while Trevor looked as fresh and pressed as the cowboy hero's hat at the end of the last reel, I looked like I'd slept in the barn with the hero's horse. Even dressed in black, under an August sun, Trevor kept his cool.

Vince conferred with the local police manning the roadblocked intersection, then returned to us. "The house is over that small rise." He shouldered a backpack and an M16. "Saddle up."

I carried a pack with water, light rations, and extra radio batteries. Trevor carried extra radios, ammunition, and his black bag.

"What's in there?" Vince asked him.

"My makeup."

We humped up the hill and over the top, a walk of about half a mile. A stand of trees gave us shade and cover and a clear view of the house at the bottom of the valley, two hundred yards away. A local cop, dressed in black SWAT fatigues, lay on his stomach and peered at the house through binoculars.

"Anything?"

"Nothing yet. There's somebody inside, but I can't tell if it's male or female or how many might be inside."

The small vacation cottage had a long porch that shaded the front windows. In the driveway was a green minivan with Maryland tags.

"Have you been able to run the plates?" I asked.

"Yeah." The cop, Officer Waters, didn't take his eyes away from the binoculars. "Belongs to a Russell Frey from Takoma."

"Have we tried to call Russell Frey in Takoma?"

Vince said, "His wife says he's at a sales retreat in the mountains—you know, that fire-walking, team-building bullshit. We tried his cell phone number and he must have it turned off."

Waters said, "Yesterday, the state police found a

body in a Dumpster off 40 that matches the general description of Russell Frey. No positive ID yet, but he's about the same age, weight, and height."

Trevor pulled his black bag toward him, unzipped the top, pulled out a Colt Python, and handed it to me. "If you'd prefer an automatic, I've got that in here, too."

"No." I swung out the cylinder, checked the rounds, and locked her back up. "This will be fine."

The sun slowly sank toward the ridge behind the house.

"Be careful of your reflections," Vince said. "He sees sunlight off a lens and we might as well walk up to the door and introduce ourselves."

Each minute that passed made me more nauseated with dread. I needed to move, and the sooner the better. I watched Waters wipe his palms on his shirt and knew we were all feeling the same way.

The cop at the intersection came through the radio. "Special Agent Andrews? I've got a Joe Ripley here. He says he's from Agent Burke's office in Washington. Should I send him up?"

Vince looked at me. "What the hell's Joe doing here?"

"Whatever it is, it's not good." Joe Ripley was a great guy, and a real warrior in the turf battles that erupt around Washington, but I could sooner see my mother storming this house with a gun in her hand.

Vince went back to the radio. "Roger that. Send him up."

Trevor zipped open his bag, removed a small case, opened it, and started to put together a sniper rifle.

Vince gave him a look that would have shattered a lesser man. "Malone, what the fuck?"

"Joe's here, it means we're on our own."

"Do not, and I repeat, do not shoot anyone with that thing unless I tell you to. You got that?"

"I got it." The rifle together, Trevor put it to his shoulder and adjusted the scope, doping out distance and wind. "But it still doesn't alter the fact that we're on our own."

Ten minutes later, Joe came huffing into the trees. "Goddamn," he said. "I've got to get out more, do a push-up or something."

"Joe," I said, "Trevor here thinks you two are our only backup. Please tell him he's wrong."

Joe wouldn't look at me. He stretched out onto his stomach and crawled up to the tree line. "That the place?"

"Jesus, Joe, you see any other place?"

Trevor muttered in blackface vaudeville, "Dis mus' be de place, boss."

Joe glared at him, eyes in a squint.

"Joe, we're getting toward dark. Are we getting any help?" Vince asked.

Joe stared through the binoculars at the house. "No. We're on our own."

"Told ya," Trevor said, eye still glued to the scope.

Vince blew out a long, patient breath.

I was not so patient. "Let me guess, Joe. The attorney general decided he needed the HRT someplace else, like his rec room, just in case some Eastern European busts in and blows up his fucking stamp collection."

That drew Trevor's attention away from the house. "Jake. Did you just use the F-word?"

I don't use rough language, as a general rule, but as Mark Twain said, sometimes prayer helps and then there are times when a man's only recourse is blue.

Joe said, "When Armstrong vetoed the HRT response, Neil wanted to come himself, and the director was ready to suit up, too, Jake, honest. But Armstrong called both of them up to Justice. So here I am."

"Neil let you do this?" Vince asked.

Joe gave us a thin, wavering grin that made him look vaguely seasick. "He wasn't in the office to stop me." I could tell that the macho Joe who had strapped on the Kevlar in Washington felt a hell of a lot different up here on the hill, facing a man whose murder of one FBI clerk wouldn't add a day to his sentence.

Waters said, "You want, I can have our team here in a couple hours."

Vince thought it over, then said, "I don't see how we have a choice, do you, Jake?"

I didn't think I could stand the wait. But I knew Eric would be safer if the assault was done by people trained for this instead of two Broken Wings, one agent, a cop, and a clerk.

As it turned out, we didn't have a choice.

Waters whispered, "Hold it."

"What?" Everyone's attention went back to the house.

"Someone's coming out," Waters said.

In my binoculars, I saw the man moving in the silence of distance. He took a small bag from the house to the van and then went back inside the house. He was in a hurry.

"Looks like he's leaving," Vince said.

"He's running scared," I said. "Look at his face."

"You want to catch him at the crossroads?" Waters asked.

Vince said, "What do you think, Malone?"

Trevor didn't hesitate. "We need to get him when he comes out. Don't wait until he has Eric in the car."

Vince looked at me. "And you, Jake?"

"Trevor, can you hit him from this distance?"

"You know I can."

"Okay."

"If you're going, go now," Trevor said.

"Right," Vince said. "Joe, you and Waters go left. Jake, you and I go right and come up on the far side of the van. Remember, we wait for him to come out and hope he doesn't have Eric. If he does, you take him down before he gets to the van, right, Malone?"

"Right."

"Everybody ready?"

We all nodded and on Vince's word we were up and running in two enveloping arcs down the hill, moving as quickly as we could while staying low. My pounding heart was so loud I felt sure the killer could hear it inside the house.

The grass was nearly to our knees and our running released clouds of insects into the air. Gnats got into my eyes and mouth and I worried about being able to make an accurate shot with the Colt, but felt better knowing Trevor was behind the scope on the hill.

As we reached the house, Vince and I pressed against the side of the van. When the man came around to the driver's side, we'd take him, hoping he'd be too surprised to clear a weapon. We knew that once he rounded the front of the van, Trevor wouldn't have a shot. It would be on us.

The hinges shrieked and heavy steps hurried across the porch and down the three steps to the grass.

My body tensed, and my finger curled into the trigger guard of the revolver. Vince was crouched below me, his Sig in two hands, ready to take the man down. I heard the soles of the man's shoes crunch gravel and stop. He slid the van's side door open and dropped something heavy inside that made the van rock slightly on its springs. My stomach lurched. We waited. The man came around the front of the van. I could see his silhouette pass across the windshield and there he was, keys in one hand, his face open in shock as Vince sprang at him, the pistol pointing at his face.

"Get down! Get Down! Get down!" Vince

hollered, and even I was shaken by the volume and force of his voice.

The man's arms shot up toward the sky, and in one motion, Vince had his weapon holstered, the cuffs out, and he was spinning the man around and down to his knees. When the man was face-down on the gravel drive, Vince planted his knee against his neck and snapped the cuffs around his wrists.

Joe and Waters were just clearing the front door when I looked up. I ran for the porch, took the three steps in one stride, and burst into the living room just as Waters cuffed a woman who, like the man outside, was on her stomach. Unlike the man, the woman was crying.

Joe came out of the bedroom. "The house is clear."

Waters helped the woman to her knees and I hollered at her, the big Colt Python's muzzle aimed between her eyes, "Where's Eric? Where'd he bury the boy?"

The woman stopped crying and her face fell open, her eyes wide, her mouth agape.

"Where's the boy? Where did he bury the boy?"

"I don't know." She began to cry again.

I ran outside and jumped off the porch. Vince had the man on his feet, his hands cuffed.

I couldn't see the man's face. The air turned red and details lost all definition. I hollered at the man's shape, "Where's my boy?"

Vince's hand was on my chest and his voice

echoed in my head. "Jake, Jake, stop. It's not the guy. It's not our guy."

"What?" My vision began to clear and I saw the man in front of me, trembling.

"Jake, this is Russell Frey. The woman is Bonnie Booth. Mr. Frey's business associate."

The man said, his voice a mere squeak, "What boy?"

33

"You should see a doctor," Toni said.

"I *am* seeing a doctor."

"You know what I mean," she said as she slowly peeled away the bandage. The wound had opened and soaked through to my shirt, making a great picture for the nightly news. As I'd made my way through the reporters, I'd heard one ask, excited nearly to the point of incontinence, "Did you get it? Did you get the blood?"

Now, standing in front of the motel room mirror, Toni inspected the through-and-through Bower'd given me in the parking garage. "Doesn't this hurt?" She gently probed the tender flesh with her fingertips.

"I'll heal," I said, smarting more from the humiliation of the balls-out assault on Russell Frey's love nest than anything as trivial as a gunshot wound.

Toni poured hydrogen peroxide on the wound, fore and aft, and the sting chased away the drowsiness that dulled my thoughts and caused my mind to wander into dark dead ends of self-recrimination and dread. When I was a younger man, I'd marched for three days without so much as a nap. But now, sleep was claiming more of my time, as if life itself was preparing me for what Chandler called the Big Sleep, that final lie-down that comes too quickly to the young and too slowly to the old.

I wondered if Eric was sleeping, or if he was awake and terrified, calling for me, and counting on his famous father to ride in with the cavalry, a father who had wasted the day chasing a software salesman from between adulterous sheets.

Toni saw my face in the mirror and knew my thoughts, as she always knew them. "You'll find him. I know you will."

"I'm running out of time. And I'm running out of ideas."

"Vince is a good agent. He's out there right now, I bet, following new leads the Bureau's turned up."

"Vince is back in Washington, explaining to the director why he should keep his job."

Toni took in a deep breath, gathering her strength so that she could hold us both up. Slowly, almost afraid to hear the answer, she asked, "So who's taking the investigation?"

"Harry Gillette."

It was my turn to read Toni's thoughts as they passed over her face. They were the same as mine.

"I know. He's not my first choice, either. Or my fifty-first. That's why I need to get back out there. Harry will spend more time on the phone, covering his ass when he fails, than he will on the case."

"You need some rest." Toni taped fresh bandages over the puckered entry and the ragged exit wounds.

"A quick shower. The bad guys will smell me coming."

"You don't want to get this bandage wet." Toni took a washcloth, soaked it in hot water, and lathered it up with soap.

Carefully, she began to wash my skin, first around the bandage, then around the sutures on my neck. She rinsed the washcloth, lathered up again, and began washing my arms and chest. The warmth of the water, and the closeness of this woman who had been my wife before murderers, rapists, and arsonists had crept into our bed, and her gentle ministrations, made me pull her closer. She kept her face turned away from me, and I could feel her hesitation and fear. When she did lift her face, it was to kiss me, her arms around my waist, her mouth open and forgiving.

I pulled her from the bathroom and we fell onto the bed. Like teenagers stealing a moment while the parents slept, we fumbled with the buttons and belts and snaps, trying not to wake Ali in the next room.

It is perhaps the least talked about kind of sex there is. Grief sex. In times of tragedy or loss we often lose ourselves, or find ourselves, in this most intimate of human connections. Perhaps it is the affirmation of life in death. Perhaps it is simply an escape from the pain and confusion. The naked truth is, funerals are almost as fertile a field for coupling as weddings.

So it was with Toni and me. We used our bodies to numb our minds, finding comfort in the ageless rhythm of flesh on flesh. We turned, through the alchemy of sex, our panic into passion. And when we returned to earth, we felt as if we should somehow feel ashamed, but we could not.

Toni, lying next to me, her body against mine, said, "Tell me it will be all right, Jake. I need to hear that."

"It will be all right, Toni." And I discovered that I needed to say it, as much as she needed to hear it.

The bedside phone rang and I fumbled to pick it up.

"Jake, this is Trevor. Dom is here and Jerry's on his way." Trevor hesitated, and in that pause, I knew that Trevor was a hell of a lot more sensitive to the truth of things than any of us had ever given him credit. "Uh, is it all right if we come up?"

I asked him for ten minutes and he said, "Take all the time you need, partner."

Toni slid out of bed and was picking her clothes up from the floor.

"Toni?"

"You don't have to say anything, Jake. I'm glad this happened. I am. But I'm not kidding myself. I'm not a schoolgirl." She pulled on her shirt and buttoned it, crooked in her haste. "You need to get back to work." She leaned over the bed, kissed me lightly on the cheek, and left by the adjoining door.

"Take all the time you need," Trevor had said.

In this case, that would be centuries.

34

Although Russell Frey was the one caught with his tail flapping in the breeze, Vince, Joe, and Officer Waters got their butts kicked in public. Our old friend Spider Urich was back on his feet, head wrapped melodramatically in a bandage, doing a stand-up in front of the Frederick courthouse. He was understandably eager to take a few shots at me, but he saved his snidely best for Vince.

Urich, his voice carrying the weight of the crumbling republic, intoned, "Special Agent Andrews, with little more than a few years' experience, took it upon himself to form a vigilante posse to smoke out a philandering software salesman from Takoma, Maryland. Is this what we pay our law enforcement officials, from the attorney general right on down to the cop on the beat, to do: to catch otherwise law-abiding software salesmen with their trousers down? I, for one, think not."

Trevor aimed the motel remote at Urich's nose and plinked him into a tiny, receding beam of light. "How does he do that?"

"Do what?"

"Raise that eyebrow up to his hairline?"

"The guy's forehead muscles must be strong enough to lift a truck. It's something I wouldn't mind investigating," Dom said, "during an autopsy."

"I mean," Trevor said, "he lifts that one eyebrow clean off his head. How does he do that? The man's a cartoon."

Dom tugged at the knee of his slacks, making sure the crease was sharp, and crossed his legs. His socks had little clocks on them. Calmly he said, "Did you know that Urich's right testicle hangs lower than his left?"

That got our attention.

Trevor stopped, an unopened beer in one hand, the opener in the other.

Dom said, "Most of us hang lower on the left, due to the spleen. However, on occasion, you'll run into someone who hangs opposite. In those cases, the body's internal organs are quite often flopped, with the liver on the left, the heart on the right, et cetera."

"How do you know this?" Dominic's knowledge of the human body always amazed me, but this bit of anatomical trivia was a new high, even for Dom.

"I'm a highly trained pathologist. Which is why you hired me."

"No," I said, "not how do you know this thing about hanging testicles. I understand that might take up an entire class in med school. I meant, how do you know this about Urich?"

"Urich was shot once."

"Just once?" Trevor arced the beer cap into the wastebasket on the far side of the room.

"He was a cub reporter covering crime in Detroit."

"I remember that," I said. "A drug dealer shot him in the chest. Everyone was surprised he lived. The Detroit PD had a pool going." I remembered a lot about Urich in those days. We were both young. We were both hungry. I was a street agent with a family, trying to carve out my place in the Bureau. Urich worked for the *Free Press* and his contacts were so good and so deep, he would often beat the cops to a crime scene. He even went undercover as a mental patient to get the scoop on a local heroin ring fronting as a VD clinic. Even with our differences, I respected Urich and always knew he had balls. Now, thanks to Dom, I knew that his right one hung lower than his left.

"Urich took a nine-millimeter right here"—Dom touched his chest, just left of the sternum—"point-blank. The gunpowder tattooed him and he's got a scar shaped like a star. The expanding gases from the pistol's muzzle exploded under the skin. Painful, I'd imagine. He calls it his sheriff's badge."

"And it didn't kill him?" Even Trevor was impressed.

"The reason he survived is because his heart is on the right side of his chest; not the left. The dope dealer assumed Urich was put together like the rest of us. He was wrong."

"Does this have a larger point, Dom?"

"You know it does, Jake."

"You think I'm making assumptions about how the Black Diamond Killer works, is that it?"

"It's a possibility," Dom said. "It's also a possibility that this isn't the Black Diamond Killer at all."

Trevor sat on the bed, elbows on his knees, his big hands folded together. "I've been thinking the same thing. Because I don't think this is the same guy at all. In fact, I think the Black Diamond Killer is dead, Jake. He's nothing more than a spook."

I sat down on one of the chairs and put my feet up on the bed. My shoulder was throbbing but I didn't want a painkiller to make me stupid and slow. "I wish I had the files."

"The files are gone, Jake. But I bet you could recall most of the pages from memory."

I took a long, slow breath and tried to see the file in my head. The case file was really a box with dozens of folders, all several inches thick. I could see the last one, the Jernigan boy.

I closed my eyes and slowed my breathing. Mentally, I pulled up individual pages. First were the photographs, the easiest to remember. I drifted past the Jernigan boy's school picture, a picture of him with a Christmas bike, and finally, the photographs of his body, curled up as though he were sleeping. I tried to concentrate on the photos of the bedroom, but there was nothing to see. The night-stand, the autographed baseballs on the bookcase, the bed with the covers pulled back as if he had just gotten up. And tucked under the corner of the pillow was the card, the black diamond. "Spook the gooks," I said aloud without thinking.

"What?"

I opened my eyes to see Trevor and Dom watching me. "It's something one of the assassin squad said in an interview. They left the black diamond card so it would spook the enemy."

"Charlie Cong was one superstitious little fucker," Trevor said.

I laughed. "I don't care who you are, Trev, if you know a killer's come into your house, done his dirty business, and then left without a sound, that'd rattle anyone."

"The card rattled you," Trevor said. "But that's the man's point, isn't it?"

Dom nodded. "Rattled you before, and he's doing it again. You're acting more from your heart than your head."

He was right, of course. I had been running since Bower showed up, with that ice cream cone in his hand and that smirk on his face. I hadn't really stopped to think about who was doing what and why. I'd just run from fight to fight, thinking with my gut. The bomb, Urich, the storming of the software salesman's hideaway, and now sleeping with my ex-wife, all were emotional responses motivated by fear. Whoever was trying to scare me stupid was succeeding.

I paced from the windows to the door and back
again. I turned the Jernigan case around in my
head, looking for something I'd missed, something
small, because the Black Diamond Killer left so few
clues, and took so little. Except for the victim, he
took so little when he left. Suddenly, a new light fell
on Eric's kidnapping.

Ali and Toni were both in the next room, lying in
the dark. Ali had fallen asleep, but Toni was awake,
her eyes open. I must have looked like a lunatic,
standing backlit in the doorway, because Toni sat
up and whispered, "Jake, what is it? What's
wrong?"

"Toni, when you came here, what did Eric bring
with him? Anything?"

"What do you mean, like his toothbrush?"

"No. I mean a toy, or a book, something of his
own."

"We moved so fast that we didn't have time to
bring much of anything." Toni thought a moment.
"He brought his book. The Harry Potter book."

"I saw that."

"And his Game Boy."

"Is that all?"

"I think so."

I would ask Vince Andrews for a list of the items
recovered from the scene tomorrow. "Try to remember the room this morning," I said.

Toni sat up on the side of the bed. "Okay." Her
eyes focused on a point in the air, searching the panicked snapshots in her mind.

"Was the Game Boy still there?"

"I think it was." Then, with more certainty: "Yes, it was." She came back to the present. "I remember it on the nightstand. I remember thinking he'd played with it after I'd told him to go to sleep. I remember."

I nodded. "That's good, Toni. That's really good."

"Why, Jake? Why is that important?"

"That makes this different from the other cases," Trevor said. "That means this isn't the Black Diamond Killer."

Toni looked confused, trying to see what Trevor and I saw.

I said, "The Black Diamond Killer always took a souvenir. Always. But whoever took Eric didn't know that."

"Whoever took Eric was targeting Jake, not your boy," Dom said.

"That means he could still be alive?"

"Yes, of course. We just have to find him."

Toni hugged my neck. "Oh, Jake, this is good news, isn't it?"

"I think so, Toni. Yes."

Dom said, his voice a rumble, "All along, all they've done is distract Jake. That was their intention."

Trevor added, "Look at Bower. The clown came out of nowhere just to mess with Jake's head."

"And it worked. I was distracted."

"But from what?" Toni asked.

"We're only working one case," Trevor said.

"So, the same people who are doing this are involved, somehow, in the Callahan case?"

"Looks like that to me," I said.

"That means, if we work our way up from North Carolina," Dom said, "we'll find who took Eric."

"Or, if we work our way from here," I said, "we'll find our North Carolina killer."

"This is no longer a series of separate crimes," Dom said. "From Durham to Beaufort, Alexandria to here, it's all one big crime scene."

"We just have to pull the right thread and the whole thing will come apart," I said.

My cell phone went off and I answered it.

"Jake, it's Rob."

"Where have you been? You disappear. You don't answer your phone. Jesus, McManus, what the hell's going on?"

"I've been working the phones all afternoon, Jake. Neil Burke assigned me to the Jason case this morning. I'm not one of your special team, remember? I can't just leave work."

"You should call Katie. She's been worried about you."

"I will. I heard about Ravan pulling you from the case . . ."

"That was Armstrong."

"Jake, you know that nothing happens around here without Ravan's blessing."

"Are you saying Ravan wanted me off this investigation?"

"You have no idea how Ravan talks about you when you're not around, do you, Jake?" Rob said it with condescending sympathy, as if I'd suffered a head injury and couldn't tie my shoes.

"You find something funny in this situation, Rob, you let me know what it is. I could use a good laugh."

"No, no, honest. I'm just amazed at how blind people can be. Me, too. I mean, if I didn't know better, I'd say there was still some lingering hostility between us. But then, why would I be busting my ass to find your son if that was true?"

The possibility that Rob had a lead trumped all of the other emotions. "You have something, Rob?"

"I think so. One of the other agents caught the follow-up on one of the fruitcake calls."

"Yeah?"

"He got some fucking yokel up in Trailerville somewhere, you know, so he didn't think much about it until the guy mentions the Holy Knights of New Jerusalem. So he asks me if maybe it has something to do with your case. And since it's up in your neck of the woods . . ."

"Did you mention this to Vince?"

"Vince isn't heading up the investigation. Harry Gillette is."

"I know. But Harry's an ass."

"I called Vince," Rob said. "I called Harry and Ravan, too. None of them thought it was worth a look."

"What makes you think different, Rob?"

"Well, I pulled up Bower's file."

"I had Vince do that before."

"But did Vince think to track down Bower's old butt buddy from Leavenworth? Did he pull the file on old Tom Smooth? Did your golden boy really do the digging he should have, Jake?"

I was suddenly so tired of Rob's frat-boy attitude that I wanted to strangle him. "Godammit, do you have something, Rob?"

"Yeah. I think I know where Bower is. Tom Smooth was the guy who recruited Bower into the Holy Knights. I had a hunch they might still be in contact. You know how old lovers are, Jake: persistent, even when they're time is gone."

I let it pass. "Where are they, Rob?"

"Tom Smooth has a training camp about an hour from where you are now, toward South Mountain. You got a map?"

35

"There it is." Trevor pointed to the small, single-story house built back in the trees. It was the kind of place that would have started as a fishing camp, then grown, room by room, into a year-round house with proper siding and paint. The front-porch light was off, but we could see the orange spark of a cigarette in the dark.

I parked at the side of the road and Trevor and I walked across the lawn toward the porch.

"Officer Waters?"

The smoker on the porch was quiet for a long time. The cigarette arced into the grass and Waters said, "Come on up before you wake the wife and get us all in trouble."

"Why the dark?" Trevor asked. He was so alert I could practically feel the tension vibrating the air. Waters could, too.

"Mr. Donovan here seems to trail reporters around."

"I'm sorry about that," I said. Officer Waters had been the target of a full-blown media attack, or as full-blown as it gets in rural Maryland. The shouts, the shoving, and the cameras trip up even the stars, and no one (or no one sane) ever gets used to it. You learn how to look natural, but that's the best you can hope for. And for those who are pushed into the glare by accident or mischief, it can make smart people stupid and stupid people forget how to walk and talk.

"My phone's been ringing so much I may have to move," Waters said.

I couldn't tell if he was serious or joking. "I'm glad you decided to help us," I said.

"I haven't decided anything. I might go back to sleep. That'd be the smart thing." He paused and lit another cigarette with a match that blasted away our night vision. "You know I'm suspended."

"I know."

"Without pay."

"We'll make it right," Trevor said, but didn't tell either of us how.

Waters seemed to think about that. "I almost didn't answer when you called."

"I'm glad you did." I sat in a rocking chair and let my eyes readjust to the dark. Trevor leaned against the porch railing.

"I still haven't decided."

"But you thought about it," I said.

"Yeah. I thought about it."

"What do you think?" Trevor asked.

"I think I'd be nuts to do this. You have no warrant. And it's out of my jurisdiction. And, after Russell Frey's lawyer gets through with me, I might be sleeping in a box under the railroad trestle."

"If you help us get my boy back, I'll get you a better job, and I'll make sure you get enough good press that no lawyer in the world will take you to court."

Waters laughed. "Like you've been so good at getting good press for yourself."

I was grateful that it was too dark for Waters to see my face redden. "It's been a bad week for a lot of things," I admitted.

"First question is, why not call the tactical boys from Quantico, or even the Baltimore office?"

Trevor and I looked at each other, aware of the glance even in the dark.

"You deserve the truth," I said. "The director's at a charity function at the White House. The assistant director's at Lincoln Center seeing *La Traviata*."

"What about the agent in charge? Vince?"

"He's been removed from the case."

"His replacement?"

"He won't take my call."

Waters laughed, but it wasn't because he'd heard anything particularly funny. "So we're on our own again, ready to bust into another software salesman's boudoir?"

"Maybe," Trevor said.

Waters stood up and walked past us, off the porch and into the yard. He looked up at the stars, the sky full of them out here in the darkness, away from the city lights. "I think I'm going to pass this time, boys. I got plenty of trouble already."

Trevor said, "Jake and I could do it in daylight, maybe. But at night we need someone who's been there."

"Where's that?"

"A militia camp near South Mountain."

"Tom Smooth's place? Yeah, I've been there. I was part of a reconnaissance team investigating weapons violations."

"Why'd the ATF choose you over one of their own?"

"Same as you. They picked me because I've hunted in and around those mountains since I was a boy. I know that camp. And I know Tom Smooth. If your son is with Tom, you need to get him out quick. Tom has a fondness for the boys."

"I heard that," I said.

"You have any tools?"

Trevor said, "They confiscated my black bag."

Waters scratched his head. "Let's see what I've got inside."

"So, are you in?"

Waters took a deep drag off his cigarette and flicked it into the darkness. "Yeah, what the hell, my career's pretty much shot in the ass anyway."

Waters took us into the mountains, the three of us jammed together in the front seat of his Chevy truck. He played cassettes of Hank Williams and Buck Owens and Dwight Yoakam until Trevor said,

"You know, sometimes quiet is good," and Waters took the hint.

We wound up into the mountains, then turned off and followed an old logging road that wasn't much more than a rutted trail through the forest. The truck rocked on its springs. Leaves and small branches closed in on all sides, making it impossible to see more than ten feet in front of us.

"We used to bring girls up here," Waters said. "That was when there was still some logging work, but I figured nobody worked on Saturday. Me and Marilyn Singer, cute little thing, were naked in the back of my four-by when a flatbed full of loggers drove up behind us. Course, I had to scramble to the front and pull into the ditch so they could get by. Those old boys hooted and waved and had a hell of a time. I never did get Marilyn to come up here after that. You suppose that's why?"

"You know," Trevor said, "those stories lose a lot of their charm when you have a daughter."

"I suppose so." Waters stopped the truck and turned off the lights. "We hump it from here."

With the truck lights off we were blind. No moon, and starlight was blocked by the forest canopy. Waters turned on a red-filtered flashlight and we gathered around the bed of the truck. I couldn't hump a regular pack because of the .22-caliber hole Bower had inconsiderately put through my trapezius muscle, so I carried a pistol, ammunition, and three canteens on a utility belt. I also carried Waters's Ruger mini-14.

When he gave it to me, Waters said, "It's semi-auto, but she'll squirt out rounds as fast as you need. The Holy Knights are probably full auto." He smiled. "It's a macho thing."

Trevor carried a 30.06 deer rifle with a scope. Waters had a Remington 870 pump with an extended magazine. We also had Motorola handheld radios, designed for camping families and vacationers traveling in more than one car.

Armed and ready, we set out in darkness so complete that I kept my fingertips on Waters's back and Trevor kept his on mine. Together, three blind men walked slowly up the mountain, one foot in front of the other. It's the infantryman's lullaby, so restful in its predictable rhythm that exhausted men often fall asleep without missing a step.

An hour into our march, Waters began to pick up the pace. "We need to be there, ready, when light comes," he said. My shoulder was on fire and my hips ached from carrying the weight of the belt, but I couldn't slow the two younger men who had come out here into the wilderness to rescue my son. When Waters broke into a jog, I did, too.

At a sign that only Waters could see, he stopped. "Malone, come with me. Donovan, you wait here. You hear gunfire, you come running."

As I waited, the birds began to stir, claiming their territory, calling to potential mates, and celebrating another day. The light gradually turned to gray and I could make out a road that had been used by a truck recently. I concealed myself in a thicket and listened. Even alone in the woods, on guard, I didn't hear Waters come up behind me.

"Come on," he said, and I followed him uphill, away from the road. He raised his fist and I stopped, keeping low. He waved me forward and we crawled up to the edge of a ridge. Below us, in a flat spot one hundred yards square, was a small camp. In the breaking gray dawn I could see two cabins, an out-house, one large tent, and far away from the buildings, in the trees, a slit-trench latrine. This was no yuppie summer camp with four-star accommodations. This was as rough as roughing it gets without sleeping in the mud.

"Any sentries?"

"None that I've seen," Waters said.

"Malone?"

"He's on the far side of the camp." Waters pointed.

I keyed the radio. "What have you got?"

"A clear shot of both cabins."

"Prepare to give us suppressing fire as needed."

"Roger that."

"What are we going to do?" Waters said.

"We're going to storm the camp. We take the men in the tent first. Then we take the cabins."

"Just like that?"

"They have my boy. I came prepared to kill men if I have to, Waters. Did you?"

Waters considered the full impact of what we were about to do. "I don't know."

"It's like the Alamo. You leave now and no one will blame you. Trevor and I will understand."

Waters shook his head. "No, I'm in. I'm in."

"But no one gets hurt unless there's no other choice, I promise."

Waters nodded, his lips pressed tightly together, his face set to the grim job ahead.

A thin line of smoke rose from the central tent and someone was already awake starting the fire. I withdrew my knife. "I'll take the men in the mess tent first."

Trevor's whispered voice came through the radio. "I got movement."

Waters and I watched as the door to the larger cabin opened and two boys dressed in camouflage pants and white T-shirts came out. They crossed the open assembly area toward the latrine, but stopped short of the trench, each boy finding a tree to wet against.

"Jesus," I whispered, "they're just kids."

Waters was as surprised as I was. "What do we do now?"

"I don't know." As I said that, a pudgy little man in full camo and black beret, Beretta on his hip and a magazine under his arm, emerged from the smaller cabin.

"That's Tom Smooth," Waters said.

The little man breathed in the morning air, hitched up his pants, and headed toward the back of the cabin.

There was our chance. "When I'm in position, you and Trevor make some noise," I said.

Waters looked from me to Smooth just as the little man turned the corner. A smile broke across his face. "You got it."

I took a wide circle around the edge of the camp, keeping to the trees. As I did, other boys came out of the larger cabin, rubbing the sleep from their eyes. Alone or in pairs, they walked into the trees to urinate. So far, Smooth was the only adult I'd seen.

I held close to the rear wall of the larger cabin. I looked through the window and saw two rows of six bunk beds and boys, none older than twelve, getting up and getting dressed. On one wall was the flag of the Third Reich. Next to it was the banner of the Holy Knights, the flaming cross with the barbed-wire halo. In the center were two photos, Hitler on top and Tom Smooth on the bottom. I couldn't see any weapons and I didn't see Eric.

The second, smaller cabin appeared to be Smooth's office and bedroom. The bunk was still rumpled. Along one wall was a rack of AK-47s, locked. Again, there was no sign of Eric.

Smooth had closed the door to the outhouse and was settling in with his magazine when I gave Waters the signal.

From two directions, Waters and Trevor fired over the camp, sounding like an entire squad of infantry. The shotgun blasted leaves overhead and bits of green flittered down like confetti. Trevor's deer rifle split the air and tore chunks from trees as the boys scattered into the woods, shrieking, their arms waving about their ears as if they were being chased by bees.

Smooth burst out of the outhouse, one hand holding up his pants, the other holding his Beretta. He saw the smoke from Waters's shotgun and aimed toward the trees.

I pressed the muzzle of my pistol against the back

of his neck, just under the hairline, and screamed, "Get down, get down, get down!" Just as I'd hoped, he did. I kicked the Beretta away, cuffed him, and hauled him toward the clearing, his pants down around his thighs.

Two of the older boys had fallen back on their training and were inside Smooth's cabin. One had unlocked the AKs and the other was loading a magazine. When they saw me with their commander, they seemed relieved to raise their hands and march into the clearing.

Trevor and Waters were rounding up the scattered kids. Many of the boys were in tears, especially those found by Trevor. He was the Holy Knights' biggest fear, a black man with a gun.

Waters checked the mess tent and found three boys under the tables and a cook, a white man in his sixties, armed with a cleaver.

I checked the cabins but found no one.

Trevor inspired the most fear so he did most of the yelling.

"I want every one of you little fascists to sit on your cracker asses, on your hands, palms up," he shouted. "Now!" He picked out one of the older boys, the one I'd caught in Smooth's cabin trying to load the AK. "Palms up, you ignorant cracker. Don't you know which part of your hand is your palm? It's the part that goes around your buddy's dick when you give him a reach-around, that's your palm, and I want you sitting on it. That's right."

With them sitting in the dirt, many of them in tears, I circled the boys and the two men. "A man named Bower came out here with a boy, ten years old, named Eric. I want to know where Bower took the boy. Who wants to be my friend and tell me first?"

"Remember the oath," Smooth shouted. "No one talks. No one!"

The boys were silent, except for those sobbing.

"Oh, tough little Nazis. Have an oath and everything." Trevor snatched up one of the older boys, one with three stripes sewed to his sleeve. "How about you, Sergeant? You got nothing to say?"

The boy spit on Trevor's boot. Trevor smiled. "This one will be a pleasure." He grabbed the boy by the arm and marched him around to the rear of the larger cabin. As the boys watched and listened, Trevor hollered, "Tell us what we want to know! Tell us!" Then a pistol shot cracked the morning air. The boys jerked as if pulled up by an invisible string; two of the boys screamed and there was a renewed round of sobbing.

"He'll do this until one of you talks," I said. "I've seen him kill people all morning, until the bodies were stacked up like cordwood. Women, children, old people, doesn't matter." I shook my head at the waste of it all. Several of the boys cried. Two of the boys wet their pants.

"But I can stop him," I said. "Just tell me what happened."

The boys whimpered, trying hard not to look at Smooth.

I shrugged. "I tried to help."

Trevor came around the cabin and headed for the group. "Who's next?"

"I'll tell," a boy blurted, his eyes panicked. He was about Eric's age, with blond hair and big, crooked teeth.

Smooth glared at him.

"What's your name, boy?"

"Cameron Conners." The boy looked at me, but kept glancing back at Trevor. "You'll keep the nigger off me, right?"

I nodded. "Just tell us what happened, son."

"Bowers come up here last night with a boy and some other man, looked like maybe he was CIA or something like that."

"What did he do with the boy?"

"I don't know. But they buried something big out in the woods. We dug the hole."

"What did they bury? A box?"

"I don't know. Some of the older boys said it was Stingers."

"Can you show me where?"

"I'll show you." The boy's eyes were fixed on Trevor. "Just don't let that big nigger man kill nobody else."

Trevor went from angry to sad in a flash. I could see it in his eyes, how the thought of another generation being raised like this broke his heart. Calmly he said, "You boys need to step into the twenty-first century. All that word does is make you sound like an ignorant peckerwood."

I pulled Cameron Conners to his feet. "Show us."

Waters watched over the prisoners while Trevor and I followed Cameron into the woods behind the cabin. As we passed, Cameron glanced over at the boy sergeant Trevor had taken first. There he was, curled up, bound and gagged with duct tape.

"You didn't . . . ," Cameron said.

"No, I try not to kill anybody before breakfast." Trevor pushed the boy forward.

"When the men left, did they take the boy with them?"

"I don't know. We was in bed when they left."

Cameron led us about fifty yards into the forest and started walking around, looking, saying, "It's right here somewheres. Here!" He stopped and pointed. "Here it is."

Cameron stood on a patch of freshly dug earth about three feet by six. The site had been hastily covered over in pine needles, but there, sticking up about a foot above the ground, were two steel pipes. Their ends were capped.

36

"Get some shovels," I said. "And some of the bigger boys with strong backs."

Trevor ran, leaving me alone with Cameron. I dropped to my knees and gripped one of the caps. At first it held, then, with a dull ringing, it turned. With the first pipe open I swung around to the second. I looked up and Cameron was pointing the rifle at me. The muzzle shook. The look in his eye made me shiver. It was determined, and clear with purpose. I could see the young soldier, trained, confronting the enemy.

"Cameron. That boy who was here last night is my son. I'm his father. And I think they buried him here."

"You saying them men killed him?"

"He might still be alive." I tried to sound more

optimistic than I felt. "But we have to get him out of this box."

Cameron hesitated.

"There's not much time," I said.

"I could shoot you."

"Yes, you could. But shooting me won't get you anywhere but prison. And you might as well be shooting my boy, too. Is that what you want? You want to kill my son, Cameron?"

The movement was so small, I didn't see it. Then the boy shook his head again. "I guess not, mister. I didn't know." He lowered the rifle.

Trevor, standing ten feet behind the boy, lowered his pistol and I felt myself begin to breathe again.

"The boys are coming," Trevor said.

When they heard it was a human in the hole, a boy who might still be alive, the three boys dug quickly. In under twenty minutes they stood on the plywood, clearing the edges so we could open it.

One of the boys put his ear to the pipe and said, "I don't hear nothing. And it smells."

"Bad?" one of the boys asked.

The boy at the pipe screwed up his face, searching for a name to put to the smell. "No. Not bad. It kinda smells like pennies."

"Maybe it's Stingers like the men told us," the boy said.

"Or maybe he's dead," said the third.

They climbed out, and on my hands and knees I pried up the nails. Each creak of wood ripped through my heart as I became more and more convinced that the third boy was right.

They all stood around the open hole, watching as Trevor and I got our fingers under the edge of the plywood sheet and lifted. When we got the cover up and off, we looked back inside the box. He was facedown and dead, without a doubt. Someone had cut his throat from behind and let him topple into the box. The box was flooded with blood, thick and black. One of the boys turned and vomited into the weeds. The others stared in horror, frozen to the spot, unable to look away.

"That must be Bower," Trevor said.

"Yeah," I said. "That's him."

37

"You don't mind waiting?"

Waters shook his head, a cigarette dangling from his lips. He sat on a camp chair, his feet up on a log bench, the twelve-gauge across his lap.

On the other side of the circle Smooth sat cross-legged on the ground, sobbing, his hands cuffed behind him. His boys sat apart from him, occasionally staring at him in disgust, the way you'd look at caterpillar guts on the bottom of your shoe.

"You send up the state patrol. Until then, I'm going to tell these boys stories about life in prison. Maybe Smooth will have a few to add, too. Like when the African brothers made him their bunk buddy. That must have been a great time, huh, Tom? Why don't you tell the boys about that?"

Smooth stopped sobbing long enough to give Waters a look that could strip the bark off a tree.

"Yessir, Tom Smooth, a man so coarse that he shames his family name just by wearing it around in public," Waters said.

Trevor and I thanked Waters, climbed into the camp truck, and took off down the mountain. The Knights' truck was a three-quarter-ton pickup, the bed covered in flapping canvas, and like me, it was a veteran of long-forgotten campaigns. Also, like me, it was maintained sporadically, if at all. The shifter would leap out of gear going on a grade, and the engine spewed a plume of blue smoke into the pine branches. In lieu of a nut, vise grips held the steering wheel to the steering column.

Trevor sat quietly, eyes straight ahead, concentrating on what I guessed was the same conclusion I'd come to. The missing evidence, the phone calls, the disappearances, the knowledge of all our movements and all our investigations.

"You're thinking about Rob, too," he said.

"Yeah. I am."

"All this time he's eating with us, watching my TV, being nice to my wife and children."

"Yeah. Not to mention Katie."

"This is going to hurt her bad, Jake."

"I know."

"All we can be is friends for her, you know that."

"I know."

"She'll need a friend more than she needs a boyfriend."

"I understand, Trevor."

"Just want to make sure you don't fuck up, start mistaking what *you* need for what *she* needs."

"Lay it all out, Trevor. Don't hold back."

"I'm just saying—"

The road made a sharp turn to the left, and as I pulled the truck around the curve, I saw a tree, its trunk as big around as my waist, lying across the road. Trevor saw it the same instant I did and gripped the dash. I hit the brake and pulled the wheel, hand over hand, to the right. The truck bounced across the ruts, over the gravel berm, and down a steep slope into the trees. All I could see was a rush of green as the truck plowed through the pines. I tried to steer but the truck was on its own, fueled more by gravity than gasoline, rocketing toward the stony creek at the bottom of this ravine. Twenty yards up, a tree stood between the truck and the creek. I tried to brake and steer around it, but the trunk caught us at the right headlight and the truck stopped cold, throwing me into the steering column, and Trevor into the dash.

I don't know how long it took me to shake the galaxy of pain-inspired stars from my head, but when I could catch my breath, I touched Trevor's shoulder. "Trevor, talk to me."

Trevor lifted his head, his face shining with blood. "I hate riding with you, man."

"Are you okay?"

"I'm bleeding all over my shirt and you ask if I'm okay?"

"You know what I mean."

"I hate that shit. Man falls off a fucking cliff and the first thing someone asks is 'Are you okay?' No, godammit, I'm not okay. I just fell off a goddamn cliff." Trevor threw the truck door open and stepped out. He looked a little wobbly.

"Maybe you should sit down."

"Fuck sitting down. I'm going to lie down."

I got out of the driver's side and looked up the hill. "Can you walk up to the road?"

Trevor leaned against the side of the truck and inspected the gash on his forehead in the mirror. "Yeah. I can walk."

I took his arm and he let me. That's how I knew he was hurt. "Come on, we need to get you to a doctor."

"What about you?"

"I'm a little bruised, but okay."

"That's why you're bleeding."

I touched my neck and felt the fabric of my shirt was wet. "It's an old wound."

"Oh, well, that's a big relief." Trevor continued to complain as we labored up the slope. Suddenly, he stopped and listened. His eyes scanned the trees. I knew enough about Trevor's training and instincts to listen, too. Quietly, without moving anything but his lips, Trevor said, "This doesn't feel too smart, Jake."

"What? You hear something?"

"No. I mean, climbing up this hill. Someone had to dump that tree across the road. Maybe he's up there waiting for us."

"Uh-huh." I searched the edge of the rise. We were still twenty yards from the road and in the cover of the trees. "You think maybe we should go off-road?"

"Yeah. That's exactly what I was thinking." Trevor pulled his pistol and racked the slide.

From above us we heard, "Trevor, throw that gun away."

"Rob?"

"Yes, Jake."

"You know this is crazy, right?" I watched for any movement on the cusp of the road and still couldn't see him.

Trevor whispered, "We should run, Jake. He can't hit us both."

I whispered back, "You're not the one sleeping with his ex-wife."

"I thought of that."

Rob said, "Don't think I can't hit you both if you run, because I was trained by the best, wasn't I, Trevor?"

"Damn," Trevor said.

"And you miss your boy, don't you, Jake?"

"Eric!"

"Daddy!"

"Eric!" I clambered up the hill on all fours, followed by Trevor. When I came up on the road, Rob let Eric run to me and I held my boy as he held me, tightly, not ever wanting to let go.

"You okay, champ? Are you hurt?"

"No, Dad. I'm okay. I'm scared, but okay."

"I wouldn't hurt the boy, Jake. You should know that." Rob held an AR-15 at port arms. Rob didn't smile. I had expected him to be wearing that Big Boy grin, and if he had, in that moment, I'm not sure I could have kept myself from trying to take that rifle and stick it into one of Rob's more secure orifices. Fortunately for us both, Rob wasn't amused by the situation.

"My car's parked just down the road. Let's go."

"Don't worry, Eric, we'll get you out of this," I said.

"You listen to me, and everyone gets out of this," Rob said.

"I wouldn't count on that," Trevor muttered.

"Come on, let's go."

Trevor walked in front of us. Eric and I took the middle and Rob followed behind us.

"Things get a little hairy last night?"

"Shut up," Rob said.

"Let me guess what happened," I said. "Whoever is on top of this thing told Bower to kill you."

"Told him to kill both of us, me and the boy."

Eric squeezed my hand.

"I saved your son, Jake. He's a good kid. I wouldn't hurt him unless I had to. You know what I'm saying?"

"Then why don't you let us go?"

"I would, Jake, honest, I would. But right now, I'm a trusted member of the FBI. I need things to stay that way for another eight to twelve hours. So, you see, I need you with me."

"They'll catch you, Rob."

"You're probably right, Jake, but I'm running out of options."

We came to the car and Rob told us to get in. Trevor slipped behind the wheel and Eric sat in the middle, between us. Rob took the backseat. We took off down the mountain toward the valley.

"If you know you'll be caught, why not give yourself up?"

Rob didn't say anything for a long time. When he did speak, he sounded resigned to his fate, whichever way it went. "I don't think I could stand the shame, Jake, and that's the truth. At the very best I'd go to jail, and how long do you think I'd survive? These people have a very long reach, Jake."

"Who are they, Rob? Who are we talking about?"

"I don't know, and that's the truth. It was while I was in Florida, you know."

"With the girl from Records," Trevor said, "thinking with your little head."

"I was spending more money than I had coming in. A lot more." Rob mumbled.

"What?"

"I said I'd done some gambling. And my career was pretty shaky after what I'd done to Katie. You know, we like to think Hoover's dead, but his ghost still carries a big stick when it comes to sexual indiscretions. So when this guy offered me a hundred thousand dollars to put him in touch with an explosives guy, I introduced him to Bower. That's all. I just made the introduction."

"How'd you know Bower?"

"I'd worked his case."

"And now they own you," I said. "For a hundred thousand dollars. Seems pretty cheap."

"Yeah, Jake. That's easy to say when you're getting that much to tech *The X-Files*."

There wasn't much sense in responding to that, so I asked, "What happened after you got the money? I mean, how'd you get here, to this place, running out of options?"

Rob settled into the rear seat, obviously as tired as I was, working on as little sleep. I could only imagine how fast he'd been running in the past week, and I hoped his fatigue would make him careless.

He sighed. "Things go fine, I get the money, and then I don't hear from them for months. One day Bower shows up on my doorstep and tells me we're partners. I tell him to take a hike, he's got everything, Jake, my bank records, everything. I ask him what he needs from me and he says all we have to do is blackmail this research scientist. No spy stuff, he says, just business. So I set up William Rush with the hooker. I honestly thought it was a blackmail scheme, Jake. But then Bower killed Rush and I staged it to look like the husband did it."

"Janice Callahan?"

"No," Rob said, his voice almost a whisper. "I did that. I was told to kill her and her boyfriend in Alexandria. By then I was in so far, I couldn't see any other way out."

We came to a macadam road and Rob told Trevor to turn left.

"Where are we going, Rob?"

"The airport in Winchester. It's not far. Bower called his people yesterday and arranged for a charter to pick us up. Extracting the troops, right?"

We rode in silence for a while, all in our own

thoughts, the sharp turns in the shaded two-lane bringing us closer to the end of the road.

Rob sat staring out the window at the trees. "I love this country." He looked at me. "I brought Katie up here last month, Jake, when you thought she was at her mother's. She and I didn't get dressed for three days. God, but I'm going to miss her most of all. But, then, there's other pussy in the world."

"How long do you think it'll be before the Bureau tracks you down?"

Rob laughed. "If it's Harry Gillette, I'll die an old man before he finds me. The guy couldn't capture his dick with both hands."

Eric tried not to look at me, embarrassed by a grown man using words like *dick* and *pussy* in front of his father.

"What do you think will happen when Bower doesn't show up?"

"I don't know, Jake. I may have to kill everyone but my pilot here." Rob poked the back of Trevor's head with the muzzle of the rifle.

"Eric," Rob said, "when I was a boy about your age, my father would come out here and rent a plane for the afternoon. We didn't have a lot of money, but Dad was a flying fanatic. He'd hock Grandma's silver to spend a few hours in the air." Rob stared into his days as a boy, before everything had gone so horribly wrong. "My father wanted me to learn how to fly, but I was too afraid to go up. So I stayed on the ground and watched him fly circles above us. He seemed like Superman, only better because he was my dad. I wish now I'd flown with him."

"Don't say it," Trevor said.

"What?"

"How things might have been different if you'd been closer to your old man. I hate when criminals say that."

Rob stared at the back of Trevor's head as if trying to see through to the man for the first time. "Yeah. Right. I guess it is a cliché among the criminal set. How was your father?"

"Dead," said Trevor. "My father was dead."

Rob turned back to the window. "That would explain the hostility."

Trevor didn't say what he was thinking, but only because Rob held the gun.

Rob didn't talk again until we reached the airfield, a busy little airstrip with several hangars and a terminal building. On the far side of the field a man was refueling a Cessna Citation.

"There," Rob said. "That's our ride out of here."

"Pretty nice plane," Trevor said. "It's got a range of what, two thousand miles?"

Rob poked the back of Trevor's head again. "You'll find out where we're going when we get there. Maybe they'll even let you fly a little, Malone. Katie told me you could fly just about anything, even that big fat piece of shit you call the *Broken Wing*. You know, of all the things I'm going to miss about Katie, her conversation certainly won't be one of them. All she talked about was 'the team' and the cases you'd worked on and how much happier she was with you guys than she was with the Bureau, blah blah blah blah blah. It was enough to make me gag. You'd have thought she'd joined a fucking cult."

As Rob rambled on, his monologue fueled by nervousness and fatigue, I caught Trevor's eye and nodded toward the terminal. Trevor looked in time to see a sharpshooter settle in on the roof. Once we knew they were there, we saw them everywhere: the man getting his bags from the trunk of his car, the two pilots talking to each other by the hangars, the woman with the carry-on standing by the terminal door, and the young man in blue pants and white shirt walking toward us. He carried a clipboard, had a nametag pinned to his shirt, and was smiling.

I heard Rob remove the magazine from his pistol and heard jacketed rounds rasp against steel. When I looked, he was tucking the .45 into his belt.

Trevor parked in the small charter lot. Rob said, "You and Malone get out. Eric, you get out with me, okay?"

Eric looked up at me and I nodded. "You do as he says, Eric, and everything will be all right."

"That's right, Jake. I could have killed you all in the woods. So let's just get through this and then you can go home. And you even think the wrong thoughts, the first one to die will be the boy. I'm not bullshitting here, Donovan. I wouldn't want to hurt the kid. I kinda like him, actually."

I nodded. "We won't do anything, will we?"

"It's your show, man."

Trevor and I got out and waited. From the corner of my eye I watched two men in full assault gear move slowly through the rows behind us, their rifles trained on the rear window of the car.

Rob got out of the backseat as Eric slid across the front. Holding Eric close to him, Rob urged us all forward.

The man in the white shirt stopped. He looked up at the rifleman on top of the terminal. Rob followed his glance and saw the man, too. The four of us stopped.

"You see 'em?" Trevor said.

"Yeah. I see 'em." Rob pulled his pistol.

For a moment, no one moved. The four of us stood in the parking lot. The man in the white shirt stood thirty feet in front of us. The sharp-shooters stationed all around us waited, listening in their headsets for the green light. The two men behind us waited, their weapons aimed at Rob. From a car parked on our right, the driver's side door opened and a woman got out. She was dressed in a green blouse and black cotton pants, and the summer sunlight captured highlights in her hair. In her hands was a Smith & Wesson .45.

"Rob, let them go."

"Hi, Katie," Rob said. "I'm really glad they sent you to do this."

"They didn't want me to, Rob, but I convinced them that you'd listen to me."

"So talk."

"Nobody has to get hurt. This doesn't have to be a bad end. Just throw the pistol away and get down on the ground."

Rob sighed. His left hand held Eric's shoulder; his right hand pointed his pistol at Eric's temple.

Eric stood as still as time.

Rob's hand tightened on the pistol. I watched the hammer of his .45 come slowly back as he squeezed the trigger.

"Don't do this, Rob."

"Rob," Katie said, "please don't do this. Please."

Rob stopped and took his left hand from Eric's shoulder. "Get away, boy."

Eric looked at me and I said, "Go." Eric walked toward Katie, his steps careful and slow, like walking across ice.

Rob smiled and in a flash of blued gunmetal, raised the pistol, and aimed straight at my face. I saw his finger tighten and the trigger break. The hammer fell as Rob was ripped apart by eight shots, all fired from different angles. Rob jumped as if struck by lightning, and he was dead before his body hit the pavement.

38

After we'd given our statements, Katie, Trevor, Eric, and I were allowed to wait inside the terminal in a small conference room, away from the press.

"Ravan's sending the *Broken Wing*," Katie said, "to fly us home." She was still swimming through waves of shock and disbelief. For the rest of her life she would replay the instant she shot a man she'd trusted and swore to love until death.

"How did you find us?"

Katie said, "I found out that Rob was Bower's Florida connection." She raised her head and she began to cry, without a sound. I put my arm around her and she let me hold her until the moment passed, then she wiped her face with the back of her hand. Eric found a box of tissues and gave her one and was rewarded with a smile.

"Thank you, Eric. You're such a gentleman. I thought you were amazingly brave out there."

"I did, too," I said. "I'm very proud of you, son."

"Me, too," Trevor said. "You can watch my six any day."

Eric sat on the other side of Katie and held her hand. He hadn't spoken since the shooting, except to tell me he wasn't hurt. It would be several days before he said anything at all, and then he would talk nonstop for hours, but only to his mother. The one time I asked if he wanted to talk about it, he said, "No, Dad. I really don't."

Katie said, "When I found out it was Rob, I called the director. He pulled Rob's phone records and there were a number of calls to that girl in Records."

Katie would never mention her name. She was always "that girl in Records."

"When Ravan confronted her, she admitted that she was the one who'd taken the Black Diamond cards from the evidence room. Early this morning, Rob called her and told her to meet him in three days on St. Thomas." Katie tore her tissue into tiny bits. "Apparently it was 'their place.' That meant a plane. Ravan pulled a dozen agents in and we called every charter on the East Coast, every one that had a plane capable of flying to the islands. About the time you guys were digging Bower up at the Holy Knights' camp, we found the flight."

The picture of all those agents finding and calling all those phone numbers reminded me that it was this kind of dogged police work that solved crimes. The Broken Wings, with all of our flashy independence and photogenic investigations, were saved by slow, methodical, one-foot-in-front-of-the-other grunt work.

Vince poked his head into the conference room. "Jake, can I see you for a minute?"

The press was held back fifty yards by a cordon of local cops. When the reporters saw me, they aimed their cameras and shouted questions about how I felt. Rob had been taken away in an EMT van, and all that was left was the dark stain of his blood on concrete. That would be gone, too, with the next rain. I kept my head down and followed Vince across the lot to the rental car. All four doors stood open and Vince took me to the rear door, where Rob had been sitting.

"What is it?"

"This." He pointed at the floor. A hard shaft of yellow sun fell onto nine .45-caliber bullets, the brass gleaming, new in the light.

"I thought it was a misfire."

"No, Jake," Vince said. "His gun was unloaded. He saw us and unloaded here, before he got out of the car."

39

The first sight of it was a spark of reflected sunlight in the sky. Then, minutes later, the big old girl barreled onto the landing strip, flying as naturally as a bumblebee. An airport shuttle took us to the plane as she slowed to a stop by the charter hangar.

Scott opened the door and helped us in. This was Eric's first trip inside the *Broken Wing*, and of all the amenities—the bunks, the head, the forensics lab, the flying morgue—the one item that held Eric's complete but silent fascination was the cat.

Jerry and Dominic were on board, and after Scott and Trish had put us back in the air, we sat at the conference table and quickly traded information, catching up. This was the first time the entire team had been together since North Carolina, and we had a lot to talk about.

I turned to Jerry first. "What did you find out about the computer?"

"Oh, right. The computer. At first, my guy at Langley wouldn't even admit he had it. So, I was like, 'Hey, man, I gave that to you,' and he was like, 'Hey, man, it's national security.' " Jerry could hardly stop his hands from flying off his wrists. "But after I promised to share my database on natural poisons with him, he told me two things."

"What did he say, Jerry?"

Jerry jumped up, unable to keep his limbs still. "This thing is, like, more secret than the vice president's war record."

"I take it we don't get Janice Callahan's computer back."

Jerry laughed and it sounded like someone rattling a stick in a bucket. "You're kidding, right? And it wasn't Janice Callahan's laptop. It was William Rush's laptop."

"So, Langley is keeping it?"

"Oh, man, they almost kept me. Do you have any idea what was on that thing?"

"No, Jerry, but you were about to tell us."

"Oh, right, but there's a lot I don't know."

Trevor muttered, "The master of understatement."

Jerry paced, pausing every now and then to open his mouth and stretch his jaw as he tried to equalize the pressure in his ears. "I don't know where to start."

"Start anywhere," Dom said, and yawned. "And stop that thing you're doing."

"What thing?"

"With your mouth," Dom said.

"You're making us all yawn," Katie said.

Trevor was recovering from his own yawn. "And you look like a damn grouper."

"Okay, okay." Jerry held his nose and swallowed. His Adam's apple bobbed up and down.

"Are you finished?"

"Yeah, Jake. Anyway, the guy said he'd tell me two things. One is EMPs."

"What are EMPs?" Dom asked.

"Electromagnetic pulses." Trevor was acutely focused on what Jerry was saying, which didn't happen often.

"Right." Jerry looked surprised for a moment, then jumped back aboard his train of thought and held on. "You know how a nuclear detonation produces large amounts of ionized matter and gamma rays? Well, under the right conditions, those ionized particles and those gamma rays produce EMPs. And EMPs can disable electronic equipment. The ionized gases can block radio signals, too. It's called a fireball blackout."

"So, William Rush was working on a nuclear bomb?"

"No, Jake. He was working on EMPs. See, we've known for a long time that a nuclear explosion would fry electrical parts, particularly chips. But the EMP is highly dependent on the altitude. It can be on the ground, which is blown up anyway, and if you're going to blow someone into the void, who cares if their Nokias work, right? But at high altitudes, like above thirty thousand meters, the EMPs generate enormous electrical currents in anything metal—wires, antennas, missiles, airplanes, skyscrapers. Anything metal, even braces." Jerry showed us his teeth.

"What would that do?" Dom asked.

"Dominic, my man, think of a commercial power grid as a giant EMP antenna. You'd get a power surge greater than lightning. Computers, fax machines, phones, everything electrical, would be toast. Now, think of this weapon on the modern battlefield."

"But the military has known about this for years," Trevor said, "and they've hardened all of their equipment."

Jerry held up one long finger. "They say they have, but have they?"

Trevor looked surprised. "I don't know."

"Realistic tests are nearly impossible to perform," Jerry said, "and EMP protection, this hardening the military talks about, can be compromised by water, sand, poor maintenance, all the things that bedevil the military in the kind of places where today's bad guys hang out."

"And given the new direction of our armed forces . . . ," Trevor said.

"Exactly." Jerry stabbed the air with his forefinger, then looked at it as if inspecting his own fingerprint. When he recovered, he said, "And think about this for a while: With a practical EMP generator, all of our high-tech, whiz-bang weaponry is just so much scrap. That includes everything from our radios to our billion-dollar Stealth bombers.

That, my friends, takes away our edge and puts our army on an equal footing with just about any army, anywhere in the world. Nothing but men and guns. No tanks, no planes, no radar. It'd be like fighting the Civil War again, but with automatic rifles."

"I can see very bad people dancing in the street over that news," Dom said.

"The trouble was"—Jerry tucked his hands into his pockets—"from a practical standpoint, nuclear bombs aren't very efficient because they carry a whole lot of other baggage, and, you know, because we're not the only ones who have them."

"What's the second thing?"

"What second thing?"

Trevor looked as if he were about to come across the table and shake it from him. "You said the guy from Langley told you two things. EMPs and what?"

"Oh, just that Rush had figured it out." Jerry sat down and folded his hands together on the table, his report done.

We all sat quietly for a moment, the drone of the plane in our ears.

Dom finally cleared his throat. "After Cassandra there, my report seems rather mundane, but I did find something out that may be of interest."

"Tell me anything, Dom, just so I can stop thinking about Iraqis with EMPs."

"It might be a coincidence, but I was reading the paper this morning about the downing of the Hawker 700. Those guys on board, with the exception of Buckholz and his staff, were all part of the same agency."

"They were civilians," Trevor said.

"Right, but they worked for the government." Dom placed his briefcase in his lap, opened it, and pulled out that day's *Washington Post*. He moved his head until he found the right spot on his bifocals and leafed through the first section. "Here it is. A column about the bombing." Dom scanned down until he found what he was looking for. "They worked for the Defense Acquisition Research Project Agency, some kind of weapons development organization."

"It is," I said. "It's set up so DOD can green-light projects on a small scale and bypass the usual layers of oversight."

"A lot like us," Katie said.

"Except they get paid," Trevor said.

"It's called DARPA," I said.

Dom removed his glasses and carefully polished them with his handkerchief. "Well, it rang a bell with me, so I checked. One of the great things about DARPA is that it's vertically organized, which means you have a lot of small, autonomous teams all working on their own projects, all at the top, hierarchically, so that each of the projects gets equal attention. Now, this vertical integration is also, in the case of our EMT project—"

"EMP," Jerry said.

"Whatever." Dom waved the distinction away with a flick of his handkerchief. "The drawback to this vertical integration is that each team works essentially alone. The entire team on this particular project was killed, all but one that is, when the congressman's plane went down. Care to venture who that one lone survivor was?"

"Ted Baker," I said.

Dom smiled. "That's right. The man who was murdered with Janice Callahan."

It was as if a light had been turned on in a dark room. Suddenly, I could see the how and the why, and with those I was so much closer to finding the who.

Knowing he followed the financial news, I gave Dom some homework. I asked Jerry to call his man at Langley to see if anyone else could have been working on the same technology. No secrets, just if anyone else in the world was researching EMPs. I had a pretty good idea what answer, if any, I would get. Katie said she would dig into public records, and even Trevor volunteered to spend time at the computer, a task he compared to dental work.

"Trevor, I want you to stay with me as backup. I have an idea I might need you."

I called the director's office and was told he'd see me at three. At four, I was still in the waiting room. I read through every issue of *Law Enforcement Bulletin*, paced in front of his secretary's desk until she asked me to please sit down, and looked at every picture on the wall, from the one of Ravan shaking hands with Hoover and Hoover looking like someone had slipped him a bad clam, to the head shot of Ravan looking pretty damn pleased with himself for outlasting his enemies.

The intercom buzzed and Ravan's secretary said, "The director will see you now." I don't know which one of us was more relieved.

Ravan was standing when I entered. He was near the door, between me and the other man in the room. The other man stood up, but made no approach and did not try to shake my hand.

Ravan cleared his throat. He gave me a quick look that asked me to behave. "You know Attorney General Armstrong."

"Yes," I said. "We met a long time ago, in New York."

I sat across from the director. The AG sat in an overstuffed armchair by the window.

Ravan sat behind his desk. It was big and uncluttered, much like Ravan's life. I'd heard that he had had the legs of all the other chairs in his office shortened so he would have an automatic height advantage, but sitting in that chair, in front of that desk and that face, I realized Ravan didn't need props. He'd have an advantage in stature in any room in Washington.

"You've had a pretty busy week, Jake."

"Yes, sir, I have."

"Me, too. I'm tired. How about you?"

"Yes, sir."

"How'd you like to go home and take a nice long vacation?"

I expected more, but Ravan apparently was willing to wait for an answer.

"No, sir, I'm not done with my investigation."

Ravan leaned back in his chair and the leather

creaked. It was the only sound in the office besides the ticking of an antique clock in the bookcase.

From the windows, the AG mumbled, "I wanted to thank you for your help in solving the murder of General Buckholz, his staff, and the research team." It was like a schoolboy forced to apologize for pulling a girl's hair.

I listened to my heartbeat for a moment, then the clock, then to the creaking of Ravan's chair, just to make sure I hadn't slipped into a coma. I tried to make out Armstrong's face, but the light behind his head made it impossible for my eyes to adjust to his features in shadow. "Thank you. I think. But how did I do that?"

"The clue you gave us."

"What clue?"

"From the TV interview you did with that reporter, that Tick fellow."

"Spider," I said. "Spider Urich."

"Same family," Armstrong said. "Arachnids."

That was as close as I'd heard the AG come to actually making a joke.

"You told Urich that if you were investigating the case, you'd start looking at the victims as the real targets, and not the First Lady."

"It was an off-the-cuff remark, sir."

"But correct. When we started looking for why someone would want to kill the army chief, his staff, and a couple of researchers, it led us to a former employee of DARPA, someone whose project had been rejected and who had been let go. He has a history of mental instability and was deemed a security risk by the chief. We have him in custody right now. I'll be announcing the arrest this evening, but I wanted you to know that the shift in the investigation came from you, Jake, and the nation is grateful for your service."

"A disgruntled employee?"

"We caught him as he was getting on a plane to go home. We found the explosives in his apartment. Semtex, same as that used on the congressman's plane."

"And my car."

"Yes," the AG said. "That's right."

The AG had always hated that car, I knew, and probably broke his face smiling when he heard it had been blown away.

"This man you've arrested."

"Yes?"

"You say he was going home."

"Yes. We caught him at the airport."

"Let me guess where home is. Uganda?"

Even in shadow I could see the AG's face open in surprise. Even Ravan blinked, then a chuckle rolled across his desk and filled the room.

"Just a lucky guess, sir," I said. "But if I were you, I'd hold off on any press conferences. I have some news."

My suit was pressed, even though I was not. I was so tired, I knew that once the adrenaline of the chase wore off, I'd sleep for twenty-four hours straight.

Katie, on the other hand, looked as though she'd

spent two weeks at a spa. In a black silk dress with a high Chinese collar, her hair piled high, and jade at her neck and earlobes, she made the solarium orchids look gaudy and rough by comparison. She held a black purse decorated with tiny black seed pearls. The purse was just big enough to hold a lipstick, a set of cuffs, and my Airweight .38.

Mrs. De Vries was as sparkling as the champagne. She appeared to be a woman untroubled by life, instead of a woman who had just lost a niece to murder. She moved about the room, rearranging groups or gently steering conversations so that everyone at the party felt brilliant and charming.

Half of the guests were politicians Joe Public would recognize from Sunday-morning talk TV if Joe Public watched Sunday-morning talk TV. The other guests were anonymous to all but Washington insiders. They were the people who made the wheels turn. With few exceptions, these were the people who persevered, regardless of who won an election. They served as the institutional memory for a city where the public face of power changed every four years and political memory went back only as far as the latest poll.

Of course, even in this crowd, the attorney general wielded the big stick. People gathered around him, hoping to get the inside scoop on the investigation.

It was close to eleven when Dom joined the party, perfectly put together in a blue three-piece pinstripe and red tie.

Dom greeted Frederick as if they were old school chums, and when I introduced him to Mrs. De Vries, he said, "Yes, we've met," and held her hand for a long time. Mrs. De Vries seemed to enjoy the attention and it made me reluctant to pull Dom away, but I did.

It took a few minutes for Dom to confirm what I'd already suspected. Trying to keep it all organized in my head when all my head wanted was a pillow was the hard part. So many strings went in so many directions, but they all came back to one person.

Katie was in the garden talking to Congressman Jason when I joined them.

"Jake," he said, and pumped my hand. "Astonishing work, truly astonishing. Figuring out that the murder of the research team was the real motive behind the bombing of my plane, well, I have to say that the entire country is in awe of your investigative abilities. Everyone thought it was a terrorist attack, but not you two. Amazing."

"Oh, well, I didn't put that together. That was the Bureau who made the connection, and it was the attorney general who arrested the man from Uganda."

"You are too modest. Both of you are." Jason sipped at a martini.

"No, really. My team came to an entirely different conclusion." I watched him, his hands in particular.

Jason drained his martini and casually snagged another from a passing waiter. "Oh, well, as long as the bad guy gets caught, isn't that right?"

"That's right."

"I was just expressing my condolences to your lovely partner. This has had to be one of the hardest days anyone's ever faced, and yet here you both are, the center of attention at one of Millicent's parties where so many try and fail. And one of you"—Jason put a modest hand to his breast—"I won't say which, but one of you looks absolutely stunning." He flashed that fund-raiser smile at Katie. "I hope this means we'll be seeing more of you at these Washington get-togethers."

Attorney General Armstrong came into the garden, his hands in his pockets. In a social setting he didn't appear to be such a bad guy. Armstrong acknowledged each of us and said, "It's getting late, Jake."

"Yes, sir."

"I think here in the garden would be best."

"Yes, sir, I agree. Should you tell him or should I?"

"You're the one with the badge, Jake."

The congressman looked from Armstrong to me and back to Armstrong. The AG said, "You should probably finish up that martini, David."

Jason tried to smile, the glass halfway to his lips. "What's this all about?"

"Katie, would you do the honors?"

"May I?"

"Sure."

Jason followed this like a child about to be surprised on his birthday.

"Well, sir, this really isn't a social occasion for us." Katie put her hand inside her purse.

"No, indeed not," the attorney general said.

I said, "We're still working."

Jason's well-groomed eyebrows shot up in vaudeville surprise. "No!"

Katie smiled. "Congressman Jason, you're under arrest for murder." She pulled the cuffs from her bag.

"Really," Jason said, playing the outraged partygoer.

"The same explosive used to blow up my car," I said. "I really liked that car, too. Do you have any idea what that will do to my premiums?"

I had to give him credit. Jason didn't even break a sweat. He laughed, and it wasn't one of those nervous, I'm-guilty-as-hell laughs, either. That's the laugh of an innocent man. But Jason wasn't an innocent man.

"Jake," he said. "I was home sleeping when my plane exploded."

Katie gently put her hand on Jason's shoulder, forcing him to turn around.

"Before you say anything else, Congressman, you have the right to remain silent—"

"I know my rights."

As I Mirandized the representative, I marveled at how easily Katie patted him down and cuffed him. I would have thought it would be awkward in heels.

Trevor stood back by the garden gate with two men who weren't guests of Mrs. De Vries but were guests of mine. I introduced them to their congressman, just in case they hadn't met.

"Representative Jason, I'd like you to meet Detectives Weller and Snead. They have some questions they need to ask about conspiracy to commit murder."

Weller said, "Thanks for the call, Donovan. And that plane of yours is a sweet ride."

Snead took Jason by the arm and jerked him. "I voted for you, you son of a bitch."

The attorney general took Jason's other arm. "Let's go meet the press, shall we? Then, after that, there are people from Virginia, the District, the Justice Department, the Maryland authorities, and, oh, yes, the SEC, who have questions for you, too. I'd say you're in for a long night."

"This is all a mistake," Jason said.

"Let me recommend a good lawyer." I tucked Larry Berman's business card into the congressman's jacket. "You can call him tonight. He won't mind."

40

The next morning, David Jason of North Carolina would be on the front page of every paper in the country. But for a while it was just between us, Mrs. De Vries's party guests, and about a hundred authorities in nearly a dozen jurisdictions.

As Mrs. De Vries said good night to the last of her guests, all of whom expressed awe and appreciation for being invited, Katie, Trevor, Dom, and I waited in her library. I had a single malt that sang of the Highlands, Katie nursed a vodka martini, Dom rolled a tumbler full of seltzer between his hands, and Trevor had a beer. From the bottle.

Jerry had gone to North Carolina to "check on things." My guess was that one of those things was Dr. Plessy. I wished him a good trip and he had the decency to blush.

Mrs. De Vries settled into a chair and put her head in her hand. "Such a night."

"Such a week."

"I know you're tired," Mrs. De Vries said, "but, Jake, I think I have a right to know just what it is my money bought this time."

"Certainly, Mrs. De Vries."

"Will this be a long report?"

"It's fairly complicated. You may want to refill your glass, ma'am."

Frederick did the honors and then hovered nearby, just in case.

I sank back into the leather library chair, almost afraid to get too comfortable for fear I'd fall asleep, and started at the most logical spot, the beginning. "William Rush developed a weapon that would change the way we fight wars. He goes to David Jason with it, and Jason introduces him to DARPA. In the meantime, smelling a lot of money, not to mention a big new defense contract in his district, Jason convinces Rush to put out an IPO, and through his brother-in-law, Jason buys up as much stock as he can persuade Rush to let go."

"That's where the SEC comes in," Dominic said. "That's illegal."

"Yes, Mr. Sanchez, so I've heard," Mrs. De Vries said.

"But," Katie said, "when DARPA sees the weapon, they know that if we developed that technology in the public eye, the big loser in the long run would be us, the United States. So they decide to pursue this technology on a very small scale."

"With very small profits," Dom said.

"This makes Jason one unhappy representative," Trevor said.

"In the meantime," I said, "another company is working on the same technology."

"Empire," Dominic said. "I believe you've heard of them."

"Yes, Mr. Sanchez. I am intimately familiar with the Empire conglomerate," Mrs. De Vries said. "The bastards."

"Empire doesn't like competition, as you know from personal experience, and they've been prepared to remove, as in murder, the competition for a while," I said. "That's why they recruited Rob McManus. Then Empire sees an opportunity to do two things: keep news of the technology to themselves, and steal Rush's work, thereby cutting out a lot of R and D. But to keep the technology a secret, they have to kill or compromise anyone who knows about this system. Jason is easy. He's already compromised himself.

"But before they can eliminate Rush, he's already briefed DARPA and the army chief of staff. General Buckholz wants to make a presentation to the president, and Empire knows that once it goes to the White House, well, even they're not prepared to assassinate the president. So they decide to stop the briefing before it happens.

"Jason offers to fly the chief and his staff, along with the DARPA team, to Florida in his own private plane. The mechanic gives Jason a bomb and Jason gives the bomb to his wife."

"Which is where he screws up," Trevor said.

"Because Jason's wife has invited the First Lady to fly to Florida with her. But now there are too many people on the plane. So, when the First Lady graciously declines the invitation, Jason's wife doesn't feel right about going without her."

"Which means that the bomb doesn't make it onto the plane," Katie picked up. "Now Jason is panicked. He has the mechanic hold up the departure with some fabricated technical problems. This gives Jason time to get to National and put the case on the plane himself. The timer was set to blow up somewhere over the Outer Banks, but because of the delay, it blows up right here."

"And Jason's plane crashes into the Mall," Dom says.

"Which actually works to Jason's advantage because now everyone thinks it was a terrorist attack on the First Lady. They don't look at who was really the target."

"The army chief of staff and the DARPA researchers," Mrs. De Vries said.

"That's right."

"And it took you how long to figure this out?"

"Once Dominic had a line on the money, it all fell into place," I said.

"I follow the financial markets," Dom said, and gave Mrs. De Vries a courtly nod. Mrs. De Vries smiled back and her eyes sparkled in a way I'd never seen before.

Katie saw it, too, and smiled.

I tried to keep my head on the train of events. "So, Jason, at the request of Empire—"

"Who is working on this technology independently," Dom said.

"—blows up his own airplane, killing everyone who knows about Rush's work."

"Except Rush," Katie said, "who is afraid to fly."

"And Janice," Mrs. De Vries says.

Dominic rises and offers his handkerchief. She clutches his hand in appreciation. There is a brief moment of shared grief and consolation, made touchingly graceful by these two dignified people, and then Dominic returns to his chair.

"Your niece was dating one of the DARPA researchers, Ted Baker, who also stayed behind. That left three people who knew about this weapon system."

"So they first target William Rush," Katie said, "but he doesn't have the computer files, your niece does. But she doesn't have them in Alexandria. And why?"

"I don't know," Mrs. De Vries said.

"Because airport security in Raleigh-Durham won't let her board the plane with a laptop. They think it could be a bomb."

"And they say irony is dead," Trevor said.

"So she gives the computer to her ex-husband, who has driven her to the airport."

"But I stick my nose into all this by asking you to investigate."

"Right. They had been counting on two police departments, in different jurisdictions, to be hindered by distance and the usual turf battles."

"But, thanks to you, Millicent," Dom said, "the

Broken Wings can fly anywhere, and voilà, instead of several different crime scenes, it all becomes one large crime scene."

"Once Empire knows that," Katie said, "they know it won't be long before we make the connection between the DARPA researchers on the plane and the one in Alexandria. That's when Fletcher files his lawsuit in an effort to ground us."

"Then they get Rob and Bower to distract me with attacks on my family, and it works for a while. But because of this team here—"

"And Jerry," Trevor said.

"—and Jerry, we're able to come out on the bright end of an otherwise dark week."

"Once Empire knew that the game was over, they cut Jason loose."

"How?"

"His wife received pictures in the mail, along with information about the bomb."

"Oh my God, that's right. He tried to kill her," Mrs. De Vries said, her hand to her mouth in shock.

"He thought it was a bonus," Trevor said. "He has a girlfriend in Georgetown."

"And the girlfriend was in the pictures. A double whammy," Trevor said.

Mrs. De Vries looked down into her soda and lime. "Money, sex, and power."

"The big three," I said. "Without them, there wouldn't be any murder."

"And without them, we'd all be out of work," Trevor said.

41

Mrs. De Vries had more questions, but I begged her to let me go home and go to sleep.

"Perhaps Mr. Sanchez wouldn't mind staying," Katie said.

Dominic bowed again. "It would be my pleasure."

Mrs. De Vries thanked us all, Katie most warmly, and we walked out into the summer night to our cars. Trevor waved good night and backed out into the quiet streets of Cleveland Park.

"I came here with Dom," Katie said. "Can you give me a ride?"

"Sure." I handed her my keys. "But maybe you should drive."

We got into the Land Rover and turned on the radio. The arrest of the congressman was all over the news, and the attorney general sounded good for a change.

"Empire still gets away," Katie said.

"But not with the weapon. That's something."

Katie adjusted the mirrors and checked all the controls.

"It's not a plane, Katie."

"Just being careful, Jake."

"Maybe you should check under the hood."

"Not funny, Jake, not funny at all."

Katie, satisfied that all systems were go, backed into the street. "Jake, I've been wondering . . ."

"Yeah?"

"Do you think J. P. Napoleon really exists or is he just a fiction for Fletcher De Vries?"

"I don't know, Katie. And I'm too tired to even think about it."

Katie reached over and found a station playing Billie Holiday. It felt right.

This was our first time alone in a long time, and we were both comfortable to let Billie fill the silence with her sad song. When the song ended, Ella came on and Katie turned the radio down.

"You don't like Ella?"

"Jake, when Ella sings about her man being gone, I get the feeling that he's just gone down the street for some milk and will be right back. But Billie . . ."

"When she says her man is gone, he's gone for good."

Katie sighed. "I'm sorry for all I've put you through lately."

"I'm sorry, too, about Rob. He made his choice, you know. It wasn't your fault."

"I know. But it still hurts like hell."

I leaned over and kissed her cheek. It was wet.

"So, what do we do now?"

"I don't know," I said.

"Are we partners or lovers, Jake? And is it possible to be both? Because I do love you, you know that."

"I know. And I love you, too, Katie. But this is hard."

"It's too hard. Maybe I should start looking for another job." She laughed and wiped away a tear. "It's a hell of a lot easier than finding another man, that's for sure."

We stopped at a red light. There were no other cars for blocks. The D.C. streets were lit up and empty, all of the bad guys holed up and sleeping. I leaned over again and kissed Katie again. This time she turned her head and kissed me back.

"Let's take this one day at a time," I said.

Katie kissed me again, parted, and whispered, "Maybe we should start with the nights."

The light turned green and a lone D.C. cab came up behind us and hit his horn.

"We should go," I said.

"Screw him," Katie said, and kissed me again.